BURN
KITCHEN
VEGAN CUISINE

Calvin & Theresa Curameng

"And God said, Behold, I have given you every herb bearing seed, which is upon the face of all the earth, and every tree, in the which IS the fruit of a tree yielding seed; to you it shall be for food." -Genesis 1:29

COPYRIGHT

4100 Edgewater Drive
Orlando, Florida 32804
liquidfireyoga.com.
(407) 999-7871

This book is not intended as a substitute for the medical advice of physicians. The reader should regularly consult a physician in matters relating to their health and particularly with respect to any symptoms that may require diagnosis or medical attention. The information in this book is meant to supplement, not replace, proper yoga or food nutrition training. Any physical activity poses some inherent risk. The authors and publisher advise readers to take full responsibility for their safety and know their limits. Before practicing the yoga skills and making the recipes described in this book, be sure that your equipment is well maintained and do not make any changes to your diet unless you are under a physicians care and observation.

All layout, design, general photography and dark room effects by Calvin and Theresa Curameng. Asana pictures on pages (154, 157, 159, 167, 171, 178, 180, 189) by Tim Barker Photography. All other photographs are taken by Calvin and Theresa Curameng, with the help of a sweet little tripod and a little bit of good ol' fashioned patience. All the photographs are also copyrighted material and cannot be used or digitally distributed without express written permission from Liquid Fire Yoga® Productions.

ISBN 978-0-9964741-0-8

Printed in the United States

Liquid Fire Yoga® Productions

DEDICATION

An offering to the students of yoga.

With blessings and love,

Calvin & Theresa Curameng

CONTENTS

PART THREE

Liquid Fire Yoga® - The System

The practice of yoga is not meant to feed our human nature, it is meant to fuel our Divine nature.

INTRODUCTIONLIBERATION

BURN Kitchen Vegan Cuisine & Liquid Fire Yoga®

This book, BURN Kitchen Vegan Cuisine, and Liquid Fire Yoga®, is about balance—the balance of your health, well-being, and peace. Every recipe, word, and posture is created with balance in mind, your balance. For you, we keep BURNing.

Liquid Fire Yoga® practice is the art of learning to create friction - tapas. The friction of the water and fire inside of our very being. The friction of opposition, action, and inaction. It's the power to discern what you love from what you think you love.

This book comprises two elements in relationship together - cooking to feed your spirit, BURN Kitchen Vegan Cuisine and the practice of Liquid Fire Yoga®. This system of food and yoga is based on the ancient lessons taught by sages of yoga that offered us a way of eating that compliments the meditation practice of yoga.

The Liquid Fire Yoga® System is a powerful structure utilizing ancient yoga methodology. It is a practical application of yoga practice that launches the practitioner to develop a higher space of consciousness. There is no doubt that any student who embarks on the path, as outlined in this book will experience a tremendous shift. This comprehensive system is easy for anyone to apply, understand, and follow.

The approach to food and yoga offered in this book allows the practitioner to see firsthand what current scientific data states about meditation, exercise, and a good diet being beneficial for healthful living.

This food and yoga practice supports the path of understanding the simple, undisguised knowledge offered by the ancient sages of yoga. What is taught is an easy approach to follow: a diet of juicy fresh food, nuts, seeds and grains, hydration of the body with fresh clean water, daily devotional movement (asana), deep breath work (pranayama) and study (svadyaya). These time-honored practices are the fundamentals of purifying oneself for the experience of yoga. This basic, integral lifestyle taught by the sages of yoga is what science, intellects, and theologians for years may have been unnecessarily complicating through categorical and divisional studies. To fully understand the practice of yoga is to recognize it simply cannot be segmented into categories. It is a unifying universal all-encompassing practice.

The Liquid Fire Yoga® System (LFYS) eliminates all the separations and divisions surrounding current yoga practices. The system offers the student an ability to make clear choices without question or doubt. Doubt impedes the experience of yoga. It can be eradicated through conscious, deep, intentional breathing (pranayama) and through the daily practice of the pancha vahanas. Pancha (panca) is Sanskrit for the number five. Vahana is also Sanskrit and one of its definitions means "that which carries". The pancha vahanas of Liquid Fire Yoga® are: food (consumption of fresh food), hydration (liquid cleansing), asana (sacred movement), pranayama (controlled movement of energy) and wisdom (application of studies and practice). Through the daily application of the five vahanas, the yoga student is instilled with an all-aware, powerful connection to a higher force. This Self-realization allows the sadhaka or spiritual aspirant to attain a high level of radiant calm confidence also referred to as blissful nature. LFYS is the unambiguous choice for a yoga student who wishes to embark on the divine path of yoga without a sense of rushing or hurdling. According to the ancient sages, lifestyle changes can take a person months, years, or lifetimes in order to fully develop their skills of enlightened living. When you can feel the positive results of your daily choices, they become a learning experience as well as a definition of your life and character. Discover that genuine peace comes from how you fuel your body. A calm approach toward yoga and life is certainly a skill you will develop through the practice of Liquid Fire Yoga®.

The levels of Liquid Fire Yoga® practice are based on the application of devotion and dedication towards yoga practice. The levels of dedication and devotion are measured as mild, medium, or intense. A mild practitioner is devoted to the physical practices and dedication towards the daily work of practice is off and on. At medium intensity, the student's practice is devotional and focused on mental well-being and healing. Their dedication is fairly consistent, usually only slipping when life becomes unusually challenging or busy. At the highest intensity, the student is devoted to seeing Divinity within themselves every breath of the day and their dedication to practice is unbroken and ever-present. All students are a mixture of these intensities. The first step on your path toward liberation starts here. Love, C&T

PARTONE

The Perfected Union Of Yoga And Food

THE BHAGAVAD GITA

"You are what you eat and you eat based on what you are."

Food is the most important
of all things for the body.
Therefore it is the best medicine
for all the body's ailments.
-The Upanishads

BURNKITCHEN

Eat small meals frequently of sattvic delicacy.

"The following qualities are surely always found in the bodies of every yogi;

Strong appetite, good digestion, cheerfulness, handsome figure, great courage,

mighty enthusiasm and full strength. " -Shiva Samhita

The food of BURN Kitchen Vegan Cuisine is beyond just a mere accidental collision of substance. Take the time to discover the pure essence of your food. Honor the world of fresh food where its natural vibrancy comes from sunlight, moonlight, and rainwater. The consumption of fresh food is an illumined experience. Mindfully consume it and understand on a conscious level how food affects your body and mind.

In the Bhagavad Gita it states: "You are what you eat and you eat based on what you are. And know, [Arjuna] that due to the subtle impact of food on one's mind, sooner or later all spiritual aspirants will have to face up to the issue of what they consume." Fresh food is a substance of the Divine. All that is needed to truly understand the nutritional value of the fresh food you consume is faith. Faith that the divine essence of it will nourish you.

Raw food: Fresh gourmet and utterly outstanding alternatives to the typical processed foods you crave. Enjoy the satisfying flavors of fresh entrees, dressings, dips, and drinks. There is also a plethora of heavenly desserts. This is pure 100% honest guilt free dining.

SolFood: Sun food recipes that satisfy your cravings and feed your soul. Made-from-scratch cooked vegan comfort food. Sol-Food is concocted with minimal amounts of processed ingredients, garden fresh vegetables, homemade dips, and sauces.

BURN 33 DAYS OF RAW

Explore the art and science of good eating.

Burn is a 33 day celebration of fresh food. Honor the spirit of gathering, creating, loving, and sharing. For 33 days of glorious life be in full control of what is on your plate and what goes into the body. Refine the choices of your food down to the basics: fresh vegetables, nuts, seeds, grains, and fruits. Your body deserves gourmet fresh raw food that is satisfying and is easy to digest.

THE KITCHEN OF BURN

To gain the full benefits of BURN, take your time learning about raw foods and their effects on your body. We suggest to become familiar with the recipes in this section. Make them a part of your daily routine. Once you build a repertoire of these raw food recipes then you will be confident to begin the 33 day process. Until then, cheerful cooking and mindful dining is what matters.

BURN 33 Days Of Raw begins with clearing the kitchen pantry, the cabinets, the refrigerator, and the freezer. Removal of these items is a necessary step that will help you prevent unhealthy food cravings. Cravings intensify when the object of desire is just within reach. Get a box and label it for the local food bank. In this box place all unopened processed foods. The canned goods and the packaged foods. Especially if it has high fructose corn syrup, sugar, soy, salt, oil, wheat, whey, corn, dairy, dye, it goes. Even if the package label says organic, all-natural, and that it's good for you, it goes. Out of the kitchen. Also, all dairy, meat, and egg products - out. Anything that is not a raw food or vegetable - out. There are no exceptions. No refined sugars, no vegan sugar, no sugar in the raw. And absolutely no beer, no wine, spirits, or candy. Nothing

passes the test unless it is a fresh, raw, non-mind-altering item. This food lifestyle is a personal commitment to only purchase products with labels that have a clear and unfiltered ingredient list. It is tremendously important to understand ingredient listings. In America, if an item is less than 10 percent of the final packaged product the company is not required to list it on the label. If two items combined create another ingredient, they don't have to list those ingredients either. Therefore, in BURN 33 Days of Raw the use of high-quality-raw ingredients is the main focus.

THE LIFESTYLE OF BURN

For 33 days eat fresh, light, and often. Drink plenty of water. Practice meditation, pranayama, and yoga asana for at least thirty-three minutes a day. Also, for another thirty-three minutes a day incorporate the following activities: walking, hiking, biking, surfing, skating, or dancing. If you are unable perform these daily then devote yourself to doing one activity a minimum of three times a week.

When practicing yoga asana use the pleasant approach as instructed in Part Three of this book. Avoid extreme yoga asana and unnaturally heated environments. Eliminate extreme sports that heighten adrenaline levels. Create an easy-going lifestyle. Stay home on rainy nights. Read inspiring books. Watch pleasant TV. Minimize electronic device activity. Spend time with the kids, the cat, the dog. Enjoy the outdoors at the beach or in the woods. If you go out for social gatherings or for work then go well-fed and bring plenty of raw snacks. Embark on a new lifestyle of yoga practice.

CLEANLINESS. Cleanliness is important for the raw food kitchen. Cross contamination is a threat to good health. Avoid potential contamination by designating a few basic kitchen utensils for only vegan and raw food recipes. We also recommend to use natural cleaners to sanitize your kitchen before and after cooking. We like to use a mixture of water, lemon juice, distilled vinegar, and tea tree oil as our kitchen cleaner.

CHOPPING METHODS. Knowing the difference between chopped, diced, minced and julienne is helpful for this cuisine. We suggest to study different methods of chopping. As you continue to make the recipes, these cutting techniques will become second nature. In some cases the use of a food processor can help to save time chopping.

BLENDING METHODS. Raw foods always vary in texture and taste. Nature is not like the common processed food that tastes exactly the same each time it is made. The consistency of all dips and dressings should always turn out creamy and smooth and never watery or coarse. Continue blending until the desired smooth texture is reached. Water helps to hydrate and move ingredients. The amount of water and salt in each recipe can also be fine tuned to your personal preference.

SHELF LIFE. When properly sealed and refrigerated, the BURN dressings and dips have a varying shelf life from 5 to 10 days. Dips or dressings made with fresh herbs or vegetables should be consumed within one to three days. We suggest chopping your veggies fresh instead of buying supermarket-chopped veggies. Fresh veggies you chop have a much longer shelf life and taste better.

MANAGE YOUR TIME. A well planned food week will give you an opportunity to have easy and fast meals to make on hand. Once a week, set aside a time to plan your weekly meals and to prepare the dressings and the dips.

THE MAIN INGREDIENT. Enjoy the process of discovering conscious dining. The most important ingredient to have always have on hand is love.

Juice

Convert your kitchen into a juice temple

Juicing is an honorable routine in our household. Juice revitalizes the cells on such deep levels, it is difficult to ignore its bounty. The opulence of the garden fills this temple like a garland of offering. As each leafy green, fruit, and veggie passes through the humming juicer, thank the plant, the gardener, and the divine for such abundance. Contemplate joyful space and the qualities of the saintly beings who grew this verdant food. Then direct your prana and honor the sacred temple of the juice.

LIQUID LUV TO LEAN & GREEN

"Juice powered by garden fresh greens." - C

HEART BEETS

Ingredients

Serves 2
Prep Time: 10 min

4x Parsley sprigs
4x Celery stalks
2x Lemons
1x Beet (with leaves)
1x Red apple
1/2tsp Ginger

1. Juice all ingredients. Stir and drink up.

   Note: Omega® Juicer is recommended when juicing citrus fruit with the peel.

CELLULAR SHIFT

Ingredients

Serves 2
Prep Time: 10 min

8x Celery stalks
1x Cucumber
1x Lime
1x Carrot
1x Apple
1/2x Lemon
2tbsp Mint

1. Juice and enjoy! Cheers!

   Note: Omega® Juicer is recommended when juicing citrus fruit with the peel.

BRILLIANCE

Ingredients

Serves 2
Prep Time: 10 min

4x Celery stalks
4x Parsley sprigs
2x Tomatoes
1x Lemon
1x Apple
1x Carrot
1x Cucumber
1/2x Garlic clove

1. Juice. Stir. Drink. Enjoy.

   Note: Omega® Juicer is recommended when juicing citrus fruit with the peel.

PINK LEMONADE

Ingredients

Serves 2
Prep Time: 10 min

4x Celery stalks
2x Lemons (fresh squeezed)
2x Red apples
3c Pineapple
1/4c Beet
1/2x Lemon (sliced, garnish)
1/2c Ice (crushed)

1. Juice all ingredients. Shake or stir. Serve in a high ball glass with crushed ice and garnish with lemon slices.

   Note: Omega® Juicer is recommended when juicing citrus fruit with the peel.

LEAN & GREEN

Ingredients

Serves 2
Prep Time: 10 min

4x Kale leaves
4x Swiss chard leaves
2x Celery stalks
1x Cucumber
1x Lime
1x Green pear

1. Juice all ingredients. Cheers!

   Note: Omega® Juicer is recommended when juicing citrus fruit with the peel.

KALI GREEN

Ingredients

Serves 2
Prep Time: 10 min

6x Kale leaves
2x Celery stalks
1c Spinach leaves
1x Lime
1x Pear

1. Run all ingredients through a juicer. Drink up!

   Note: Omega® Juicer is recommended when juicing citrus fruit with the peel.

CRIMSON PUNCH

Ingredients

Serves 2
Prep Time: 10 min

3x Parsley sprigs
1x Red beet with leaves
1x Green apple
1x Carrot
1x Orange
1x Lemon
1/4tsp Ginger

1. Juice. Stir. Drink.

   Note: Omega® Juicer is recommended when juicing citrus fruit with the peel.

CARROT TOP

Ingredients

Serves 2
Prep Time: 10 min

3x Carrots (with tops)
2x Celery stalks
1x Apple
3x Parsley sprigs
1x Lemon

1. Juice. Stir. Drink.

   Note: Omega® Juicer is recommended when juicing citrus fruit with the peel.

LIQUID LUV

Ingredients

Serves 2
Prep Time: 10 min

4x Rainbow chard
3x Celery stalks
3x Parsley sprigs
1x Cucumber
1x Green apple
1/2x Lemon

1. Juice. Stir. Drink. Enjoy!

   Note: Omega® Juicer is recommended when juicing citrus fruit with the peel.

BERRY IN LUV

Ingredients

Serves 2
Prep Time: 10 min

1x Apple
1x Cucumber
1x Lime juiced (fresh squeezed)
1c Florida strawberries
1/2c Florida blueberries

1. Run all ingredients through a juicer.

   Note: Omega® Juicer is recommended when juicing citrus fruit with the peel.

SOUTHERN STAR

Ingredients

Serves 2
Prep Time: 10 min

2x Star fruit
1x Lime
1x Orange (whole)

1x Orange juiced (fresh squeezed)

1. Run all ingredients through a juicer shake and serve over ice!

   Note: Omega® Juicer is recommended when juicing citrus fruit with the peel.

DRAGON FRUIT

Ingredients

Serves 2
Prep Time: 5 min

2x Asian pears
2x Dragon fruit

1. Juice. Stir. Drink. Enjoy this vibrant beverage!

   Note: Asian pears have the appearance of a pear and apple with a similar texture and taste.

Drinks

Satisfy the inner longing

Drinks in general are sugary, alcoholic, or just filled with unnecessary ingredients. For something that enters the body with such satiny ease its baffling that so many will settle for the sugar rush of ordinary beverages lining supermarket shelves. In the pleasant abode of your kitchen savor the calm energy that comes from stirring and shaking your own luminous energy.

The beverages in this section range from milk to icy smoothies to the nightly virgin cocktail. These liquid offerings have no adverse side effects and no long recovery time. There is no need to overcome the desire or longing for these little glasses of perfected light.

MACA LATTE

"Make love your daily dose." - T

MILK FRESH ALTERNATIVES

ALMOND JOY MILK

Ingredients

Makes Approx. 16 oz
Prep Time: 5 min (plus soak time)

2c Water
1/4c Raw almonds (soaked)
2x Dates (pitted)

1. Soak almonds in filtered water for 8 hours or overnight.

2. Peel and discard almond skins.

3. Blend all ingredients on high (in a regular blender or VitaMix®) until the fully blended and froth begins to form on surface of the milk.

Note: When using a regular blender a milk bag or fine strainer may be used to separate milk from the almond sediment.

MACA LATTE

Ingredients

Makes Approx. 16 oz
Prep Time: 5 min

2c ALMOND JOY MILK (recipe above)

3x Medjool dates (pitted)
2tbsp Pecans
2tbsp Cacao powder raw
1tbsp Maca powder
1tbsp Coconut sugar crystals
1tsp Vanilla extract (non-alcohol)

1. Blend on high (in a VitaMix®) until hot and frothy. Pour into your favorite mug and enjoy!

CHOCOLATE MILK

Ingredients

Makes Approx. 16 oz
Prep Time: 5 min (plus soak time)

2c ALMOND JOY MILK (recipe on left)

2x Medjool dates (pitted)
2tbsp Raw cacao powder
2tbsp Tahini
2tbsp Hemp seeds
1tbsp Maca powder
1tsp Vanilla extract (non-alcohol)

1. Blend all ingredients on high (in a regular blender or VitaMix®) until the fully blended and froth begins to form on surface of the milk. Serve chilled or over ice.

THE MILKY WAY

Ingredients

Makes Approx. 16 oz
Prep Time: 5 min

2c Water
1/4c Hemp seed
1tsp Vanilla extract (non-alcohol)
1tsp Maca powder
1tsp Chia seeds
1x Medjool date (pitted)

1. Blend all ingredients on high (in a regular blender or VitaMix®) until the fully blended and froth begins to form on surface of the milk. Serve chilled or over ice.

RISE UP AND DRINK UP

Surya Sunrise

Fruit is a sattvic (pleasant) delicacy. It is light, tasty, and easy to digest. Fruit is known in the East to promote a jovial spirit and a light body. Fresh fruit is unlike the powdery white and refined sugary substance over-used in shelved products. Fresh fruit is sweet, peaceful, and the food of choice for yoga masters. To be sattvic, make sattvic choices. Dine on fruit that grows naturally where you live, in small harmonious doses, and when in season. Fuel your sattvic nature with true food.

SUCCULENT SMOOTHIES

STAR GAZER

Ingredients

Makes Approx. (2) 16 oz
Prep Time: 6 min

2x Star Fruit
1x Mango (peeled & sliced)
1x Tangerine (peeled)
1x Banana
1tsp Hemp seeds
1c Ice

1. Blend star fruit, mango, tangerine, banana and hemp seeds until liquefied. Then add ice and blend again until desired smoothie consistency is reached. The planets have aligned! Enjoy!

HARVEST GROVE

Ingredients

Makes Approx. (2) 16 oz
Prep Time: 5 min

1c Sunflower sprouts
1x Peach
1x Pear
2x Bananas (frozen)
1c Ice

1. Blend sunflower sprouts, peach, and pear until smooth. Then add frozen bananas and blend again. Add 1 cup of ice and blend on high until desired smoothie consistency is reached.

BANANA BERRY BLISS

Ingredients

Makes Approx. (2) 16 oz
Prep Time: 5 min

2c Strawberries
3x Medjool Dates (pitted)
2tbsp Hemp seed (hulled)
2x Bananas
2c Ice

1. Blend strawberries, dates, and hemp seeds until liquefied. Then add banana and blend again. Add ice and blend on high until desired smoothie consistency is reached.

ELECTRIC MELON

Ingredients

Makes Approx. (2) 16 oz
Prep Time: 5 min

3c Watermelon (chopped)
1/2c Coconut water
1tsp Coconut sugar crystals
1c Ice

1. Blend watermelon, coconut water, and coconut sugar until smooth. Then add 1 cup of ice and blend on high until desired smoothie consistency is reached.

FIELD OF GREENS

Ingredients

Makes Approx. (2) 16 oz smoothies
Prep Time: 15 min

1/2c **The Milky Way (recipe below)**

1tbsp **Hemp seed**
2tsp **Spirulina**
2x **Kale (chopped)**
1x **Green apple**
1x **Pear**
2x **Oranges (fresh squeezed)**
1c **Ice**

THE MILKY WAY

Ingredients

Makes Approx. 16 oz
Prep Time: 5 min

2c **Water**
1/4c **Hemp seed**
1tsp **Vanilla extract (non-alcohol)**
1tsp **Maca powder**
1tsp **Chia seeds**
1x **Medjool date (pitted)**

1. Blend all ingredients on high (in a regular blender or VitaMix®) until the fully blended and froth begins to form on surface of the milk. Serve chilled or over ice.

Method

1. Follow recipe below for The Milky Way fresh milk alternative.

2. Blend ½ cup of The Milky Way with hemp seed and spirulina. Then add kale, green apple, pear, and orange juice. Blend until smooth. Then add 1 cup of ice and blend on high until desired smoothie consistency is reached.

BLUEMOON

Ingredients

Makes Approx. (2) 16 oz
Prep Time: 5 min

2c Blueberries
1x Banana
1/4c Orange juice (fresh squeezed)
3x Medjool Dates (pitted)
1tbsp Maca powder
2c Ice

1. Blend blueberries, orange juice, dates, and maca powder until liquefied. Then add banana and blend again. Then add ice and blend on high until desired smoothie consistency is reached.

CHOCOLATE FROSTY

Ingredients

Makes Approx. (2) 16 oz
Prep Time: 5 min

1c Almond Joy Milk (recipe below)
2x Bananas (frozen or fresh)
3x Medjool dates (pitted)
3tbsp Cacao powder raw
1tsp Vanilla extract (non-alcohol)
1tbsp Coconut sugar
1tbsp Maca powder
2-1/2c Ice

1. Blend Almond Joy Milk, dates, raw cacao, vanilla, coconut sugar, and maca until liquefied. Then add frozen bananas and blend again. Then add ice as needed and blend on high into a Chocolate Frosty consistency.

ALMOND JOY MILK

Ingredients

Makes Approx. 16 oz
Prep Time: 5 min (plus soak time)

2c Water
1/4c Raw almonds (soaked)
2x Dates (pitted)

1. Soak almonds in filtered water for 8 hours or overnight.

2. Peel and discard almond skins.

3. Blend all ingredients on high (in a regular blender or VitaMix®) until the fully blended and froth begins to form on surface of the milk.

   Note: When using a regular blender a milk bag or fine strainer may be used to separate milk from the almond sediment.

SUBLIME CHERRY

Ingredients

Makes Approx. (2) 16 oz
Prep Time: 5 min

2x Bananas (frozen)
1c Cherries (pitted)
1/2c Coconut water
1tbsp Almond butter
1tsp Vanilla extract (non-alcohol)
1tsp Maca powder
1c Ice

1. Blend all bananas, cherries, coconut water, almond butter, vanilla, and maca together on high. Then add ice and blend until desired smoothie consistency is reached.

TROPICAL SUNSHINE

Ingredients

Makes Approx. (2) 16 oz
Prep Time: 5 min

1/2c The Milky Way (recipe below)
1x Banana
1c Pineapple (peeled & chopped)
1/2c Orange juice (fresh squeezed)
2c Ice

1. Blend The Milky Way, banana, pineapple, and orange juice together. Then add 2 cups of ice and blend on high until desired smoothie consistency is reached.

THE MILKY WAY

Ingredients

Makes Approx. 16 oz
Prep Time: 5 min

2c Water
1/4c Hemp seed
1tsp Vanilla extract (non-alcohol)
1tsp Maca powder
1tsp Chia seeds
1x Medjool date (pitted)

1. Blend all ingredients on high (in a regular blender or VitaMix®) until the fully blended and froth begins to form on surface of the milk. Serve chilled or over ice.

VIRGIN COCKTAILS

BAILEY'S DOUBLE

Ingredients

Makes Approx. (2) 12 oz beverages
Prep Time: 5 min

8oz Water
1/3c Cashews (soaked 4 hrs.)
4tbsp Coconut sugar crystals
3tbsp Raw almonds (soaked 4-6 hrs.)
2tbsp Hazelnuts (soaked 4-6 hrs.)
2tsp Cacao powder raw
1tsp Maca powder
2tsp Vanilla extract (non-alcohol)
1/2tsp Almond extract (non-alcohol)
2tsp Hemp seed (hulled)
Pinch Himalayan or Celtic sea salt
1c Ice

1. Soak almonds and hazelnuts in filtered water for 4 to 6 hours or overnight. Peel and discard almond and hazelnut skins.

2. Blend all ingredients except for ice. When all the ingredients are fully blended into an even color then add ice and blend until smooth.

3. Pour over a cup of ice in a rocks glass. Cheers!

SURYA SUNRISE

Ingredients

Makes Approx. (2) 8 oz beverages
Prep Time: 8 min

2c Orange juice (fresh squeezed)
4oz Grenadine (recipe below)
2x Orange slices (garnish)

1. Pour orange juice into a chilled highball glass and add ice. Tilt glass and slowly add Grenadine syrup. Allow syrup to slide down the inside of glass and sink to the bottom. Then stand glass upright. Witness how the distinct red contrasts beautifully with the orange to paint a sunrise color scheme. Garnish with sliced oranges. Revel in this drinkable liquid Surya Sunrise. Rise and shine.

GRENADINE

Makes Approx 6 oz
Prep Time: 5 min

1/2c Pomegranate juice (fresh squeezed)
1/4c Maple syrup
2tbsp Lemon juice (fresh squeezed)

1. Mix pomegranate juice, maple syrup, and fresh squeezed lemon juice on high until fully blended into a syrup.

Note: To make pomegranate juice, roll fresh pomegranates onto a tabletop. This will gently pop the small segments of the interior fruit under the thick-skinned shell. Once the majority of segments are opened, the outside of fruit will feel soft and almost moldable. Then puncture a small hole in the skin with a knife and squeeze out juice into a glass.

MOJITO

Ingredients

Makes Approx. (2) 16 oz beverages
Prep Time: 10 min

1/2c Lime juice (fresh squeezed)
2tbsp Coconut sugar crystals
1c Ice (crushed)
2c Kombucha tea (unflavored)
12x Mint leaves

1. In a shaker add lime juice, coconut sugar, and ice. Shake. Pour even amount into 2 highball glasses and mix in 1 cup of kombucha tea into each glass. Stir in 6 mint leaves as garnish.

Note: If purchasing kombucha tea, buy from a trusted brand and make sure there are no added flavors. Most manufacturers call this original or natural flavored. If kombucha tea is unaccessible replace it with sparkling mineral water instead.

STRAWBERRY DAIQUIRI

Ingredients

Makes Approx. 20 oz
Prep Time: 5 min

1/4c Coconut sugar crystals
2x Medjool dates (soaked 15 min)
1x Orange juiced (fresh squeezed)
1x Lime juiced (fresh squeezed)
2pints Strawberries (destemmed)
2c Ice
2x Strawberries (garnish)

1. Blend coconut sugar, dates, orange juice, and lime juice together. Once all the dates are blended, add strawberries and blend again. Then add ice and blend on high until it reaches a thick daiquiri consistency. Pour into a margarita glass and garnish with a strawberry. Savor this cocktail where the only side effect is from vitamin C.

Note: An alternate way to make this is to use frozen strawberries. This will lessen the amount of ice required as listed in ingredients.

Sauces

Liquid luminous energy

Succulent, luscious, lip licking bliss. Any raw foodist will tell you that sauces are the heart and soul of raw food cuisine. The stars, the light, the luminous fortitude of extraordinary delights. Even the most fearful, uncertain cook can build a new database of pure confident structure by making these savory sauces everyone will absolutely love to lick up. Go ahead, pick up your plate and lick every last drop, we won't tell anyone, we promise.

RADICAL RANCH DRESSING

"An original organic shift of an old style country dressing." - C

LIQUID FIRE SAUCES

PICANTE

Ingredients

Makes Approx. 12 oz
Prep Time: 5 min

1c Mexican chili peppers (dried)
1/2c Tomato (chopped)
2x Medjool dates (pitted)
1x Chipotle pepper dried
1x Garlic clove (peeled)
1/2x Lemon juiced (fresh squeezed)
1tsp Apple cider vinegar
1tsp Oregano fresh
1tsp Cumin
1/2tsp Himalayan or Celtic sea salt
1/8tsp Black peppercorn (fresh ground)

1. Soak Mexican chili peppers and chipotle peppers in water for 15 minutes. Drain and discard water. Blend all ingredients together on high until liquefied into a sauce.

   Note: Be cautious when blending hot peppers as strong vapors can irritate your eyes. Thoroughly wash hands when handling hot peppers. Avoid contact with eyes for several hours.

HAUTE SALSA VERDE

Ingredients

Makes Approx. 20 oz
Prep Time: 5 min

2c Jalapeños fresh (destemmed)
3/4c Cilantro fresh
1/2c Parsley fresh
1/4c Tomato (chopped)
1/4c Extra virgin olive oil (cold pressed)
1x Lemon juiced (fresh squeezed)
1x Garlic clove (peeled)
2tbsp Onion (chopped)
1x Habanero (destemmed)
1-1/2tsp Apple cider vinegar
1tsp Himalayan or Celtic sea salt
1/2tsp Black peppercorn (fresh ground)

1. Blend all ingredients on high. Allow sauce to have a slightly chunky texture.

   Note: Be cautious when blending hot peppers as strong vapors can irritate your eyes. Thoroughly wash hands when handling hot peppers. Avoid contact with eyes for several hours.

PHANTOM FIRE

Ingredients

Makes Approx. 12 oz
Prep Time: 5 min

1/3c Ghost peppers (dried)
2x Medjool dates (pitted)
2x Carrots small (chopped or grated)
1/2c Pineapple fresh (chopped)
2x Lime juiced (fresh squeezed)
1x Lemon juiced (fresh squeezed)
2tsp Apple cider vinegar
1x Garlic clove (peeled)
1tsp Himalayan or Celtic sea salt

1. Soak ghost peppers in filtered water for 15 minutes. Drain and discard water. Blend all ingredients on high until mixed into a smooth thick sauce that is even in color.

   Note: Be cautious when blending hot peppers as strong vapors can irritate your eyes. Thoroughly wash hands when handling hot peppers. Avoid contact with eyes for several hours.

HABANERO HOTTIE

Ingredients

Makes Approx. 20 oz
Prep Time: 5 min

2c Habanero peppers (destemmed)
1x Carrot small (chopped)
1/4c Onion (chopped)
1/4c Sunflower oil (cold pressed)
1/4c Apple cider vinegar
1tbsp Coconut sugar crystals
1x Garlic clove (peeled)
1-1/2tsp Paprika
1tsp Himalayan or Celtic sea salt

1. Blend all ingredients on high until completely liquefied. The Habanero Hottie sauce has an appearance that is bright in color and thick in texture.

   Note: Be cautious when blending hot peppers as strong vapors can irritate your eyes. Thoroughly wash hands when handling hot peppers. Avoid contact with eyes for several hours.

CREAM CHEESE

CREAM CHEESE

Ingredients

Makes Approx. 20 oz
Prep Time: 5 min

1c Cashews (soaked 4 hrs.)
1c Macadamia nuts (soaked 2 hrs.)
3/4c Water (filtered)
1/2c Lemon juice (fresh squeezed)
1/2x Garlic clove (peeled)
1tsp Himalayan or Celtic sea salt

1. Blend all ingredients on high until a smooth and thick cream cheesy consistency is reached. Use tamper to frequently move ingredients around during the blending process. Spread on your favorite cracker, use on a wrap, or as veggie dip.

Note: A Vita Mix® brand or high speed blender is recommended for the best results.

For the best consistency serve dressing chilled.

GARDEN HERB SPREAD

Ingredients

Makes Approx. 8 oz
Prep Time: 5 min

1c Cream cheese (recipe on left)
1/4c Onion (minced)
2tsp Dill fresh (minced)
1/2tsp Oregano fresh (minced)
1/2tsp Rosemary fresh (minced)
1/2tsp Chives fresh (minced)

1. Remove leaves of herbs from their stems. Mince all herbs and onions in a food processor or by hand with a sharp knife.

2. Then, in a small mixing bowl fold all ingredients into cream cheese to make the Garden Herb Spread.

Note: For the best consistency serve dressing chilled.

If using dried herbs lessen the quantity to 1/3 of the amount listed above. For example, if the recipe calls for 1 tablespoon of fresh herbs, use 1 teaspoon of dried.

VEGGIE DIP

Ingredients

Makes Approx. 12 oz
Prep Time: 10 min

1c Cream Cheese (recipe on pg. 34)
2x Celery stalks (chopped small)
1x Carrot (chopped small)
2tbsp Parsley fresh (minced)
2tbsp Onion (minced) (optional)
1/4c Red Bell Pepper (chopped small)
1/2tsp Chives fresh (minced)
1-1/2 tsp Dill Sprigs fresh (minced)

1. In a food processor add pre-chopped celery and pulse until shredded into smaller pieces. Then separately process carrot in the same fashion. Next process onions and parsley. Then place shredded ingredients into a mixing bowl. Then stir in red bell pepper, chives, and dill.

2. In the mixing bowl stir in the cream cheese with all fresh ingredients. Mix well together to create the Veggie Dip.

SWEET CREAM

Ingredients

Makes Approx. 10 oz
Prep Time: 5 min

1c Cream cheese (recipe on pg. 34)
3tbsp Raisins (chopped)
3x Dates (chopped)
2tbsp Walnuts (chopped coarsely)
2tbsp Coconut sugar crystals

1. Chop raisins, dates, and walnuts into small pieces.

2. In a medium mixing bowl, fold all ingredients together to create the Sweet Cream Cheese.

   Note: For the best consistency serve dressing chilled.

SAVORY DRESSINGS

CRÈME LA BLANC

Ingredients

Makes Approx. 12 oz
Prep Time: 5 min

3/4c Cashews (soaked 4 hrs.)
1/4c Macadamia nuts (soaked 1 hr.)
3/4c Water (filtered)
1/2c Avocado oil (cold pressed)
1x Lemon juiced (fresh squeezed)
2tbsp Apple cider vinegar
1tsp Yellow mustard seeds
1tsp Brown mustard seeds
1tsp Himalayan or Celtic sea salt

1. Blend all ingredients until a thick and creamy consistency is reached.

   Note: A VitaMix® brand or high speed blender is recommended for the best results.

   For the best consistency serve dressing chilled.

CAESAR DRESSING

Ingredients

Makes Approx. 16 oz
Prep Time: 10 min

2/3c Cashews (soaked 4 hrs.)
1/2c Macadamia nuts (soaked 1 hr.)
1/2c Water (filtered)
1/3c Sesame oil (organic, cold pressed)
2x Lemons juiced (fresh squeezed)
1tbsp Dijon mustard (apple cider vinegar based)
1tsp Apple cider vinegar (unfiltered)
1/2tsp Himalayan salt
1/4tsp Onion powder

2x Garlic clove (peeled & minced)
1tsp Himalayan or Celtic sea salt
1/4tsp Paprika

1/4tsp Black peppercorn (fresh ground)

1. Combine into a blender: cashews, macadamias, water, sesame oil, lemon juice, dijon mustard, apple cider vinegar, salt, and onion powder. Blend on high into a creamy dressing consistency.

2. Use a mortar and pestle to mash the garlic and salt into a paste. Hand mix garlic paste, paprika and pepper into the creamy dressing base. Then serve Caesar Dressing onto a bed of freshly torn romaine lettuce.

   Note: A VitaMix® brand or high speed blender is recommended for the best results.

   For the best consistency serve dressing chilled.

NICOISE

Ingredients

Makes Approx. 8 oz
Prep Time: 5 min

1c Extra virgin olive oil (organic)
1x Lemon juiced (fresh squeezed)
3tbsp Dijon mustard (acv based)
1tsp Apple cider vinegar (unfiltered)
1/2tsp Himalayan or Celtic sea salt
1/4tsp Paprika
1/2tsp Garlic powder
1/4tsp Onion powder
1/4tsp Black peppercorn (ground)

1. Blend all ingredients together into a thick dressing consistency. The Nicoise Dressing is pronounced nee-swahz, but you don't have to speak French to love it!

Note: Apple cider vinegar based mustard can be found in your local health food store.

RADICAL RANCH

Ingredients

Makes Approx. 16 oz
Prep Time: 5 min

3/4c Cashews (soaked 6 hrs.)
3/4c Macadamia nuts (soaked 30 min.)
2x Lemons juiced (fresh squeezed)
2/3c Sesame oil (first cold pressed)
1/2c Water (filtered)
1x Garlic clove (peeled)
1tsp Yellow mustard seeds
1/2tsp Apple cider vinegar
1tsp Himalayan or Celtic sea salt
1/4c Italian parsley fresh, flat leaf (minced)
1tbsp Chives fresh (minced)
2tbsp Dill fresh (minced)
1tsp Onion powder
1/2tsp Paprika
1/4tsp Black peppercorn (fresh ground)

1. In a blender combine: cashews, macadamias, lemon juice, sesame oil, water, garlic, mustard seeds, apple cider vinegar, and salt. Blend into a thick creamy dressing.

2. Then, in medium size mixing bowl add: creamy dressing, Italian parsley, dill, chives, onion powder, paprika, and black pepper. Stir well together. Radical Ranch Dressing is primal.

Note: A VitaMix® brand or high speed blender is recommended for the best results.

For the best consistency serve dressing chilled.

BLEU CHEESE DRESSING

Method

1. Blend all ingredients thoroughly into a thick creamy dressing. In a stainless steel mixing bowl combine Bleu Cheese with creamy dressing and stir well.

   Note: A VitaMix® brand or high speed blender is recommended for the best results.

   For the best consistency serve dressing chilled.

BLEU CHEESE

Makes Approx. 1/2 cup
Prep Time: 5 min (plus dehydration time)

1/4c Macadamia nuts (soaked 30 min.)
3tbsp Pine nuts
2tbsp Cashews (soaked 4 hrs.)
2tbsp Water (filtered)
1tsp Apple cider vinegar (unfiltered)
1tsp Nutritional yeast flakes
3/4tsp Himalayan or Celtic sea salt

1/8tsp Spirulina

1. In a food processor combine all ingredients, except spirulina. Process into a thick batter.

2. Next, spread batter flat onto a non-stick dehydrator sheet approximately ¼ inch thick. Then sprinkle spirulina randomly over top of batter. Swirl in spirulina into surface of batter with a fork.

3. Then dehydrate for 8 hours on a non-stick sheet at 108 degrees. Flip onto dehydrator screen and dehydrate for another 3 hours. Next, break up cheese into large crumbles and place back onto an non-stick sheet. Dehydrate for 3 more hours until cheese is firm with minimal moisture.

Ingredients

Makes Approx. 12 oz
Prep Time: 10 min (plus dehydration time)

1/2c Blue Cheese (recipe on left)

1/2c Macadamia nuts (soaked 30 min.)
1/4c Cashews (soaked 4 hrs.)
3/4c Water (filtered)
1x Lemon juiced (fresh squeezed)
1/4c Extra virgin olive oil (organic)
1tsp Apple cider vinegar (unfiltered)
1tsp Himalayan or Celtic sea salt
1/8tsp Yellow mustard seeds
1/8tsp Black peppercorn (ground)

THOUSAND ISLAND DRESSING

Ingredients

Makes Approx. 16 oz
Prep Time: 15 min

1c Crème La Blanc (recipe on pg. 36)
1/2c Sweet relish (recipe on right)

1/4c Water (filtered)
3x Medjool dates (pitted & soaked 15 min.)
1/4c Roma tomato (chopped)
1/4c Sun dried tomatoes (soaked 30 min.)
1/4x Lemon juiced (fresh squeezed)
1/2x Garlic clove (peeled)
1tsp Coconut sugar crystals
1tsp Apple cider vinegar (unfiltered)
1tsp Maple syrup
1/2tsp Himalayan or Celtic sea salt
1/4tsp Paprika
1/4tsp Onion powder
1/4tsp Black peppercorn (ground)

Method

1. Combine in a blender: 1 cup of Crème La Blanc, water, date, tomato, sun dried tomatoes, lemon juice, garlic, coconut sugar, apple cider vinegar, maple syrup, salt, paprika, onion powder, and black peppercorn. Blend into a thick dressing. Appearance of dressing should be even in color.

2. Strain ½ cup of sweet relish from its liquid. Stir relish into 1 cup of dressing to create the Thousand Island Dressing.

Note: For the best consistency serve dressing chilled.

To extend shelf life only mix the amount of dressing and Sweet Relish that will be consumed within 3 days.

SWEET RELISH

Makes 12 oz
Prep Time: 5 min

1x Cucumber (minced)
1/2c Red bell pepper (minced)
1/2c Sweet onion (minced)
1/3c Coconut sugar
1/4c Apple cider vinegar
1tsp Celery seed
1/4tsp Brown mustard seed

1. Combine all ingredients into a jar. Seal with an airtight lid. Allow to pickle for 30 min or longer.

Note: Lasts in fridge for up to 10 days.

If available use a food processor to mince vegetables. Deseed cucumbers before mincing with a food processor.

HONEY MUSTARD

Ingredients

Makes Approx. 12 oz
Prep Time: 5 min

6x Honey dates (pitted & soaked)
3/4c Water (filtered)
1/3c Carrot (chopped)
1/4c Sunflower oil (cold pressed)
2tbsp Cashews (soaked 2 hrs.)
2tbsp Coconut sugar crystals
2tbsp Maple syrup
2tbsp Apple cider vinegar
1tsp Yellow mustard seed
1-1/2tsp Himalayan or Celtic sea salt
1/2tsp Paprika

1. Combine all ingredients into a blender.
   Blend into a thick creamy dressing. This
   Honey Mustard is taste bud gratification.

   Note: Pit and soak dates in filtered water
   for approximately 15 minutes. Drain and
   discard water.

   For the best consistency serve dressing
   chilled.

STRAWBERRY VINAIGRETTE

Ingredients

Makes Approx. 12 oz
Prep Time: 5 min

1/2c Strawberries
1/2c Sunflower oil (organic, first cold pressed)
1/4c Champagne vinegar
1x Orange juiced (fresh squeezed)
1/2tsp Rosemary fresh (minced)
1/4tsp Himalayan or Celtic sea salt
1/8tsp Black peppercorn (fresh ground)

1. Lightly purée ½ cup strawberries in a food processor. Keep
   texture slightly chunky.

2. In a stainless steel mixing bowl combine all ingredients.
   Whisk together rapidly until fully blended. Briskly whisk
   again before serving. Pour the Strawberry Vinaigrette over
   any of your favorite greens.

LEMON PEPPERCORN

Ingredients

Makes Approx. 16 oz
Prep Time: 5 min

1/2c Cashews (soaked 4 hrs.)
1/2c Macadamia nuts (soaked 2 hrs.)
3/4c Water (filtered)
1/2c Lemon juice (fresh squeezed)
1x Garlic clove
1/2tsp Black peppercorn
1tsp Himalayan or Celtic sea salt

1. Combine all ingredients into a blender. Blend on high into a creamy dressing.

   Note: For the best consistency serve dressing chilled.

TANGY TAHINI

Ingredients

Makes Approx. 18oz
Prep Time: 5 min

1/2c Lemon juice (fresh squeezed)
1/2c Tahini
1x Garlic (peeled)
2tbsp Extra virgin olive oil (organic)
1tsp Himalayan or Celtic sea salt
1/4tsp Black peppercorn (fresh ground)

1. Combine all ingredients into a blender. Blend on high into a creamy dressing.

   Note: For the best consistency serve dressing chilled.

Snacks

Fragments of Freedom

F reedom from the paper tearing, bag crumpling, too salty, super sugary pre-packaged snacks. Marvel at the joy of raw nuts and spices. Have chocolate covered bananas for dinner. Or let a kale chip explosion embolden the inner self to animate into full being. No longer hiding under the clutter of cellophane bags and cardboard boxes, the shelves are free for your own containers of wrapped goodies and treats. You could give these away as gifts or presents, but you will probably end up eating them all before you even finish tying the ribbon.

CRANBERRY PECAN & CHOCOLATE GOJI BISCOTTI

"Awake and move into your daily groove" - C

SWEET CREAM FRUIT CREPES

Method

1. Spread Sweet Cream Cheese onto crepes. In a medium size bowl carefully toss bananas, blueberries, and strawberries with maple syrup. Then spoon fruit mix onto cream filled crepes. Roll up, serve up, and love up!

CREPES

Makes Approx. 12
Prep Time: 10 min (plus dehydration time)

2c Thai coconut meat
1-1/3c Yellow squash (chopped)
1c Golden flaxseeds ground
1c Water (filtered)
2tbsp Maple syrup
2tbsp Coconut sugar crystals
1tsp Cinnamon powder
1tsp Vanilla extract (non-alcohol)
1tsp Himalayan or Celtic sea salt
Pinch Coriander ground

1. Blend all ingredients into a high speed blender.

2. Spread onto non-stick dehydrator sheets into 5 inch round shapes approximately ¼ inch thick. Dehydrate 6 to 8 hours at 120 degrees. Flip onto dehydrator screen. Dehydrate for another 2 to 4 hours at 108 degrees until texture is dry but soft.

Ingredients

Makes Approx. 12 crepes
Prep Time: 25 min (plus dehydration time)

6x Crepes (recipe below)
1c Sweet Cream Cheese (recipe below)

1x Banana (sliced)
6oz Blueberries
5x Strawberries (wedges)
2tbsp Maple syrup

SWEET CREAM CHEESE

Makes Approx. 12
Prep Time: 10 min (plus dehydration time)

1c Cream cheese (recipe below)

3tbsp Raisins (chopped)
3x Dates (chopped)
2tbsp Walnuts (chopped)
2tbsp Coconut sugar crystals

1. Chop dates, raisins, and walnuts. In a medium size mixing bowl fold all ingredients to create the Sweet Cream Cheese.

CREAM CHEESE

Makes Approx. 14 OZ
Prep Time: 5 min

1c Cashews (soaked 4 hrs.)
1c Macadamia nuts (soaked 2 hrs.)
3/4c Water (filtered)
1/2c Lemon juice (fresh squeezed)
1/2x Garlic clove (optional)
1tsp Himalayan or Celtic sea salt

1. Blend all ingredients into a smooth and thick cream cheese consistency. For the best consistency serve chilled.

Note: A VitaMix® brand or high speed blender is recommended for the best results.

CHOCOLATE FROZEN BANANAS

Ingredients

Makes Approx. 4 oz
Prep Time: 20 min (plus freeze time)

4x Bananas (frozen)
2c Chocolate Candy Shell (recipe below)

CHOCOLATE CANDY SHELL

Makes 12 oz
Prep Time: 15 min

1/3c Cacao butter
1/3c Cacao powder raw
1/4c Coconut oil (first cold press)
3/4c Coconut sugar
1tbsp Sunflower lecithin
Pinch Himalayan or Celtic sea salt
1/2tsp Vanilla extract (non-alcohol)

1. In a small sauce pan, melt cacao butter into a liquid using the lowest temperature setting. If available use the warming feature on stove top to slowly melt butter.

2. In a blender combine: melted cacao butter, cacao powder, coconut sugar, sunflower lecithin, salt, and vanilla extract. Blend together well to create a smooth chocolate mixture.

3. Pour chocolate sauce into a shallow dish or a small shallow baking pan. Allow sauce to cool for several minutes before dipping bananas.

Method

1. Remove peels from 4 ripe bananas. Cut bananas in half. Spear sliced end of the bananas with a popsicle stick. Then place in freezer for several hours until completely frozen.

2. Make Chocolate Candy Shell recipe and pour into a shallow dish or baking pan.

3. Dip frozen bananas into the chocolate mixture. Chocolate Frozen Bananas will be ready to eat once dipped into chocolate. Place all Chocolate Frozen Bananas onto natural parchment paper to prevent sticking. Immediately place in freezer. Keep frozen in a freezer-safe container to devour at a later time.

Note: Chopsticks can be used in place of popsicle sticks.

FLORIDA CRACKER & VEGGIE DIP

Method

1. In a food processor grind sunflower seeds and almonds into coarse granules. Then place into a large mixing bowl with flaxseeds and hempseeds. Next, grind carrots in food processor until chopped small and add to mixing bowl. Then add sun dried tomatoes and tomatoes to the food processor and pulse into a chunky consistency. Add onions, parsley, and oregano to tomato mixture and pulse. Then add to mixing bowl.

2. Then add all remaining ingredients into mixing bowl. Mix well together into a batter. Divide batter equally onto two non-stick sheets into a 12x12 inch square, ¼ inch thick. Dehydrate 10 to 12 hours at 115 degrees. Score the dough into 2x2 inch squares. Flip onto dehydrator screen and dehydrate for another 12 to 16 hours at 108 degrees until crunchy.

VEGGIE DIP

Makes Approx. 12 oz
Prep Time: 10 min

1c Cream Cheese (recipe on right)
2x Celery stalks (chopped small)
1x Carrot (chopped small)
2tbsp Parsley fresh (minced)
2tbsp Onion (minced) (optional)
1/4c Red Bell Pepper (chopped small)
1/2tsp Chives fresh (minced)
1-1/2 tsp Dill Sprigs fresh (minced)

1. In a food processor add pre-chopped celery and pulse until shredded into smaller pieces. Then separately process carrot in the same fashion. Next process onions and parsley. Then place shredded ingredients into a mixing bowl. Then stir in red bell pepper, chives, and dill.

2. In the mixing bowl stir in the cream cheese with all fresh ingredients. Mix well together to create the Veggie Dip.

Ingredients

Serves 6 - 12
Prep Time: 10 min (plus dehydration time)

1-1/4c Sunflower seeds (ground)
3/4c Almonds (coarsely ground)
1-1/4c Golden flaxseeds (whole)
1c Hempseeds (whole)
2x Carrots (chopped)
6x Sun dried tomatoes (soaked 20 min.)
1x Tomato (chopped)
3tbsp Onions (minced)
2tsp Parsley fresh (minced)
1/4tsp Oregano fresh
1x Lemon juiced (fresh squeezed)
1/2c Water (filtered)
2tbsp Coconut sugar crystals
1-1/2tsp Himalayan or Celtic sea salt
1/8tsp Dill (dried)
1/8tsp Thyme (dried)

CREAM CHEESE

Makes Approx. 14 OZ
Prep Time: 5 min

1c Cashews (soaked 4 hrs.)
1c Macadamia nuts (soaked 2 hrs.)
3/4c Water (filtered)
1/2c Lemon juice (fresh squeezed)
1/2x Garlic clove (optional)
1tsp Himalayan or Celtic sea salt

1. Blend all ingredients into a smooth and thick cream cheese consistency. For the best consistency serve chilled.

Note: A VitaMix® brand or high speed blender is recommended for the best results.

SOUTHERN RANCH TORTILLA CHIPS

Ingredients

Serves 4
Prep Time: 25 min (plus dehydration time)

3x Corn ears fresh
1x Lime juiced (fresh squeezed)
1x Yellow bell pepper
1/2c Golden flax seed (ground)
1/3c Hemp seed
1/4c Sunflower seeds (soaked 30 min.)
1/4c Yellow onion (diced)
1/2x Jalapeño pepper (minced)
1-1/2tsp Himalayan or Celtic sea salt
1/2tsp Black peppercorn (fresh ground)

Southern Ranch Chip Season Mix

2tsp Onion powder
2tsp Garlic powder
1tsp Paprika powder
1tsp Dill (dried)
1tsp Chives (dried)
1tsp Himalayan salt

Sour Cream & Onion Season Mix

2tbsp Onion (minced)
2tbsp Chives fresh (chopped)
1/2tsp Himalayan or Celtic sea salt
1/4tsp Garlic powder
1/4tsp Onion powder
1/4tsp White peppercorn (ground)

Method

1. In a blender add: corn, lime juice, bell pepper, flax seed, hemp seed, sunflower seed, onion, jalapeño pepper, salt, and black pepper. Blend on medium speed into a slightly chunky batter. Pour batter into equal parts onto two non-stick dehydrator sheets. Use an off-set rubber spatula to spread evenly into two 12x12 inch squares, ⅛ inch thick.

2. Combine all ingredients for the Southern Ranch Chip season mix in a spice shaker with an adjustable sifter (or one with large holes in the lid). Dust entire top of the formed batter with seasoning mix. Dehydrate 8 to 12 hours at 120 degrees.

3. Score the dehydrated squares into small triangle shaped chips. Then flip onto dehydrator screens and season other side of chips. Dehydrate for another 10 to 14 hours at 115 degrees or until crispy.

SOUR CREAM & ONION DIP

Makes Approx. 8 oz
Prep Time: 8 min

3/4c Macadamia nuts (soaked 30 min.)
1/4c Cashews (soaked 4 hrs.)
1/2c Avocado oil (first cold pressed)
1/2c Lemon juice (fresh squeezed)
1/4c Water (filtered)

1x Sour Cream & Onion Season Mix (on left)

1. In a VitaMix® brand or high speed blender, blend all ingredients above into a Sour Cream.

2. Then in a bowl stir in Sour Cream & Onion seasoning mix on the right. Mix well together with Sour Cream to make the Sour Cream & Onion Dip.

GO NUTS

CANDIED PECANS

Ingredients

Makes Approx. 2 cups
Prep Time: 5 min (plus dehydration time)

2c Pecans (soaked 2 hrs.)
1/4c Maple syrup
2tbsp Maple sugar
1/4tsp Cinnamon
1/8tsp Himalayan salt (fine ground)

1. Drain soaked pecans and discard water. Place nuts into a medium size mixing bowl. Stir in all other ingredients with pecans and mix well.

2. Lay nuts flat onto a non-stick dehydrator sheet. Dehydrate at 108 degrees for 18 to 24 hours. Remove from sheet and place onto dehydrator screen. Dehydrate for another 18 to 24 hours until dry, crunchy, and a candy shell forms on nuts.

Note: Convection ovens can be used at low temperatures for 10 to 15 minutes or until nuts are dry and crunchy.

SWEET WALNUTS

Ingredients

Makes Approx. 2 cups
Prep Time: 10 min (plus dehydration time)

2c Walnuts (soaked 30 min.)
5x Medjool dates (pitted & soaked 15 min.)
2tbsp Maple syrup
1/4c Water (filtered)
1tbsp Coconut sugar crystals or maple sugar
1/8tsp Himalayan salt (fine ground)

1. Drain soaked walnuts and discard water. Place nuts into a medium size mixing bowl.

2. In a blender add: dates, maple syrup, water, sugar, and salt. Blend on high into a smooth sauce. Then stir sauce with walnuts and mix well.

3. Lay nuts flat onto a non-stick dehydrator sheet. Dehydrate at 108 degrees for 18 to 24 hours. Remove from sheet and place onto dehydrator screen. Dehydrate for another 18 to 24 hours until dry and crunchy.

Note: Convection ovens can be used at low temperatures for 10 to 15 minutes or until nuts are dry and crunchy.

CAJUN CASHEWS

Ingredients

Makes Approx. 2 cups
Prep Time: 10 min (plus dehydration time)

2c Cashews (soaked 1 hr.)
3tbsp Maple syrup
1tsp Paprika
1tsp Himalayan salt (fine ground)
1/2tsp Onion powder
1/2tsp Garlic powder
1/4tsp White peppercorn (fine ground)
1/4tsp Cayenne pepper
1/8tsp Oregano (dried)
Pinch Thyme (dried)

1. Drain soaked cashews and discard water. In a mixing bowl whisk all other ingredients into a sauce. Place cashews into sauce and mix well until fully covered.

2. Lay nuts onto a non-stick dehydrator sheet. Dehydrate at 108 degrees for 18 to 24 hours. Flip onto dehydrator screen and dehydrate at 108 degrees for 18 to 24 hours or until dry and crunchy.

Note: Convection ovens can be used at low temperatures for 10 to 15 min or until nuts are dry and crunchy.

SPICY THAI ALMONDS

Ingredients

Makes Approx. 2 cups
Prep Time: 10 min (plus dehydration time)

2c Almonds (soaked 8 hrs.)
2tbsp Maple syrup
1tbsp Lime juice (fresh squeezed)
1tsp Cayenne pepper
1tsp Himalayan salt (fine ground)
1/8tsp Habanero pepper (powder)

1. Drain soaked almonds and discard water. Use a towel to pat nuts dry.

2. In a mixing bowl whisk all other ingredients into a sauce. Place almonds into sauce and mix well until fully covered.

3. Lay nuts onto a non-stick dehydrator sheet. Dehydrate at 108 degrees for 18 to 24 hours. Flip onto dehydrator screen and dehydrate at 108 degrees for 18 to 24 hours or until dry and crunchy.

Note: Convection ovens can be used at low temperatures for 10 to 15 min or until nuts are dry and crunchy.

HALE THE KALE

PLAIN JANE KALE

Ingredients

Makes Approx. 6 oz
Prep Time: 12 min (plus dehydration time)

1x Kale bunch
1/2x Lemon juiced (fresh squeezed)
2tbsp Extra virgin olive oil (organic)
1/2x Garlic clove (minced)
1/2tsp Himalayan salt

1. Wash kale thoroughly. Remove excess stem and cut into four inch lengths. Then toss into a large mixing bowl. Cover with lemon juice, olive oil, garlic, and salt. Mix well and massage gently together for 5 minutes until kale is entirely covered with dressing.

2. Place kale onto two dehydrator screens and dehydrate for 12 to 16 hours on 108 degrees until crispy. The kale should be a crispy chip-like consistency. These Plain Jane Kale Chips are extraordinary!

RANCHERO KALE

Ingredients

Makes Approx. 6 oz
Prep Time: 15 min (plus dehydration time)

1x Kale bunch
1/2c Cashews (soaked 6 hrs.)
1/4c Sunflower seeds (soaked 2 hrs.)
1/4c Macadamia nuts (soaked 1 hr.)
1x Lemon juiced (fresh squeezed)
1x Garlic clove (peeled)
1c Water (filtered)
2tbsp Extra virgin olive oil (organic)
1-1/2tsp Himalayan or Celtic sea salt
1/2tsp Parsley fresh (minced)
1/2tsp Chives (dried)
1/8tsp Onion powder (optional)
1/8tsp Paprika
1/8tsp Black peppercorns (fresh ground)
1/8tsp Yellow mustard seed (ground)
1/8tsp Dill (dried)

1. In a high-speed blender add: lemon juice, garlic, water, olive oil, salt, onion powder, paprika, black peppercorn, and mustard seed. Blend into a thick sauce.

2. Wash kale thoroughly and remove excess stem. Then cut into four inch lengths. Next, toss kale into a large mixing bowl with the sauce. Then add minced dill, parsley and chives and mix well. Place onto two non-stick sheets and dehydrate for 8 to 12 hours on 108 degrees. Flip onto dehydrator screen and dehydrate for another 6 to 10 hours into a crispy kale chip.

ZESTY KRUNCH KALE

Ingredients

Makes Approx. 6 oz
Prep Time: 15 min (plus dehydration time)

1x Kale bunch
1/2c Cashews (soaked 6 hrs.)
1/4c Macadamia nuts (soaked 1 hr.)
1/4c Sunflower seeds (soaked 2 hrs.)
1x Lemon juiced (fresh squeezed)
1/2x Garlic clove (peeled)
1-1/2tsp Himalayan or Celtic sea salt
1/8tsp Onion powder
1/4tsp Paprika
1/8tsp Cayenne pepper
Pinch Habanero pepper powder

1. In a high-speed blender add: nuts, sunflower seeds, lemon juice, garlic clove, salt, onion powder, paprika, cayenne, and habanero pepper. Blend into a thick sauce.

2. Wash kale thoroughly and remove excess stem. Then cut into four inch lengths. Next, toss kale into a large mixing bowl with the sauce. Mix well until fully covered. Place onto two non-stick sheets and dehydrate for 12 to 16 hours on 108 degrees. Flip onto dehydrator screen and dehydrate for another 8 to 12 hours until crispy. The kale should be a crispy chip-like consistency. Zesty Krunch Kale Chips are savory and satisfying. Hale to the kale!

CHEESEY KALE

Ingredients

Makes Approx. 6 oz
Prep Time: 15 min (plus dehydration time)

1x Kale bunch
1/2c Cashews (soaked 6 hrs.)
1/4c Macadamia nuts (soaked 1 hr.)
1/4c Sunflower seeds (soaked 2 hrs.)
1/4x Red bell pepper (chopped)
1x Lemon juiced (fresh squeezed)
1/2x Garlic clove (peeled)
1c Water (filtered)
1/4c Nutritional yeast flakes
1-1/2tsp Himalayan or Celtic sea salt
1/4tsp Paprika
1/8tsp Onion powder
1/8tsp Black peppercorns (ground)

1. In a high-speed blender add: nuts, sunflower seeds, red bell pepper, lemon juice, garlic, water, nutritional yeast flakes, salt, paprika, onion powder, and black pepper. Blend into a thick cheese sauce.

2. Wash kale thoroughly and remove excess stem. Then cut into four inch lengths. Next, toss kale into a large mixing bowl with the cheese sauce. Mix well until fully covered. Place onto two non-stick sheets and dehydrate for 12 to 16 hours on 108 degrees. Flip onto dehydrator screen and dehydrate for another 8 to 12 hours until crispy. The kale should be a crispy chip-like consistency. Cheesey Kale Chips are a perfect on-the-go snack!

HUMMUS & SUN CHIPS

Method

1. Slice all cucumbers, zucchini, and root vegetables into medallions. Arrange Sun Chips on a chip-and-dip platter and serve with Hummus as a party platter or appetizer.

HUMMUS

Makes Approx. 24 oz
Prep Time: 8 min

3/4c Sesame seeds
1c Water (filtered)
1-1/4c Cashews (soaked 6 hrs.)
1/4c Macadamia nuts (soaked 30 min.)
1/3c Lemon juice (fresh squeezed)
2tbsp Extra virgin olive oil (first cold pressed)
1x Garlic clove
1tsp Himalayan or Celtic sea salt

1tbsp Parsley (minced)
1/8tsp Paprika (garnish)

1. In a blender combine sesame seeds with ½ cup of filtered water. Blend until seeds breakdown into a chunky consistency.

2. Then add to blender: cashews, macadamia nuts, lemon juice, olive oil, garlic clove, salt, and remaining filtered water. Blend down into a thick Hummus dip. Top Hummus with minced parsley and paprika. A delicious dip with texture indistinguishable from the traditional version.

   Note: A VitaMix® brand or high speed blender is recommended for the best results. For the best consistency serve chilled.

Ingredients

Serves 2 - 4
Prep Time: 15 min

16oz Hummus (recipe below)

1/2x Cucumber (sliced medallions)
1/2x Zucchini (sliced medallions)
1/2x Daikon root (sliced medallions)
1/2x Chioggia beet (sliced medallions)

CUCUMBER SNACKER

Ingredients

Serves 2 - 4
Prep Time: 10 min

1/4c Sour Cream (recipe below)

1x Cucumber (slice thin)
1/4x Onion (sliced thin)
2tbsp Apple cider vinegar
2tbsp Coconut sugar crystals
1/4tsp Himalayan or Celtic sea salt
Pinch Paprika

SOUR CREAM

Makes Approx. 16 oz
Prep Time: 5 min

3/4c Macadamia nuts (soaked 30 min.)
1/4c Cashews (soaked 4 hrs.)
1/2c Avocado oil (first cold pressed)
1/2c Lemon juice (fresh squeezed)
1/4c Water (filtered)
1tsp Himalayan or Celtic sea salt

1. Soak cashews and macadamia nuts for the suggested amount of time in filtered water then drain. Blend nuts with remaining ingredients into a smooth Sour Cream texture.

   Note: A VitaMix® brand or high speed blender is recommended for the best results.

Method

1. Slice cucumber and onion thin. In a bowl add: Sour Cream, apple cider vinegar, coconut sugar, salt, and paprika. Whisk until the sugar crystals dissolve.

2. Marinate cucumbers and onions in sauce for 20 minutes.

Note: Best when served chilled.

CRANBERRY PECAN BISCOTTI

Method

1. Combine all ingredients in a KitchenAid® mixer or by hand in a stainless steel mixing bowl. Mix into a dough-like consistency.

2. Flatten out dough onto a cutting board using a rolling pin. Create two 12x12 inch squares, ½ inch thick. Then slice into bars 1½ inch wide by 4 inches long. Place bars onto dehydrator screens. Set dehydrator to 108 degrees and dehydrate for 8 to 12 hours or until crispy like a biscotti. Snack on these Cranberry Pecan Biscotti treats with a cup of Cranberry Pomegranate Tea.

Note: If you do not own a dehydrator keep bars refrigerated to maintain their taste and shape.

Ingredients

Makes Approx. 20 bars
Prep Time: 20 min (plus dehydration time)

2-1/2c Almond Flour (coarse)
2/3c Maple syrup
1/3c Coconut oil
1/2c Coconut flakes (dried)
1/4c Coconut sugar crystals
1/4c Pecans (coarsely chopped)
1tsp Vanilla extract (non-alcohol)
1/2c Cranberry (dried, chopped)
Pinch Himalayan salt

CRANBERRY POMEGRANATE TEA

Makes 16 oz
Steep Time: 3-4 min

2tsp Sencha green tea
1tbsp Cranberries (fresh)
1tbsp Pomegranites (dried)
2c Water (filtered, 160 degrees)

1. Use loose leaf tea in a traditional cast iron tea pot. Steep for 3 to 4 minutes and remove tea strainer. Drink with sheer pleasure one sip at a time.

CHOCOLATE GOJI BISCOTTI

Ingredients

Makes Approx. 20 bars
Prep Time: 20 min (plus dehydration time)

2-1/2c Almond Flour (coarse)
1/2c Maple syrup
1/2c Coconut flakes (dried)
1/2c Goji berries (dried)
1/3c Coconut oil
1/4c Coconut sugar crystals
1tsp Vanilla extract (non-alcohol)
1/4c Chocolate nibs
Pinch Himalayan salt

Method

1. Combine all ingredients in a KitchenAid® mixer or by hand in a stainless steel mixing bowl. Mix into a dough-like consistency.

2. Flatten out dough onto a cutting board using a rolling pin. Create two 12x12 inch squares, ½ inch thick. Then slice into bars 1½ inch wide by 4 inches long. Place bars onto dehydrator screens. Set dehydrator to 108 degrees and dehydrate for 8 to 12 hours or until crispy like a biscotti. Chocolate Goji Biscotti and Japanese Cherry Tea is a heavenly way to spend the afternoon.

Note: If you do not own a dehydrator keep bars refrigerated to maintain their taste and shape.

CHOCOLATE AND GOJI BERRY TEA

Makes 16 oz
Steep Time: 3-5 min

1tbsp Chocolate nibs
1tbsp Goji Berries
2c Water (filtered,160 degrees)

1. Place goji berries and chocolate nibs in a traditional ceramic tea pot. Cover with water and steep for 3-5 minutes. Remove tea strainer and drink with sheer pleasure one sip at a time.

TEA TIME

OOLONG

Ingredients

Makes 16 oz
Steep Time: 3-4 min

2c Water (filtered, boiled 190 degrees)
1tbsp Loose leaf oolong tea

1. Boil filtered water to about 190 degrees. Fill a yixing clay pot with 1 tablespoon of tea. Pour heated water over the tea leaves until the pot is filled. Let steep for 3 to 5 minutes. Remove tea strainer. Drink tea slowly. One sip at a time.

Note: For the best flavor of tea we recommend a high grade tea that is fair trade or organic. Use a timer to avoid over-steeping as it causes tea to become bitter.

GREEN

Ingredients

Makes 16 oz
Steep Time: 3-4 min

2c Water (filtered, boiled 180 degrees)
1tbsp Loose leaf Sencha

1. Boil filtered water to about 180 degrees. In a cast iron pot fill the tea strainer with 1 tablespoon of tea. Pour heated water over the tea leaves until the pot is filled. Let steep for 2 to 3 minutes. Remove tea strainer. Drink tea slowly. One sip at a time.

Note: For the best flavor of tea we recommend a high grade tea that is fair trade or organic. Use a timer to avoid over-steeping as it causes tea to become bitter.

WHITE

Ingredients

Makes 16 oz
Steep Time: 3-4 min

2c Water (filtered, boiled 180 degrees)
1tbsp Loose leaf white tea

1. Boil filtered water to about 180 degrees. In a cast iron pot fill the tea strainer with 1 tablespoon of tea. Pour heated water over the tea leaves until the pot is filled. Let steep for 2 to 3 minutes. Remove tea strainer. Drink tea slowly. One sip at a time.

Note: For the best flavor of tea we recommend a high grade tea that is fair trade or organic. Use a timer to avoid over-steeping as it causes tea to become bitter.

ROSE & CORIANDER

Ingredients

Makes 16 oz
Steep Time: 3-4 min

2c Water (filtered, boiled 205 degrees)
2tsp Rose Petals
2tsp Coriander seeds

1. Boil filtered water to about 205 degrees. In a ceramic pot fill the tea strainer with 1 tablespoon of tea. Pour heated water over the tea leaves until the pot is filled. Let steep for 5 to 7 minutes. Remove tea strainer. Drink tea slowly. One sip at a time.

Note: For the best flavor of tea we recommend a high grade tea or spice that is organic or fair trade. Use a timer to avoid over-steeping as it causes tea to become bitter.

Soup

Liquid Love

There is nothing that can replace the steaming warmth of a hot soup on a cold rainy night. When it comes to winter cuisine or rainy day provisions we like to affect the heart and warm our souls. Many of our soups are old family recipes passed down for generations. When you serve these time-honored meals, send gratitude to the praiseworthy mothers of your own families heritage and celebrate the abundance of mother earth. Love your hot steaming soups as they warm your heart, just as divine women do.

"Serenity and tranquility in every bowl." - T

MISO

MISO LIGHT

Ingredients

Serves 4
Prep Time: 10 min

2pcs **Wakame sea weed (soaked)**
4c **Water (filtered)**
1x **Green onion (chopped)**
2tbsp **White miso**

1. Seaweed prep: soak in warm water for 30 minutes. Remove rib from seaweed and cut into bite-size square pieces.

2. In a pot add 4 cups of water. Heat on high just before it reaches a full boil. Then add green onion and set heat to lowest warming temperature.

3. Remove 1 to 2 cups of the hot water and mix in a separate bowl with miso. Stir until miso is completely dissolved. Stir blended miso back into the pot.

4. Next add seaweed and let simmer for a few minutes. To keep soup hot, pot can be set on a warming burner until ready to serve. Sip this soup before you indulge in the next course . . . Sushi!

   Note: Avoid boiling miso soup to maintain living enzymes in the miso.

VEGETABLE MISO

Ingredients

Serves 4
Prep Time: 15 min

4c **Water (filtered)**
1x **Napa cabbage leaf**
1x **Bok choy leaf (chopped)**
1/2c **Celery stalks (sliced thin)**
1/4c **Sweet onion (sliced thin)**
Handful **Bean sprouts**
1tbsp **Brown barley miso**
1tbsp **Red miso**
1tsp **Dulse flakes**
Pinch **Ground black peppercorn**

1. In a pot add 4 cups of water. Heat until it reaches a boil. Then reduce heat to low and add all fresh vegetables. Allow to simmer for a few minutes.

2. Remove 1 to 2 cups of the hot water and mix in a separate bowl with miso. Stir until miso is completely dissolved. Stir blended miso back into the pot.

3. Then add dulse flakes and pepper. Rejoice as you absorb the goodness and experience miso happiness rise within you!

   Note: Avoid boiling miso soup to maintain living enzymes in the miso.

PAPAYA & POTATO MISO

Ingredients
Serves 4
Prep Time: 15 min

4c Water filtered
2c Green papaya (chopped)
1x Japanese potato small (diced)
1x Carrot (sliced thin)
1/4x Onion (sliced thin)
1/2c Bok choy (chopped)
2tbsp Arame seaweed (soaked)
2tbsp White miso

1. Arame seaweed prep: soak in warm water for 10 minutes.

2. In a pot add 4 cups of water. Heat until it reaches a boil. Then add green papaya and boil for about 15 minutes or until it is soft. Next, add potato and carrot and allow to boil for a few minutes. Then lower heat. Then add bok choy, onion, and seaweed. Allow to simmer on low for several minutes.

3. Remove 1 to 2 cups of the hot water and mix in a separate bowl with miso. Stir until miso is completely dissolved. Stir blended miso back into the pot. Serve hot! Savor as a light meal or as a starter before your next munchin' morsal.

Note: Avoid boiling miso soup to maintain living enzymes in the miso.

If Arame seaweed is not available use wakame.

THAI LEMONGRASS

Ingredients
Serves 4
Prep Time: 25 min

4c Veggie Broth (pg. 68)

3x Lemongrass stalks (chopped)
2x Red Thai chilies (whole)
1x Garlic clove (minced)
1tbsp Ginger (julienne)
1c Bok choy (chopped)
1tbsp Nama Shoyu
2tsp Coconut sugar crystals
4x Kaffir lime leaves
2x Kaffir limes juiced (fresh squeezed)
1/4c Cilantro leaves (chopped)
1/8c Basil leaves (chopped)

1. Set pot on medium-high heat and add Veggie Broth. Stir in lemongrass, chili, garlic and ginger. Let flavors meld for 5 minutes.

2. Stir in bok choy, nama shoyu, coconut sugar crystals, kaffir leaves and kaffir lime juice. Simmer and allow flavors to marry for 10 minutes.

3. Use a straining spoon to remove chopped lemongrass stalks from broth.

4. Use a ladle to spoon soup into a single serving soup bowl. Top with fresh basil and cilantro. Honor the intoxicating flavors of the east!

BROCCOLI & CHEDDAR SOUP

Method

1. Chop broccoli into small bite-size flowerets and set aside.

2. In a VitaMix® blender or heavy duty blender combine the following ingredients: cashews, macadamia nuts, red bell pepper, garlic, nutritional yeast flakes, water, salt, paprika, and black peppercorns. Blend evenly into a thick creamy soup. Continue to blend on high until the VitaMix® container feels warm to the touch.

3. Distribute broccoli evenly into two hefty soup bowls. Stir in warmed soup into broccoli filled bowls. Enjoy the creamy-cheesy taste filled with richness and love.

Note: Steam broccoli flowerets until bright green, if desired. Save stems of broccoli for Veggie Broth.

Ingredients

Serves 2
Prep Time: 10 min

2x Broccoli heads (chopped)

1c Cashews (soaked 4 hrs.)
1/4c Macadamia nuts (soaked 1 hr.)
1x Red bell pepper (chopped)
1x Garlic clove (peeled)
1/4c Nutritional yeast flakes
1c Water (filtered)
1/2tsp Himalayan or Celtic sea salt
1/8tsp Paprika powder
1/8tsp Black peppercorns

GREEN AND GOLD

The perfect alchemy.

Nature is perfect.
Cheese, glorious cheese (when it's vegan) makes everything scrumptious!

MAMA'S MUNGO SOUP

Method

1. Remove any foreign objects from mung beans. Wash beans in a large mixing bowl with ½ teaspoon of Himalayan salt and water. Then rinse again and drain.

2. In a large pot cook beans in 10 cups of filtered water. Bring to a boil then reduce to medium heat. Cover pot and cook beans for 45 minutes or until beans are soft.

3. Create spice mix with Himalayan salt, cumin, turmeric, coriander, paprika, black peppercorn, and cayenne powder. Place into a small bowl.

4. In a separate medium size pot, add 2 tablespoons of olive oil. On medium-low heat sauté garlic. Then stir in ginger and onions together with garlic until browned. Once the onions are soft and sweet, stir in spices and mix well. Then immediately add tomatoes and reduce heat. Allow to simmer until tomatoes cook into almost a saucy texture.

5. Then add beans and turn up heat to medium-high. Cook until beans are hot and married with the sautéed onions and tomatoes. More water can be added if a soupier consistency is desired.

6. In a soup bowl, serve Mama's Mungo Soup over a handful of fresh arugula and The Perfect Rice. It is super delicious with fresh squeezed calamondin juice. This Asian citrus, (also known as kalamansi) completes the Mama's Mungo dish. This ultimate vegan style Philippine cuisine is more than a soup; it's a meal!

Note: As an option mung beans can be sprouted before cooking. They can also can be purchased pre-sprouted. The benefits of sprouting increases nutritional value and also reduces starch levels.

Ingredients

Serves 6
Prep Time: 40 min

2c Mung beans
10c Water (filtered)
1x Arugula bunch
1x Roma tomato (chopped)
3x Garlic clove (minced)
1/2x Onion (sliced)
1/4tsp Ginger fresh (minced)
2tbsp Extra virgin olive oil (organic)
1-1/2tsp Himalayan or Celtic sea salt
1tsp Cumin powder
1/4tsp Turmeric powder
1/2tsp Coriander (ground)
1/2tsp Paprika
1/2tsp Black peppercorn (ground)
1/8tsp Cayenne pepper

6x Calamondin juice fresh (garnish)

THE PERFECT RICE

Serves 6
Prep Time: 35 min (plus cook time for broth)

1/3c Sweet brown rice
1/3c Red rice
1/3c Forbidden rice
2c Water

1. In a pot combine rice mix and water and bring to a boil. Then lower to medium heat. Allow rice to absorb liquid until reduced down just above the surface of rice. Then cover and simmer on low for 20 to 25 minutes until soft.

ADZUKI BEAN SOUP

Ingredients

Serves 4-6
Prep Time: 35 min

2c Adzuki beans (soaked 4 hrs.)
10c Water (filtered)
1c Onions (chopped)
1/2c Tomatoes (chopped)
1/2x Green bell pepper (chopped)
1x Poblano pepper (chopped)
1x Garlic clove (minced)
1x Jalapeño (chopped)
2tbsp Extra virgin olive oil (organic)
1tsp Himalayan or Celtic sea salt
1tsp Cumin powder
1/2tsp Onion powder
1/2tsp Black peppercorn (fresh ground)
1/4tsp Cayenne pepper
1/8tsp Coriander powder

Dollop Sour Cream (recipe below)

SOUR CREAM

Makes Approx. 16 oz
Prep Time: 5 min

3/4c Macadamia nuts (soaked 1 hr.)
1/4c Cashews (soaked 4 hrs.)
1/2c Avocado oil (cold pressed)
1/2c Lemon juice (fresh squeezed)
1/4c Water (filtered)
1tsp Himalayan or Celtic sea salt

1. Blend all ingredients until creamy and smooth.

Method

1. Soak 2 cups of adzuki beans in 10 cups of filtered water for approximately 4 hours. Then drain. In a pot add 8 cups of fresh water to slow cook beans until soft. This may take up to 4 hours. Remove pot from burner and set aside. Allow beans to remain in water they were cooked in.

2. Create Latin spice mix. In a small bowl combine following spices: salt, cumin, onion powder, black pepper, cayenne pepper, and coriander.

3. In a large pot heat 2 tablespoons of olive oil on medium-low heat. Sauté garlic first. Next add onions. Then add poblano, jalapeño, and bell peppers. Then add Latin spice mix. Immediately stir in chopped tomatoes. Next add cooked adzuki beans (with the water they were cooked in). Allow Adzuki Bean Soup to simmer on medium-high heat for 10 minutes. For the supreme Adzuki Bean Soup experience, add a dollop of Sour Cream and melt into comfort.

Note: As an option adzuki beans can be sprouted before cooking or purchased pre-sprouted.

GAZPACHO

TOMATO

Ingredients

Serves 2
Prep Time: 10 min

2x Tomatoes (diced)
3/4c Basil fresh
2tbsp Lemon juice (fresh squeezed)
2tbsp Extra virgin olive oil (organic)
1x Garlic clove (minced)

Dollop Sour Cream (recipe below)

1. In a food processor add tomatoes, basil, lemon juice, olive oil, and garlic. Lightly pulse to create a chunky texture but be careful not to purée. This fresh Tomato Gazpacho Soup is sensational topped with Sour Cream!

SOUR CREAM

Makes Approx. 16 oz
Prep Time: 5 min

3/4c Macadamia nuts (soaked 1 hr.)
1/4c Cashews (soaked 4 hrs.)
1/2c Avocado oil (cold pressed)
1/2c Lemon juice (fresh squeezed)
1/4c Water (filtered)
1tsp Himalayan or Celtic sea salt

1. Blend all ingredients until creamy and smooth.

WATERMELON

Ingredients

Serves 2
Prep Time: 10 min

2c Watermelon (chopped)
1/2c Tomatoes (diced)
1x Fennel sprig fresh (minced)
1/8tsp Coconut sugar crystals
4x Mint leaf sprigs

1. In a food processor lightly pulse tomatoes. Create a chunky texture but be careful not to purée. Then place into a large mixing bowl. In the food processor lightly pulse watermelon separately. Add watermelon with the processed tomatoes.

2. Next, stir in minced fennel and sugar. Mix well together. Then serve the Watermelon Gazpacho topped with mint leaves and enjoy with great enthusiasm.

Note: Dice the chopped watermelon smaller as an alternative to the use of a food processor.

BUTTERNUT SQUASH SOUP

Ingredients

Serves 4
Prep Time: 25 min

4c Butternut squash (chopped)
2c Almond Joy Milk (recipe below)
1/2tsp Ginger (minced)
2tsp Extra virgin olive oil (cold pressed)
1x Garlic clove (minced)
1/4x Onion (diced)
1/2tsp Himalayan or Celtic sea salt
1/2tsp Black peppercorn (fresh ground)
1/4tsp Cumin powder
1/8tsp Turmeric
1/8tsp Paprika
Pinch Coriander (ground)
Pinch Cayenne pepper

1x Sour Cream dollop (prev. pg.)

ALMOND JOY MILK

Makes 16 oz
Preparation Time: 5 min

1/4c Raw almond butter
2c 10c Water (filtered)

1. Blend until evenly mixed and liquid begins to froth.

Method

1. Cut butternut squash vertically down the middle (removing skin and seeds from squash is optional- be sure to scrub and wash skin well). Chop into medium size pieces. In a medium size pot bring 6 cups of water to a boil. Add 4 cups of chopped squash. Then lower to medium-high heat and cook until squash is soft. Drain water and remove squash from pot.

2. In a blender add: butternut squash, Almond Joy Milk and ginger into a blender. Blend on high until squash mixture is even in color.

4. Heat olive oil in a large pot on a medium-low temperature. Sauté minced garlic. Then add diced onions and stir until caramelized. Immediately mix salt, black peppercorn, cumin, turmeric, paprika, coriander, and cayenne powder. Add the seasoned sautéed garlic and onions to the squash mixture in blender container and blend until smooth.

3. Stir butternut squash mixture in pot over low-medium heat until evenly hot. Serve Butternut Squash Soup hot with the Colorful Quinoa (recipe on right) and a swirl of Sour Cream. May your heart and soul be warm from the very first bite to the last.

Note: VitaMix® brand blender is recommended for a raw version. Also cut garlic and onion amount in half. Blend using tamper to move ingredients until temperature is warm.

VEGGIE BROTH

Method

1. Place vegetables in a crock pot and add water. Set crock pot to high. Cook vegetables 6 to 8 hours or until soft.

2. Once cooked, separate the vegetables from the stock using a wire mesh strainer.

3. If desired the Veggie Broth can be thickened by blending a small portion of cooked veggies with broth. To create a thicker consistency, increase the ratio of vegetables to broth. If necessary strain remaining fiber from soup using a wire mesh strainer. Serve with The Perfect Rice.

Note: As an alternative make Veggie Broth in stock pot. On the stove top bring water to boil with vegetables. Then reduce heat to medium-low or simmer. Allow to cook for 2 to 4 hours or until vegetables are soft. Stir and occasionally check to make sure water levels do not evaporate.

Freeze unused broth in freezer safe container.

THE PERFECT RICE

Serves 6
Prep Time: 35 min (plus cook time for broth)

1/3c Sweet brown rice
1/3c Red rice
1/3c Forbidden rice
2c Water

1. In a pot combine rice mix and water and bring to a boil. Then lower to medium heat. Allow rice to absorb liquid until reduced down just above the surface of rice. Then cover and simmer on low for 20 to 25 minutes until soft.

Ingredients

Makes Approx. 3 quarts
Prep Time: 10 min (plus cook time)

3qt Water (filtered)
3x Celery stalks
2x Carrots
2x Swiss chard
2x Lacinato kale (dinosaur kale)
2x Garlic cloves (peeled, cut in half)
1x Broccoli stem
1/2x Onion (chopped)
1x Cauliflower stem
1/4x Cabbage (wedge with heart)
1/2inch Ginger fresh
1/2tsp Paprika
1/2tsp Black peppercorn (ground)
2tsp Himalayan or Celtic sea salt

HEARTY VEGGIE

Ingredients

Serves 6
Prep Time: 35 min (plus cook time for broth)

8c Veggie Broth (prev. pg.)

1/2x Green papaya (peeled, chopped)
1x Potato (chopped)
1/4x Green cabbage (sliced wedges)
2c Green beans
1x Chayote (peeled, chopped)
1/2x Sweet onion (chopped)
2x Garlic cloves (minced)
1/2inch Ginger (minced)
1/2x Lemon juiced (fresh squeezed)
1/2tsp Himalayan or Celtic sea salt

Method

1. Fill a stock pot, set to medium-high temperature, with Veggie Broth and papaya. Cook for ten minutes. Then add potatoes and cabbage. Cook until potatoes can be pierced with a fork without resistance.

2. Then add to pot: green beans, chayote, onions, garlic, ginger, lemon juice, and salt. Stir and allow to cook for another 5 to 10 minutes.

3. Serve in large soup bowls over The Perfect Rice . The Hearty Veggie Soup is our version of our mothers traditional soups, merged as one.

THE PERFECT RICE

Serves 6
Prep Time: 35 min (plus cook time for broth)

1/3c Sweet brown rice
1/3c Red rice
1/3c Forbidden rice
2c Water

1. In a pot combine rice mix and water and bring to a boil. Then lower to medium heat. Allow rice to absorb liquid until reduced down just above the surface of rice. Then cover and simmer on low for 20 to 25 minutes until soft.

Salad

The liberated plate

Salads deserve their own special place in the culinary world. They are vibrant, smart, and secretly sexy. Instead of showing everything up front, they conserve their appeal. They show off a little bit with the alluring light of their bright yellow tomatoes. The dashing red pepper compliments the sultry greens. The sensation of eating salad cannot be imagined in the mind. It must be explored every single bite. Taste the flavours melt together as the tongue moves and meanders around the dressing drenched kale.

The yogis say we will be strong, handsome figured, and well energized if we eat fresh foods. Salads are packed with protein. The dark greens, nut dressings, and seeds will have you outlasting even the greatest of athletes. Fresh chopped foods easily become a part of your daily life. You will discover a love that is both powerful and sweet. Be captivated by the salad.

AVOCADO CABBAGE CRUNCH

"Crunch and munch protein punch." - C

THE GREAT SALAD TRINITY

HERBAN SALAD

Method

1. Toss fresh salad mix together in a large salad bowl. Then add Herban Salad Dressing and mix well. Serve salad in bowls and drizzle with flax oil. Then sprinkle with nutritional yeast flakes, hemp seeds, and chia seeds. Serve it and luv it!

HERBAN SALAD DRESSING

Makes Approx. 4 oz
Prep Time: 5 min

1/2c Crème La Blanc (recipe on right)

1/2tsp Rosemary (minced)
1/2tsp Oregano (minced)
1/2tsp Parsley (minced)
1/4tsp Onion (granulated)

1. In a mixing bowl, combine all ingredients and mix well.

Ingredients

Serves 2
Prep Time: 15 min

1/2c Herban Salad Dressing (recipe on left)

5x Kale leaves (chopped)
3x Chard leaves (chopped)
1x Tomato (sliced half medallions)
1/2x Cucumber (sliced half medallions)
1/2x Onion (sliced thin)
1tbsp Flaxseed oil
1tsp Nutritional yeast flakes (garnish)
1tsp Hemp seeds (garnish)
1tsp Chia seeds (garnish)

CRÈME LA BLANC

Makes Approx. 16 oz
Prep Time: 5 min

3/4c Cashews (soaked 4 hrs.)
1/4c Macadamia nuts (soaked 30 min.)
1/2c Avocado oil (cold pressed)
3/4c Water (filtered)
1x Lemon juiced (fresh squeezed)
2tbsp Apple cider vinegar
1tsp Yellow mustard seeds
1tsp Brown mustard seeds
1tsp Himalayan or Celtic sea salt

1. Blend all ingredients thoroughly until thick and creamy.

   Note: A VitaMix® brand or high speed blender is recommended for the best results.

PUNJABI TWIST SALAD

Ingredients
Serves 2
Prep Time: 8 min

1/2c Punjabi Twist Dressing (recipe below)

5x Lacinato kale leaves (chopped)
3x Romaine leaves (chopped)
1x Tomato (sliced wedges)
1/2x Cucumber (sliced half medallions)
1/2x Sweet onion (sliced thin)
1/2x Lemon juiced (fresh squeezed)
2tsp Chia oil (garnish)
1/2tsp Chia seeds (garnish)
1/4c Cilantro (coarsely chopped, garnish)

1. Toss fresh salad mix together in a large salad bowl. Then add Punjabi Twist Dressing and mix well. Next, drizzle with fresh lemon juice and chia oil. Finally, top with chia seeds and cilantro. Do the Punjabi Twist!

THE PUNJABI TWIST DRESSING

Makes Approx. 4 oz
Prep Time: 5 min

1/2c Crème La Blanc (prev. pg.)

1/2tsp Cumin powder
1/8tsp Turmeric powder
1/8tsp Black peppercorn (fresh ground)
1/8tsp Cayenne pepper

1. In a mixing bowl, combine all ingredients and mix well.

ASIAN FUSION SALAD

Ingredients
Serves 2
Prep Time: 8 min

1/2c Asian Fusion Dressing (below)

8x Chinese cabbage leaves (shredded)
1/2x Daikon radish (matchsticked)
1x Tomato (sliced wedges)
2x Spring onions (sliced diagonally)
1/2x Onion (sliced thin)
1x Asian Pear (matchsticked)
1/2x Lime juiced (fresh squeezed)
1tbsp Black sesame oil (garnish)
1tsp Black sesame seeds (garnish)

1. Toss fresh salad mix together in a large salad bowl. Then add Asian Fusion Dressing and mix well. Next, drizzle with fresh lime juice and black sesame oil. Finally sprinkle with black sesame seeds. Enjoy!

ASIAN FUSION DRESSING

Makes Approx. 4 oz
Prep Time: 5 min

1/2c Crème La Blanc (prev. pg.)

1tbsp Nama shoyu
1/2tsp Red pepper flakes
1/8tsp Cayenne pepper

1. In a mixing bowl, combine all ingredients and mix well.

AVOCADO CABBAGE CRUNCH

Method

1. In a medium size stainless steel mixing bowl add: green cabbage, red cabbage, sweet onion, and spring onion.

2. Pour Sweet Coconut Vinaigrette over cabbage mix. Then add goji berries and toss evenly together to create the Cabbage Crunch mix.

3. Slice avocado vertically in half and remove pit and shell. Then, place each halved avocado on single serving dishes. Top each avocado generously with Cabbage Crunch mix. Serve garnished with chia seeds, salt and pepper to taste. Avocado Cabbage Crunch is a balanced food fit for a king.

SWEET COCONUT VINAIGRETTE

Makes Approx. 16 oz
Prep Time: 5 min

1/4c Avocado oil (first cold pressed)
1/4c Coconut vinegar
1tbsp Coconut sugar crystals
1/4tsp Celery seed
1/4tsp Himalayan or Celtic sea salt
1/4tsp Black peppercorn (ground)

1. In a mixing bowl, whisk all ingredients together. Mix together until blended into a saucy vinaigrette dressing.

   Note: Always whisk vinaigrette before serving.

Ingredients

Serves 4
Prep Time: 12 min

1/4x Green cabbage (shredded)
1/4x Red cabbage (shredded)
1/4x Vidalia sweet onion (sliced thin)
2x Green onions (sliced)
1/4c Goji berries

2x Haas avocados (halved & peeled)

1tsp Chia seeds (garnish)
Pinch Himalayan or Celtic sea salt
Pinch Black peppercorn (ground)

CAESAR SALAD

Ingredients

Serves 4
Prep Time: 10 min

1c Caesar Dressing (recipe on right)

2x Romaine lettuce heads
1/4x Onion sweet (sliced)
1/2pt Cherry tomatoes

1/4c Parmesan cheese (recipe below)

PARMESAN CHEESE

Makes Approx. 3 oz
Prep Time: 5 min

1/4c Macadamia nuts raw
2tbsp Pine nuts raw
1tsp Nutritional yeast flakes
1/4tsp Himalayan or Celtic sea salt

1. Grind macadamia nuts into uniform crumbles in a food processer. Remove and place into a small mixing bowl. Next, grind pine nuts into uniform crumbles in food processor and add to the macadamia nut crumbles.

2. Stir in Himalayan salt and nutritional yeast flakes into crumbles. Mix evenly.

Method

1. Hand tear romaine lettuce. Slice onions thin. Toss together in a salad bowl. Pour Caesar Dressing over the salad mix. Top with whole cherry tomatoes and Parmesan Cheese. Savor the Caesar Salad, an incidental creation still famous for its classic character and distinguished taste!

CAESAR DRESSING

Makes Approx. 16 oz
Prep Time: 10 min

2/3c Cashews (soaked 4 hrs.)
1/2c Macadamia nuts raw (soaked 30 min.)
1/2c Water (filtered)
1/3c Sesame oil
2x Lemons juiced (fresh squeezed)
1tbsp Dijon mustard (apple cider based)
1tsp Apple cider vinegar (unfiltered)
1/2tsp Himalayan salt
1/4tsp Onion powder
2x Garlic clove (minced)
1tsp Himalayan or Celtic sea salt
1/4tsp Paprika
1/4tsp Black peppercorn (fresh ground)

1. Combine into a blender: cashews, macadamias, water, sesame oil, lemon juice, dijon mustard, apple cider vinegar, salt, and onion powder. Blend on high into a creamy dressing consistency.

2. Use a mortar and pestle to mash the garlic and salt into a paste. Then mix garlic paste, paprika, and pepper into the creamy dressing base.

Note: For the best consistency serve dressing chilled.

BEAUTY IS IN THE EYE OF THE BEHOLDER

There is nothing ugly about an heirloom tomato. Imperfection is perfection!

HEIRLOOM TOMATO SALAD

Ingredients

Serves 4
Prep Time: 10 min

3oz Balsamic Vinaigrette (recipe on right)

1x Red heirloom tomato (sliced)
1x Yellow heirloom tomato (sliced)
1x Green heirloom tomato (sliced)
1/2pt Yellow pear tomato (half sliced)
1/2pt Cherry heirloom tomato (halved)
1x Rosemary sprig fresh (minced, garnish)

Method

1. Slice all large heirloom tomatoes and arrange on a large serving dish. Then place yellow pear and cherry heirlooms on same serving dish.

2. Whisk Balsamic Vinaigrette just before drizzling over sliced tomatoes. Sprinkle with minced rosemary. Explore and taste the history and tradition in every bite of Heirloom Tomato Salad.

BALSAMIC VINAIGRETTE

Makes Approx. 6 oz
Prep Time: 5 min

1/2c Extra virgin olive oil (first cold pressed)
1/4c Balsamic vinegar
1/2tsp Garlic clove (minced)
1tsp Dijon mustard (acv based)
1/4tsp Himalayan or Celtic sea salt
1/4tsp Black peppercorn (fresh ground)

DRAGON FRUIT SALAD

Method

1. Slice dragon fruit with skin. Peel Asian pear and dice. With a paring knife remove skin from orange and slice into wedges. Cut open pomegranate and remove edible seeds (arils) from shell. Peel pineapple and slice into half medallions.

2. In a bowl whisk lime and coconut sugar crystals.

3. On two salad plates arrange the fruit. Drizzle lightly with lime sauce and top with whole cherries for garnish. Dragon Fruit Salad is a sweet, smooth, and refreshing treat.

Ingredients

Serves 2
Prep Time: 15 min

1x Dragon fruit (sliced)
1x Asian pear (diced)
1x Orange (peeled, sliced wedges)
1/2c Pomegranate seeds
1/4c Pineapple (sliced)

1x Lime juiced (fresh squeezed)
1tbsp Coconut sugar crystals
2x Cherries

DRAGON FRUIT SALAD

"The quintessential fierce fruit salad." - C

KIM CHI

Method

1. Chop Chinese cabbage (Napa cabbage) and place into a large mixing bowl.

2. Grate carrots, julienne turnips and dice red bell pepper and place into a separate bowl from cabbage.

3. In a food processer grind peeled garlic clove and minced ginger with red pepper flakes to create a red paste. Then merge paste with carrots, turnips, red bell pepper and mix well.

4. Add red paste mixture into bowl with Chinese cabbage. Massage gently together for 5 minutes until cabbage is fully covered with red paste. Allow vegetables to sweat until a brine is created. If no brine appears after 10 minutes then gently massage again.

5. Sanitize jars by washing on the highest heat setting of dishwasher. This will ensure there is no contamination during fermentation process. Place Kim Chi into the clean glass jars with sealable lids. Leave a couple of inches of air space from the top of jar to the surface of brine. Then lightly cover jars without tightening lid.

6. Allow jars of Kim Chi to remain in a cool, dark space up to 3 days for the process of fermentation. Check once or twice a day until it has reached the taste you love. Then seal tightly and place jars into refrigerator. Get your Kim Chi flowing.

Ingredients

Makes Approx. 2 jars
Prep Time: 30 min (plus fermentation)

2x Chinese cabbage heads (chopped)
4x Carrots (chopped)
1x Turnip or daikon radish (julienne)
1x Red bell pepper (diced)
1/4c Chili pepper flakes(optional)
5x Garlic cloves (peeled)
1tbsp Ginger (minced)
3tbsp Himalayan or Celtic sea salt

Note: Fermentation times vary from state to state. In warm, humid regions usually 24 hours is the perfect amount of time. Cooler and drier climates may require a full 3 days for fermentation.

GREEN PAPAYA SALAD

Ingredients

Serves 2
Prep Time: 15 min

1/2x Green papaya (shredded long)
1x Daikon radish (spiralized)
3x Spring onions (sliced diagonally)
4x Chinese cabbage leaves (sliced)
1x Tomato (sliced wedges)
4x Cilantro sprigs fresh
1/2tsp Black sesame seeds (garnish)

GREEN PAPAYA DRESSING

Makes Approx. 4 oz
Prep Time: 5 min

2tbsp Coconut sugar crystals
2tbsp Sesame oil (first cold pressed)
2tbsp Lime juice (fresh squeezed)
2tbsp Nama shoyu

1. Whisk all ingredients together for dressing. Set aside for salad mix.

Method

1. Cut papaya down the middle lengthwise and deseed. Then slice into quarters. To keep papaya stable while peeling skin, place the flat cut-side down on chopping board. Use a mandoline to shred into thin strips. The Miracle Knife can also be used to cut into long strips.

2. Use a spiralizer or The Miracle Knife to create long noodles out of the daikon radish. Then add the following to a salad bowl: papaya, daikon, and green onions.

3. Then create the Green Papaya Dressing (recipe on left). Whisk together briskly. Then pour over salad and mix well.

4. Spoon one serving of salad mixture onto a bed of Chinese cabbage. Add tomato wedges and several sprigs of fresh cilantro. Sprinkle black sesame seeds on top of the Green Papaya Salad. Serve up and sanuk (sanuk is a common word used in Thailand for enjoy)!

Note: The other half of the papaya can be used in the Hearty Veggie Soup (see soups).

ALLIGTOR PEAR PICNIC SALAD

Method

1. Choose avocados that are firm and ripe, but not too soft. Peel and chop avocado into medium size cubes. Place into mixing bowl and squeeze fresh lemon juice over avocados.

2. Dice celery and onion. Mince dill. Add all chopped ingredients with cubed avocados and mix in Crème La Blanc. Stir lightly. Be careful not to mash the avocados. Sprinkle salt, black peppercorn, and paprika onto salad. Gently mix together.

3. Serve on a bed of hand torn romaine lettuce. Enjoy fresh raw goodness in the Alligator Pear Picnic Salad, our divergence of the all American potato salad.

   Note: Best when served chilled and consume within 1 day.

Ingredients

Serves 4
Prep Time: 15 min

1/4c Crème La Blanc (recipe below)

3x Haas avocados (chopped)
1/2x Lemon juiced (fresh squeezed)
3x Celery stalks (diced)
1/2c Onion (diced)
2tbsp Dill fresh (minced)
1/2tsp Himalayan or Celtic sea salt
1/8tsp Paprika
1/8tsp Black peppercorn (ground)
1x Romaine lettuce head

CRÈME LA BLANC

Makes Approx. 16 oz
Prep Time: 5 min

3/4c Cashews (soaked 4 hrs.)
1/4c Macadamia nuts (soaked 30 min.)
1/2c Avocado oil (cold pressed)
3/4c Water (filtered)
1x Lemon juiced (fresh squeezed)
2tbsp Apple cider vinegar
1tsp Yellow mustard seeds
1tsp Brown mustard seeds
1tsp Himalayan or Celtic sea salt

1. Blend all ingredients thoroughly until thick and creamy.

   Note: A VitaMix® brand or high speed blender is recommended for the best results.

ALLIGATOR PEAR PICNIC SALAD

"Tame and satisfy the most ferocious hunger." - C

BERRY BLEU CHEESE SALAD

"The perfect marriage." - C

BERRY BLEU CHEESE SALAD

Ingredients

Serves 4
Prep Time: 15 min (plus dehydration time)

1c **Bleu cheese Dressing (recipe on right)**

1x **Romaine lettuce head**
1/2pt **Blueberries fresh**

BLEU CHEESE

Makes Approx. 12 oz
Prep Time: 10 min

1/4c **Macadamia nuts (soaked 30 min.)**
2tbsp **Cashews (soaked 4 hrs.)**
3tbsp **Pine nuts**
2tbsp **Water (filtered)**
1tsp **Apple cider vinegar (unfiltered)**
3/4tsp **Himalayan or Celtic sea salt**
1tsp **Nutritional yeast flakes**
1/8tsp **Spirulina**

1. In a food processor combine all ingredients, except spirulina. Process into a thick batter.

2. Next, spread batter flat onto a non-stick dehydrator sheet approximately ¼ inch thick. Then sprinkle spirulina randomly over top of batter. Swirl in spirulina into surface of batter with a fork.

3. Then dehydrate for 8 hours on a non-stick sheet at 108 degrees. Flip onto dehydrator screen and dehydrate for another 3 hours. Next, break up cheese into large crumbles and place back onto an non-stick sheet. Dehydrate for 3 more hours until cheese is firm with minimal moisture.

Method

1. Pour Bleu Cheese Dressing over a bed of romaine lettuce. Top with whole fresh blueberries. Eat your Berry Bleu Cheese Salad and jump the blues.

BLEU CHEESE DRESSING

Makes Approx. 2 oz
Prep Time: 5 min (plus dehydration time)

1/4c **Bleu Cheese (recipe on left)**
1/2c **Macadamia nuts (soaked 30 min.)**
1/4c **Cashews (soaked 4 hrs.)**
1x **Lemon juiced (fresh squeezed)**
1/2c **Water (filtered)**
1/4c **Extra virgin olive oil (first cold pressed)**
1tsp **Apple cider vinegar**
3/4tsp **Himalayan or Celtic sea salt**
1/8tsp **Yellow mustard seeds**
1/8tsp **Black peppercorn (fresh ground)**

1. Blend all ingredients thoroughly into a thick creamy dressing. In a stainless steel mixing bowl combine Bleu Cheese with creamy dressing and stir well.

Note: A VitaMix® brand or high speed blender is recommended for the best results.

For the best consistency serve dressing chilled.

STRAWBERRY CHAMPAGNE SALAD

Method

1. Thoroughly wash arugula and remove roots and any organic debris. Spin in a salad spinner until completely free from water. Then place into a large salad bowl.

2. Then add all fresh ingredients to arugula salad and toss together. Next, generously cover salad with Strawberry Champagne Vinaigrette and mix well. Serve immediately. Increase your fiber and vitamin C and celebrate your berry existence.

STRAWBERRY CHAMPAGNE VINAIGRETTE

Makes Approx. 8 oz
Prep Time: 5 min

1/4c Strawberries fresh
1/2c Sunflower oil (organic first cold pressed)
1/4c Champagne vinegar
1x Orange juiced (fresh squeezed)
1/2tsp Rosemary fresh (minced)
1/4tsp Himalayan or Celtic sea salt
1/8tsp Black peppercorn (fresh ground)

1. Lightly purée ½ cup strawberries in a food processor. Keep texture slightly chunky.

2. In a stainless steel mixing bowl combine all ingredients. Whisk together rapidly until fully blended. Briskly whisk again before serving.

Ingredients

Serves 4
Prep Time: 15 min

1c Strawberry Champagne Vinaigrette (recipe on left)

1x Arugula bunch
1/2c Sunflower sprouts
1/2x Cucumber (sliced half medallions)
1/4c Sweet onion (sliced)
4x Strawberries (sliced)
1x Orange (peeled, sliced wedges)

SOUTHERN SLAW

Ingredients

Serves 4
Prep Time: 15 min

3/4c Crème La Blanc (recipe on right)
1/2x Cabbage green (shredded)
1/4x Cabbage red (shredded)
3x Celery stalks (diced)
1x Carrot (grated)
1/2x Onion sweet (diced)
2tbsp Parsley fresh (chop coarsely)
1/2c Thompson raisins
1/8tsp Himalayan or Celtic sea salt
1/8tsp Black peppercorn (ground)

Method

1. Shred cabbage and place into a large mixing bowl. Combine all fresh ingredients with cabbage and toss together.

2. Add Crème La Blanc, salt, and pepper with fresh ingredients and mix well. Before serving toss in raisins. Savor the Southern Slaw as a small meal or as a great side item with The Fat Burger recipe.

CRÈME LA BLANC

Makes Approx. 16 oz
Prep Time: 5 min

3/4c Cashews (soaked 4 hrs.)
1/4c Macadamia nuts (soaked 30 min.)
1/2c Avocado oil (cold pressed)
3/4c Water (filtered)
1x Lemon juiced (fresh squeezed)
2tbsp Apple cider vinegar
1tsp Yellow mustard seeds
1tsp Brown mustard seeds
1tsp Himalayan or Celtic sea salt

1. Blend all ingredients thoroughly until thick and creamy.

   Note: A VitaMix® brand or high speed blender is recommended for the best results.

Entrée

Annapoorna, the perfected food

The perfect meal is one that can be shared amongst many. This section offers an array of recipes that will twist and dance on the palate. These main course meals are complimentary when paired with a virgin cocktail, a delectable dessert, and of course, with utopian company.

Raw food entrees are not always the usual neat fork and plate food the west has grown accustomed to. These handheld scrumptious meals are messy, drippy, and heavenly. They are tiny slices of paradise. Every meal will take you across exotic seas to the islands of east Asia, to the charming hills of Italy, and to the all American backyard bar-b-que. These dishes have a history of making people so joyful, that at times they have mistaken this radiant energy with the full bliss of samadhi.

THE FAT BURGER

"All the right fat without the cholesterol." - C

WRAPPERS DELIGHT

HUMMUS WRAP

Method

1. Wash collard greens and remove excess stem. To assemble wrap, place Hummus down center of leaf. Top Hummus with fresh black pepper and Habanero Hottie sauce. Then add chopped romaine. Arrange tomato wedges, cucumbers, and sweet onion over lettuce. Finally, top with sliced olives. This Middle Eastern treat is true nourishment for your body and soul.

HUMMUS

Makes Approx. 16 oz
Prep Time: 8 min

3/4c Sesame seeds
1c Water (filtered)
1-1/4c Cashews (soaked 6 hrs.)
1/4c Macadamia nuts (soaked 30 min.)
1/3c Lemon juice (fresh squeezed)
2tbsp Extra virgin olive oil (first cold pressed)
1x Garlic clove
1tsp Himalayan or Celtic sea salt

1tbsp Parsley (minced)
1/8tsp Paprika (garnish)

1. In a blender combine sesame seeds with 1/2 cup of filtered water. Blend until seeds breakdown into a chunky consistency.

2. Then add to blender: cashews, macadamia nuts, lemon juice, olive oil, garlic clove, salt, and remaining filtered water. Blend down into a thick Hummus dip. Top Hummus with minced parsley and paprika. A delicious dip with texture indistinguishable from the traditional version.

Ingredients

Serves 4
Prep Time: 15 min

4x Collard greens
1c Hummus (recipe on left)
2tsp Habanero Hottie (recipe below)

Pinch Black peppercorn (ground)
2x Romaine lettuce leaves (chopped)
1x Tomato (sliced wedges)
1/2x Cucumber (sliced qtr. medallions)
1/4x Onion sweet (sliced)
8x Kalamata olives (pitted & sliced)

HABANERO HOTTIE

Makes Approx. 16 oz
Prep Time: 5 min

2c Habanero (destemmed)
2x Carrots small (chopped)
1/4c Onion (chopped)
1/4c Sesame oil
1/4c Apple cider vinegar (unfiltered)
2tsp Coconut sugar crystals
1-1/2tsp Paprika
1-1/2tsp Himalayan or Celtic sea salt
1/2tsp Garlic clove (peeled)

1. Blend all ingredients on high until completely liquefied. The Habanero Hottie sauce is bright in color and thick in texture.

ALL-AMERICAN WRAP

Ingredients
Serves 2
Prep Time: 8 min

2x Chard leaves
4tbsp Crème La Blanc (pg. 87)

2tbsp Yellow mustard (acv based)
1x Pickle (speared)
2x Romaine lettuce leaves (chopped)
1/2x Cucumber (sliced half medallions)
1/4x Onion (sliced)
1/4x Red bell pepper (sliced)
1x Tomato (sliced wedges)
Pinch Himalayan salt
Pinch Black peppercorn (fresh ground)
2tsp Hemp seeds (garnish)

1. Spread Crème La Blanc and yellow mustard down the middle rib of chard leaf. Add pickle, lettuce, cucumber, onion, red bell pepper, tomato. Top with Himalayan salt, black peppercorn, and hemp seeds. The All-American Wrap is a quick fix for hungry beings with little time.

   Note: ACV: apple cider vinegar

EGG SALAD WRAP

Ingredients
Serves 4
Prep Time: 20 min

4x Romaine leaves
4tbsp Crème La Blanc (pg. 87)

1x Avocado (peeled & diced)
1/2c Young Thai coconut (sliced)
4x Celery stalks (diced)
1/4c Red onion (diced)
1/2c Red bell pepper (diced)
2tbsp Parsley (minced)
2tbsp Yellow mustard (acv based)
1/2tsp Himalayan salt (ground)
1/8tsp Paprika
1/8tsp Black pepper (ground)

1. Open coconut and drain water into a glass (save water for another recipe or drink it). Spoon coconut meat from shell. Then slice meat into narrow strips.

2. Combine diced celery, red onion, bell pepper, and parsley into a medium mixing bowl. Stir in Crème La Blanc sauce, yellow mustard, salt, paprika, and black pepper. Mix thoroughly into veggies. Next, add avocado and coconut meat. Mix lightly together with veggies.

3. Place a generous scoop of Egg Salad on a romaine leaf. Fold the edges and enjoy!

WALNUT "CHICKEN" SALAD

"Pound-for-pound walnuts are equal in protein to chicken. Hands down walnuts are the true champ." -C

WALNUT "CHICKEN" SALAD

Ingredients

Serves 4
Prep Time: 20 min

3/4c Crème La Blanc (recipe on right)

1c Walnuts (chopped coarsely)
4x Celery stalks (diced)
3/4c Red bell pepper (diced)
1/4c Red onion (diced)
1x Carrot (grated)
1/4c Parsley fresh (minced)
1tbsp Dill fresh (minced)
1tbsp Chives fresh (minced)
1/4tsp Garlic powder
1/4tsp Himalayan or Celtic sea salt
1/8tsp Paprika
1/8tsp Black peppercorn (ground)

8x Green leaf lettuce (chopped)
1x Tomato (sliced wedges)
1/2x Red delicious apple (sliced)
1/4x Red onion (sliced)
1c Micro greens

Method

1. Coarsely chop walnuts and place into a medium size mixing bowl. Then add celery, bell pepper, onion, and carrot. Mix Crème La Blanc sauce evenly into walnuts and vegetables. Then stir in fresh herbs, garlic powder, salt, paprika, and black pepper into the mix.

2. Place a large scoop of Walnut Chicken Salad onto a bed of green leaf lettuce. Top with tomato, red apple, red onions, and micro greens. This dish will be eaten up with such gusto you'll rarely have any left over to refrigerate.

Note: For the best consistency serve salad chilled.

CRÈME LA BLANC

Makes Approx. 16 oz
Prep Time: 5 min

3/4c Cashews (soaked 4 hrs.)
1/4c Macadamia nuts (soaked 1 hr.)
1/2c Avocado oil (cold pressed)
3/4c Water (filtered)
1x Lemon juiced (fresh squeezed)
2tbsp Apple cider vinegar
1tsp Yellow mustard seeds
1tsp Brown mustard seeds
1tsp Himalayan or Celtic sea salt

1. Blend all ingredients until a thick and creamy consistency is reached.

Note: A Vita Mix® brand or high speed blender is recommended for the best results. For the best consistency serve dressing chilled.

MEXICAN BURRITO

Ingredients

Serves 4
Prep Time: 35 min

3/4c Walnut Meat (recipe below)
1c Guacamole (next pg.)
1/2c Pico De Gallo (recipe on right)
4tbsp Sour Cream (next pg.)
1/2tbsp Habanero Hottie (next pg.)

4x Collard greens
4x Romaine lettuce (chopped)
4x Cucumber (sliced half medallions)
1/4tsp Chia seeds (garnish)

WALNUT MEAT

Makes 1 cup
Prep Time: 5 min

1c Walnuts
1/2tsp Cumin powder
1/4tsp Chili powder
1/8tsp Coriander seed (ground)
2tbsp Nama Shoyu

1. In a food processor grind walnuts into small uniform size crumbles. Process ½ cup at a time to prevent turning nuts into a butter.

2. Place walnuts in a small bowl. Thoroughly mix in cumin, chili powder, and coriander. Then mix in nama shoyu. Then stir until nut crumbles become a little moist and meld together. Set aside as filler for burrito.

Method

1. Cut off excess stems of collards. Spoon Walnut Meat down the center rib of collard leaf. Then in the same fashion top with chopped romaine and sliced cucumbers.

2. Then, spoon on Guacamole, Pico De Gallo, Sour Cream and Habanero Hottie sauce. Sprinkle with chia seeds. Finally wrap into a burrito. Forgo the napkins and be moved by the fiesta of flavors on your tongue!

PICO DE GALLO

Makes Approx. 12 oz
Prep Time: 10 min

2x Tomatoes (diced)
1/4c Onions (diced)
1/2c Cilantro bunch fresh (coarsely chopped)
1x Jalapeño (minced)
1tsp Paprika
1/2tsp Himalayan or Celtic sea salt
1/4tsp Black peppercorn (fresh ground)

1. Dice tomatoes and onions. Coarsely chop cilantro and place into a mixing bowl. Then add minced jalapeño pepper. Next, mix in paprika, salt, and black pepper. Lightly pulse all ingredients in a food processor to meld the flavors into the Pico De Gallo.

Note: Maintain a thick and chunky sauce consistency.

Entrée

GUACAMOLE

Serves 4
Prep Time: 8 min

2x Haas avocados (chopped)
1/4c Cilantro (chopped coarsely)
1x Lime juiced (fresh squeezed)
1/4c Red onion (diced)
2x Green onions (sliced thin)
1x Serrano chili pepper (minced)
1x Garlic clove (minced)
1/2tsp Himalayan or Celtic sea salt (fine)
1/8tsp Black peppercorn (fresh ground)

1. Slice two ripe Haas avocados down the center and remove pit. Use a blunt knife to slice into medium sized cubes while in the shell. Then spoon out avocado meat and place into a mixing bowl. Mix and lightly mash together with a wooden spoon or fork. Immediately pour freshly squeezed lime juice onto mashed avocados to help preserve their freshness.

2. Combine cilantro, onion, garlic, and serrano pepper with mashed avocados. Top with salt and black pepper. Serve immediately or chill in refrigerator in a sealed container.

Note: If available, use a mortar & pestle to mash avocados.

HABANERO HOTTIE

Makes Approx. 16 oz
Prep Time: 6 min

2c Habanero (destemmed)
2x Carrots small (chopped or grated)
1/4c Onion (chopped)
1/4c Sesame oil
1/4c Apple cider vinegar (unfiltered)
2tsp Coconut sugar crystals
1/2tsp Garlic clove (peeled)
1-1/2tsp Paprika
1-1/2tsp Himalayan or Celtic sea salt

1. Blend all ingredients on high until completely liquefied into the Habanero Hottie sauce.

Note: Be cautious when blending hot peppers as strong vapors can irritate your eyes. Thoroughly wash hands when handling hot peppers. Avoid contact with eyes for several hours.

SOUR CREAM

Makes Approx. 16 oz
Prep Time: 5 min

3/4c Macadamia nuts (soaked 1 hr.)
1/4c Cashews (soaked 4 hrs.)
1/2c Avocado oil (cold pressed)
1/2c Lemon juice (fresh squeezed)
1/4c Water (filtered)
1tsp Himalayan or Celtic sea salt

1. Blend all ingredients into a smooth and creamy Sour Cream texture.

Note: A VitaMix® brand or high speed blender is recommended for the best results.

MAHA TACO SALAD

Method

1. In a large bowl toss: romaine, cucumber, tomato, and onion.

2. Add salad mixture into a single serving bowl. Then top with a scoop of Bean Dip. Then add avocado. Then pour Saucy Salsa Rojo and add a dollop of Sour Cream. Finally top with touch of Picante Sauce.

3. Use Southwest Ranch Tortilla Chips to dip into the Maha Taco Salad.

SPICY BEAN DIP

Makes Approx. 16 oz
Prep Time: 25 min (plus dehydration time)

3/4c Saucy Salsa Rojo (recipe on next pg.)

1/2c Sunflower seeds (soaked 2 hrs.)
1c Sun dried tomatoes (soaked 15 min.)
1/2c Water (filtered)
2x Green onions (chopped)
1x Jalapeño (minced)
2tbsp Extra virgin olive oil (first cold press)
1tbsp Barley red miso
2tsp Cumin powder
2tsp Chili powder
2tsp Coconut sugar crystals
1tsp Cayenne pepper
1tsp Himalayan or Celtic sea salt
1/2tsp Coriander
1/2tsp Garlic powder
1/8tsp Black peppercorn (fresh ground)
1c Cilantro fresh (coarsely chopped)

1. In a VitaMix® blend all ingredients, except for cilantro, into a thick dip. In a large mixing bowl stir fresh cilantro evenly into bean dip mix. Spread bean mixture onto a dehydrator sheet and dehydrate at 115 degrees for 6 hours. Flip the mixture and dehydrate for another 6 hours.

2. In a large stainless steel mixing bowl, stir ¾ cup Saucy Salsa Rojo with bean dip mixture. Mix together into a beautiful thick Spicy Bean Dip.

Ingredients

Serves 4
Prep Time: 35 min

16oz Spicy Bean Dip (recipe on left)
1c Saucy Salsa Rojo (next pg.)
1/4c Picante Sauce (recipe below)
1/4c Sour Cream (next pg.)
1batch S. Ranch Tortillas (next pg.)

6x Romaine lettuce leaves (chopped)
1x Tomato yellow (sliced)
1x Cucumber (sliced)
1/2x Onion (sliced)
1x Florida avocado (diced)
8x Cilantro sprigs fresh (garnish)

PICANTE SAUCE

Makes Approx. 16 oz
Prep Time: 10 min

1c Mexican chili peppers (dried)
1x Chipotle pepper
1/2c Tomato (chopped)
2x Medjool dates (pitted)
1x Garlic clove
1/2x Lemon juiced (fresh squeezed)
1tsp Apple cider vinegar (unfiltered)
1tsp Oregano fresh
1tsp Cumin powder
1/2tsp Himalayan or Celtic sea salt
1/8tsp Black peppercorn (fresh ground)

1. Soak Mexican chili peppers and chipotle peppers in water for 15 minutes. Drain and discard water. Blend all ingredients together on high until liquefied into a sauce.

Note: Be cautious when blending hot peppers as strong vapors can irritate your eyes. Thoroughly wash hands when handling hot peppers. Avoid contact with eyes for several hours.

SAUCY SALSA ROJO
Makes Approx. 24 oz
Prep Time: 10 min

3x Tomatoes (chopped)
1/2x Red bell pepper (diced)
1/2x Yellow bell pepper (diced)
1/4x Onion (diced)
1c Cilantro fresh (coarsely chopped)
1x Garlic clove (minced)
1x Jalapeño (minced)
1x Lime juiced (fresh squeezed)
1tbsp Extra virgin olive oil (organic)
1/2 tsp Red pepper flakes
1/4tsp Cumin powder
1/8tsp Coriander
1/8tsp Himalayan or Celtic sea salt
1/8tsp Paprika
1/8tsp Black peppercorn (fresh ground)
1/8tsp Cayenne pepper

1. In a large bowl place tomatoes, bell peppers, onion, cilantro, garlic, and jalapeños. Combine to create a chunky salsa mix. Then add lime juice and olive oil. Add the following spices to salsa: red pepper flakes, cumin, coriander, salt, paprika, black pepper, and cayenne. Mix well to create the Saucy Salsa Rojo.

Note: For a saucy consistency, lightly pulse a portion of the salsa in a food processor.

SOUR CREAM
Makes Approx. 16 oz
Prep Time: 5 min

3/4c Macadamia nuts (soaked 1 hr.)
1/4c Cashews (soaked 4 hrs.)
1/2c Avocado oil (cold pressed)
1/2c Lemon juice (fresh squeezed)
1/4c Water (filtered)
1tsp Himalayan or Celtic sea salt

1. Blend all ingredients until creamy and smooth.

SOUTHERN RANCH TORTILLA CHIPS
Serves 4
Prep Time: 25 min (plus dehydration time)

3x Corn ears fresh
1x Lime juiced (fresh squeezed)
1x Yellow bell pepper
1/2c Golden flax seeds (ground)
1/3c Hemp seeds
1/4c Sunflower seeds (soaked 1 hr.)
1/4c Yellow onion (diced)
1/2x Jalapeño pepper (minced)
1-1/2tsp Himalayan or Celtic sea salt
1/2tsp Black peppercorn (ground)

Southern Ranch Season Mix
2tsp Onion powder
1-1/2tsp Garlic powder
1tsp Paprika
1-1/2tsp Dill (dried)
1-1/2tsp Chives (dried)
1-1/2tsp Himalayan or Celtic sea salt

1. In a blender add: corn, lime juice, bell pepper, flax seed, hemp seed, sunflower seed, onion, jalapeño, salt, and black pepper. Blend on medium speed into a slightly chunky batter.

2. Pour batter into equal parts onto two non-stick dehydrator sheets. Use an off-set rubber spatula to spread evenly into two 12x12 inch squares approximately ⅛ inch thick.

3. In a spice shaker combine all ingredients for the Southern Ranch season mix. Use an adjustable spice shaker or one with large holes in the lid. Dust entire top of the formed batter with season mix. Dehydrate 8 to 12 hours at 120 degrees.

4. Score the dehydrated squares into small triangle shaped chips. Then flip onto dehydrator screens to season other side of chips. Dehydrate for another 10 to 14 hours at 115 degrees or until crispy.

PASTA PUTTANESCA

Method

1. Slice summer squash into long spaghetti-like strips using a spiralizer. Other kitchen tools like the miracle knife or mandolin can be used to create a similar noodle-like effect. Set aside noodles in a bowl and refrigerate until ready to use.

2. Deseed and dice tomatoes. Soak sun dried tomatoes and one date for 15 minutes. Drain and save water. In a food processor add: ½ cup of diced tomatoes, sun dried tomatoes, date, and lemon juice. Purée into a thick tomato paste with ¼ cup of the saved water.

3. Lightly pulse the remaining diced tomatoes in a food processer. Leave them slightly chunky. Then combine with tomato paste in a large bowl.

4. Stir the following into the tomato sauce: garlic, basil, rosemary, oregano, parsley, olive oil, salt, black pepper, red pepper flakes, capers, and olives. Mix well together to create the Puttanesca Sauce.

5. Generously spoon Puttanesca Sauce over a serving of noodles. Garnish with whole basil leaves. Pasta Puttanesca is the perfect accidental dish. Once you taste this raw version it will seem like it was always meant to be.

Note: To deseed tomatoes slice into quarters and remove seeds with a small spoon.

Zucchini can be used in combination with or in place of summer squash if desired.

Ingredients

Serves 4
Prep Time: 35 min

2x Summer squash (spiralized noodles)

2c Tomatoes (de-seeded & diced)
1/2c Sun dried tomatoes (soaked 15 min.)
1x Medjool date (soaked 15 min.)
1/4x Lemon (fresh squeezed)
1x Garlic clove (minced)
1tbsp Basil leaves (sliced thin)
1tsp Rosemary fresh (minced)
1tsp Oregano fresh (minced)
1tsp Italian parsley fresh (minced)
2tbsp Extra virgin olive oil
1/2tsp Himalayan or Celtic sea salt
1/2tsp Black pepper (fresh ground)
1/2tsp Red pepper flakes
2tbsp Capers
1/4c Kalamata olives (sliced)
1/4c Green olives (sliced)
1/4c Black olives (sliced)
4x Basil leaves (garnish)

PASTA PUTTANESCA

"This after-hours, full-of-life Italian dish has minimal ingredients and tons of flair." - C

SPINACH WALNUT TORTELLONI

Method

1. Slice whole cucumber into wide and thin strips using a mandolin or potato peeler.

2. Place a fresh spinach leaf onto one end of cucumber strip. Add a small disher scoop of Formaggio Bianca (white cheese) onto spinach leaf. Next a small scoop of Walnut Meat on top of cheese. Fold cucumber strips with filling into triangles. Generously top Spinach Walnut Tortelloni with Marinara Fresco and a sprinkle of Parmesan Cheese.

WALNUT MEAT

Makes 1 cup
Prep Time: 3 min

1c Walnuts
2tbsp Nama Shoyu
1/2tsp Cumin powder
1/4tsp Chili powder
1/8tsp Coriander ground

1. In a food processor grind walnuts into small uniform size crumbles.

2. Then mix in nama shoyu. Then stir until nut crumbles become a little moist and meld together. Set aside as filler for Spinach Walnut Tortelloni.

FORMAGGIO BIANCO

Makes Approx. 8 oz
Prep Time: 8 min

1/2c Macadamia nuts (soaked 30 min.)
1/2c Cashews (soaked 2 hrs.)
1/2c Water (filtered)
2tbsp Lemon juice (fresh squeezed)
1x Garlic clove (peeled)
1/2tsp Himalayan or Celtic sea salt
2tbsp Pine nuts
1tbsp Nutritional yeast flakes

1. In a blender add: macadamia nuts, cashews, water, lemon juice, garlic and salt. Blend into a creamy white cheese sauce.

2. Next, grind pine nuts with nutritional yeast flakes in a food processor. Process into small evenly sized granules. In a bowl stir granules into the cheesy white sauce. Allow to chill in refrigerator for 20 minutes until firm.

Ingredients

Serves 4
Prep Time: 15 min

2x Cucumbers (wide thin strips)
1/2c Spinach leaves fresh

1c Formaggio Bianco (on left)
1/2c Walnut Meat (on left)
2c Marinara Fresco (recipe below)
3oz Parmesan Cheese (next page)

MARINARA FRESCO

Makes Approx. 16 oz
Prep Time: 20 min

1/4c Sun dried tomatoes (soaked 15 min.)
1x Medjool date (soaked 15 min.)
1x Garlic clove (minced)
2tbsp Extra virgin olive oil (cold pressed)
1tsp Lemon juice (fresh squeezed)
1/2tsp Black peppercorn (fresh ground)
1/2tsp Himalayan or Celtic sea salt
Pinch Cayenne pepper

2c Roma tomatoes (de-seeded, diced)
1c Basil leaves (coarsely chopped)
1/4c Italian parsley fresh (coarsely chopped)
1/2tsp Oregano fresh (minced)
1/2tsp Rosemary fresh (minced)

1. Soak sun dried tomatoes and one date for 15 minutes. Drain and save water. In a food processor add: sun dried tomatoes, date, garlic, olive oil, lemon juice, black pepper, salt, and cayenne pepper. Purée into a thick tomato paste with 2 tablespoons of the saved water.

2. Then deseed and dice tomatoes. In a bowl combine tomatoes, tomato paste, and herbs. Mix well together into a savory marinara sauce.

Note: To deseed tomatoes slice into quarters and remove seeds with a small spoon.

PASTA EN BIANCO

Ingredients

Serves 4
Prep Time: 15 min

2x Summer Squash (spiralized)

1c Cashews (soaked 4 hrs.)
1/2c Macadamia nuts (soaked 30 min.)
2tbsp Pine nuts (soaked 2 hrs.)
1-1/4c Water (filtered)
1x Lemon juiced (fresh squeezed)
1x Garlic clove (peeled)
1-1/2tsp Himalayan or Celtic sea salt
1/4tsp Black peppercorn

1tbsp Oregano fresh (minced)
1tbsp Chives fresh (minced)
1-1/2tsp Rosemary fresh (minced)
1tsp Dill fresh (minced)

4x Italian parsley sprigs (garnish)
Pinch Red pepper flakes (garnish)

PARMESAN CHEESE

Makes Approx. 3 oz
Prep Time: 3 min

1/4c Macadamia nuts
2tbsp Pine nuts
1tsp Nutritional yeast flakes
1/4tsp Himalayan or Celtic sea salt

1. In a food processor first grind macadamia nuts. Process nuts into small uniform crumbles. Then place into a small mixing bowl. Next, grind pine nuts and combine with macadamia nut crumbles. Mix in nutritional yeast flakes and salt into the crumbles.

Method

1. Slice summer squash or zucchini into long spaghetti-like strips using a spiralizer. Other kitchen tools like the miracle knife or mandolin can be used to create a similar noodle-like effect. Set noodles aside in a bowl and refrigerate until ready to use.

2. In a blender add: cashews, macadamias, pine nuts, water, lemon juice, garlic, salt, and black peppercorn. Blend into smooth and creamy white sauce. Then blend herbs into the creamy white sauce.

3. Pour sauce onto noodles. Toss noodles until fully covered with white sauce.

4. Garnish a single serving with Italian parsley and red pepper flakes. Pasta En Bianco satisfies every desire for creamy Italian fare.

Note: For the sauce a Vita Mix® brand or high speed blender is recommended for the best results.

If using dried herbs lessen the quantity to 1/3 of the amount listed above. For example, if the recipe calls for 1 tablespoon of fresh herbs, use 1 teaspoon of dried.

FRESCO PIZZA FLATS

Method

1. Spread Formaggio Bianco generously over a single serving of Living Flatbread. Then spoon on Marinara Fresco.

2. Next, garnish with toppings and finish with Parmesan Cheese. The raw goodness of the Fresco Pizza Flats will feed you and will end the craving for pizza take-out forever.

FORMAGGIO BIANCO

Makes Approx. 8 oz
Prep Time: 8 min

1/2c Macadamia nuts (soaked 30 min.)
1/2c Cashews (soaked 2 hrs.)
1/2c Water (filtered)
2tbsp Lemon juice (fresh squeezed)
1x Garlic clove (peeled)
1/2tsp Himalayan or Celtic sea salt

2tbsp Pine nuts
1tbsp Nutritional yeast flakes

1. In a blender add: macadamia nuts, cashews, water, lemon juice, garlic and salt. Blend into a creamy white cheese sauce.

2. Next, grind pine nuts with nutritional yeast flakes in a food processor. Process into small evenly sized granules. In a bowl stir granules into the cheesy white sauce to create the Formaggio Bianco. Allow to chill in refrigerator for 20 minutes until firm for final assembly.

Ingredients

Serves 8
Prep Time: 30 min (plus dehydration)

8x Living Flatbread (next pg.)
1c Formaggio Bianco (recipe on left)
1c Marinara Fresco (next pg.)

Toppings

1/2x Green bell pepper (chopped)
1/2x Red bell pepper (chopped)
2tbsp Green olives (sliced)
1x Roma tomato (sliced thin)
1/4c Sweet onion (minced)
1tbsp Parsley (coarsely chopped)
1tsp Rosemary fresh (minced)

3oz Parmesan Cheese (below)

PARMESAN CHEESE

Makes Approx. 3 oz
Prep Time: 15 min

1/4c Macadamia nuts
2tbsp Pine nuts
1tsp Nutritional yeast flakes
1/4tsp Himalayan or Celtic sea salt

1. In a food processor first grind macadamia nuts. Process nuts into small uniform crumbles. Then place into a small mixing bowl. Next, grind pine nuts and combine with macadamia nut crumbles. Mix in nutritional yeast flakes and salt into the crumbles.

MARINARA FRESCO

Makes Approx. 16 oz
Prep Time: 10 min

1/4c Sun dried tomatoes (soaked 15 min.)
1x Medjool date (soaked 15 min.)
1x Garlic clove (minced)
2tbsp Extra virgin olive oil (cold pressed)
1tsp Lemon juice (fresh squeezed)
1/2tsp Black peppercorn (fresh ground)
1/2tsp Himalayan or Celtic sea salt
Pinch Cayenne pepper

2c Roma tomatoes (de-seeded, diced)
1c Basil leaves (coarsely chopped)
1/4c Italian parsley fresh (coarsely chopped)
1/2tsp Oregano fresh (minced)
1/2tsp Rosemary fresh (minced)

1. Soak sun dried tomatoes and one date for 15 minutes. Drain and save water. In a food processor add: sun dried tomatoes, date, garlic, olive oil, lemon juice, black pepper, salt, and cayenne pepper. Purée into a thick tomato paste with 2 tablespoons of the saved water.

2. Then deseed and dice tomatoes. In a bowl combine tomatoes, tomato paste, and herbs. Mix well together into a savory marinara sauce.

Note: To deseed tomatoes slice into quarters and remove seeds with a small spoon

LIVING FLATBREAD

Makes Approx. 12 pieces
Prep Time: 30 min (plus dehydration)

1-1/2c Sunflower seeds (soaked 30 min.)
1c Walnuts (soaked 15 min.)
1c Carrots (chopped)
3/4c Golden flax seed (ground)
1/2c Hemp seeds
4x Medjool dates (soaked 10 min.)
1/4c Onion (minced)
2tbsp Lemon juice (fresh squeezed)
2tbsp Maple syrup
1tsp Garlic clove (minced)
1/2x Jalapeño (minced)
1-1/2tsp Himalayan or Celtic sea salt
1tbsp Parsley (dried)
1tbsp Oregano (dried)
1/4tsp Thyme
1/4tsp Marjoram
1/2tsp Fennel seed (whole)
3/4tsp Garlic powder
2tbsp Nutritional yeast flakes
3/4tsp Onion powder
1tsp Coconut sugar crystals
1/2tsp White peppercorn (fresh ground)
1/8tsp Cayenne pepper
1-1/2c Water (filtered)

1. Soak nuts and seeds for the suggested amount of time. Drain and discard water.

2. In a VitaMix® blender process all ingredients into a thick doughy batter. Blend at medium to high speed. Continuously moving ingredients around with tamper.

3. Form dough into two 10 x 10 inch squares one inch thick. Place onto non-stick dehydrator sheets and dehydrate for 10 to 14 hours on 115 degrees. Flip onto dehydrator screens and dehydrate for another 4 to 6 hours on 115 degrees. Then cut into approximately 3x5 inch pieces. Then dehydrate for another 10 to 14 hours at 115 degrees until a crispy crust is created on both sides. Bread should be firm and hold their shape.

Note: To make the blending process easier, split ingredients into 2 equal parts before processing them.

PAD THAI

Method

1. Rinse kelp noodles with water then drain in a colander and set aside.

2. Slice summer squash and daikon radish into long fettuccini-like strips using a spiralizer. Other kitchen tools like the miracle knife or mandolin can be used to create a similar noodle-like effect.

3. Marinate mushrooms in tamari and lime juice for 15 minutes. Drain and discard marinade. As an option, dehydrate for 20 minutes at 108 degrees.

4. Slice bok choy, spring onion, carrot, and celery stalk diagonally. Slice orange bell pepper and red onion thin.

5. In a bowl toss noodles, fresh vegetables and mushrooms together. Then stir in Almond Sauce (recipe below) and lime juice and combine well. Top with basil and almond slivers. Drizzle Hot Black Sesame Oil over the Pad Thai noodles for a little added spice.

ALMOND SAUCE

Makes Approx. 16 oz
Prep Time: 5 min

1/2c Almonds (soaked 6 hrs.)
1/2c Cashews (soaked 2 hrs.)
1/4c Extra virgin olive oil (cold pressed)
3/4c Water (filtered)
4x Medjool dates (soaked 10 min.)
1tbsp Tamari sauce
1-1/2tsp Himalayan or Celtic sea salt
1/2tsp Red pepper flakes
1/8tsp Cayenne pepper

1. Blend all ingredients on high into a thick and creamy sauce. Set sauce aside for Pad Thai noodle dish.

Ingredients

Serves 4
Prep Time: 30 min

1x Kelp noodles (12 oz. package)
2c Summer Squash (spiralized)
1-1/2c Daikon (spiralized)

2c Crimini mushrooms (sliced)
1/4c Tamari sauce
2x Limes juiced (fresh squeezed)
2tbsp Extra virgin olive oil (cold pressed)

2x Bok choy leaves (sliced diagonally)
2x Spring onions (sliced diagonally)
1x Carrot (sliced diagonally)
1x Celery stalk (sliced diagonally)
1/2c Orange bell pepper (sliced thin)
1/4c Red onion (sliced thin)

1x Lime (sliced wedges, garnish)
4x Basil leaves (garnish)
1/2c Almond slivers (garnish)

1c Almond Sauce (recipe on left)
1/4c Hot Black Sesame Oil (below)

HOT BLACK SESAME OIL

Makes Approx. 1/4 c
Prep Time: 3 min

1/4c Black sesame oil
1/4tsp Cayenne pepper
1/4tsp Red pepper flakes
1/4tsp Paprika
1/8tsp Himalayan salt

1. In a small mixing bowl whisk all ingredients briskly. Drizzle over the Pad Thai dish for a spicy topping.

PAD THAI

"A remarkable raw rendition of a popular dish in Asian cuisine." - C

MINDANAO NOODLE DISH

"An elegant dish inspired from the Island paradise of home." - C

The Mindanao noodle dish is our version of a time-honored family meal. This dish is also known as pancit (pahn-seet). In our version we use kelp noodles and summer squash noodles in place of the traditional glass and egg noodles. In addition, we swap the fish sauce out with nama shoyu. Instead of chicken and shrimp, we use vibrant vegetables. The colors of red, gold, and green add to the lively-ness of this Filipino dish. Feel comfort and feel at home. Love to Mom. - C.

MINDANAO NOODLE DISH

Ingredients

Serves 4
Prep Time: 35 min

1x Kelp noodles (12 oz. package)
2x Summer squash (spiralized)

2x Bok choy stalks (sliced diagonally)
1/2x Yellow bell pepper (sliced)
1/2x Red bell pepper (sliced)
1/2c Red onion (sliced)

1x Garlic clove (minced)
1tsp Ginger (minced)
1x Lime juiced (fresh squeezed)
1/3c Sesame oil
1/4c Nama shoyu
1/2tsp Coconut sugar crystals
1/2tsp Black pepper (fresh ground)
1/4tsp Cumin powder
1/8tsp Himalayan or Celtic sea salt
Pinch Turmeric powder

1tsp Chili pepper flakes (garnish)
1/4c Cilantro (garnish)

Method

1. Rinse kelp noodles with filtered water then drain in a colander and set aside. Slice summer squash into long noodle-like strips using a spiralizer. Other kitchen tools like the miracle knife or mandolin can be used to create a similar noodle-like effect.

2. Then add noodles into a large bowl and mix noodles together evenly. Mixing the noodles evenly can be accomplished by using two forks. Draw the noodles upward little by little until kelp noodles and squash noodles are completely intertwined.

3. Use entire bok choy (with leaves) and chop diagonally. Slice onion and bell pepper. Then place into a large bowl.

4. In a blender add: garlic, ginger, lime juice, sesame oil, nama shoyu, coconut sugar, black pepper, cumin, salt, and turmeric. Blend well into a thick sauce. Then stir chilli pepper flakes into the sauce.

5. Stir sauce into veggies. Allow to marinate 10 minutes. Gently toss marinated veggies evenly into the noodles to create the Mindanao Noodle Dish. If desired add a few more dashes of nama shoyu and top with fresh cilantro. This garnish will add to your appreciation for this raw-inspired Philippine Island cuisine.

Note: Zucchini can be used in combination with or in place of summer squash if desired.

RAINBOW SUMMER ROLL

Method

1. Spiralize daikon radish and summer squash into long noodle-like strips. Other kitchen tools like the miracle knife or mandolin can be used to create a similar noodle-like effect.

2. In a large bowl mix: daikon radish, summer squash, onion, lime juice, salt, and pepper. Then combine evenly into a noodle mix. Mixing the noodles evenly can be accomplished by using two forks. Draw the noodles upward little by little until daikon noodles, squash noodles, and onions are completely intertwined.

3. Cut excess stems from rainbow chard. Spoon ½ cup of noodle mix onto the center of each chard leaf. Top with a few sprigs of cilantro and basil leaves. Then roll into a firm summer roll. Then pierce with toothpicks to hold roll in place. Slice diagonally in center and garnish with sesame seeds.

4. Deliver this Asian plate drizzled with Almond Sauce and Spicy Chili Garlic Sauce. Find joy at the end of the Rainbow Summer Roll!

SPICY CHILI GARLIC SAUCE

Makes 4 oz
Prep Time: 8 min

1/4c Black sesame oil (first cold press)
1/4c Water (filtered)
3x Medjool dates (soaked 10 min.)
1tbsp Apple cider vinegar
3/4tsp Himalayan salt
3/4tsp Paprika
1/2tsp Cayenne pepper

2tbsp Red pepper flakes
1x Garlic clove (minced)

1. In a blender add: black sesame oil, water, dates, apple cider vinegar, salt, paprika, and cayenne pepper. Then blend into a thick sauce.

2. Pour sauce into a small jar. Then stir red pepper flakes and minced garlic into sauce. Use the Spicy Chili Garlic Sauce sparingly to give your meals a little kick.

Note: Store and refrigerate in a sealed jar.

Ingredients

Makes 4 rolls
Prep Time: 10 min

4x Rainbow chard (whole leaf)

2c Daikon radish (spiralized)
1c Summer squash (spiralized)
1/4x Onion (sliced)
1/4x Lime juiced (fresh squeezed)
1/4tsp Himalayan or Celtic sea salt
1/8tsp Black peppercorn (fresh ground)
8x Cilantro sprigs fresh
8x Basil leaves fresh
1/8tsp Black sesame seeds

2oz Spicy Chili Garlic Sauce (recipe on left)
4oz Almond Sauce (recipe below)

ALMOND SAUCE

Makes Approx. 16 oz
Prep Time: 5 min

1/2c Almonds whole (soaked 6 hrs.)
1/2c Cashews (soaked 2 hrs.)
1/4c Extra virgin olive oil
3/4c Water (filtered)
4x Medjool dates (soaked 10 min.)
1tbsp Tamari sauce
1/2tsp Himalayan or Celtic sea salt
1/2tsp Red pepper flakes
1/8tsp Cayenne pepper

1/2c Almond slivers (chopped)

1. In a blender add: whole almonds, cashews, olive oil, water, dates, tamari, red pepper flakes, and cayenne pepper. Blend on high into a smooth sauce.

2. Pour sauce into a small mixing bowl. Then fold coarsely chopped almond slivers into sauce.

Note: Store and refrigerate in a sealed jar.

ENLIGHTENMENT

Awaken the soul from slumber.

Calvin was a lot more adventurous with Asian food than I. When we went out for our first Asian meal, he was shocked to see I picked the driest items on the menu. White rice and salad. He discovered quickly I wasn't keen on the oily, salty, fried Americanized version of Asian food. So, he reintroduced Asian cuisine to me in our kitchen. This is where I discovered wasabi, nut sauce, fresh bean sprouts, basil, and cilantro. Also, some of my favorite savory Asian sauces like Spicy Chili Garlic Sauce and Almond Sauce. These authentic sauces pair fantastically with fresh Asian rolls, sushi, wraps, noodles, and salads too. - T

FRESH SPRING ROLL

"This mouth-watering wrap is as fresh as spring." - C

FRESH SPRING ROLL

Ingredients

Makes 4 rolls
Prep Time: 10 min

4x Collard greens (whole leaf)

2c Cabbage green (shredded)
1c Daikon radish (spiralized)
1x Carrot (spiralized)
1/4x Onion (sliced thin)
1/2x Lime juiced (fresh squeezed)
2tsp Black sesame oil (cold pressed)
1/4tsp Himalayan or Celtic sea salt
1/8tsp Black pepper (fresh ground)

1/8tsp Black sesame seeds

2oz Spicy Chili Garlic Sauce (prev. recipe)
4oz Almond Sauce (prev. recipe)

Method

1. Shred 2 cups of green cabbage. Spiralize daikon radish and carrots into long noodle-like strips. Other kitchen tools like the Miracle Knife or mandolin can be used to create a similar noodle-like effect.

2. In a large mixing bowl add: cabbage, daikon, carrots, onions, lime juice, black sesame oil, salt, and black pepper. Toss evenly together into a noodle mix.

3. Next, strain noodle mix of liquid in a colander. Then remove excess stems from collard leaves. Spoon ½ cup of noodle mix onto the center of each collard. Roll tightly into a spring roll. Then pierce with toothpicks to hold roll in place. Slice diagonally in center and garnish with sesame seeds.

4. Enjoy the Spring Roll with Almond Sauce and Spicy Chili Garlic Sauce. Drift into a tropical jungle of flavor.

Note: If black sesame oil is not available then substitute with regular sesame oil.

THE FAT BURGER

Method

1. Soak nuts and seeds in water for the suggested amount of time. Then drain and discard water. Mix nuts and seeds in a medium size bowl. Use a food processer to grind mixed nuts and seeds into small crumbles. For ease grind ½ cup at a time. Add small portions of minced garlic and ginger to nuts and seeds during the grinding process. For a doughier consistency use the Champion or Omega® juicer with the blank plate feature.

2. Next, combine diced crimini mushrooms into a small bowl with 1/4 cup nama shoyu and 1 tablespoon of olive oil. Soak mushrooms in marinade for 15 minutes. Discard liquid and set aside for next step.

4. Then combine processed nuts with the following ingredients: mushrooms, beet, carrot, bell pepper, onion, olive oil, parsley, rosemary, oregano, black pepper, and salt. Mix together in a large bowl. For an easier mixing method use a Kitchen Aid® mixer to evenly meld into a dough.

5. Form dough into 4 inch round patties ¾ inch thick. Place onto a dehydrator screen and dehydrate for 4 to 6 hours at 120 degrees. Flip burgers and dehydrate for another 8 to 12 hours at 115 degrees until patties turn darker brown in color. Burgers should be soft and moist on the inside.

6. Assemble The Fat Burger starting with a cabbage leaf, a lettuce leaf, then the burger patty. Spread the Special Sauce on the patty and top with Real Mayo. Then top with onion, tomato, and sliced pickle. Soak up some sun while you devour this backyard style grilling grub.

Note: Store burgers in a sealed container and refrigerate. Consume within 3 days .

Ingredients

Makes Approx. 12 burgers
Prep Time: 40 min (plus dehydration)

1c Walnuts (soaked 15 min.)
1c Almonds (soaked 8 hrs.)
1c Sunflower seeds (soaked 2 hr.)
1x Garlic clove (minced)
1tbsp Ginger (minced)
1c Crimini mushrooms (diced)
1/4c Nama Shoyu
1tbsp Extra virgin olive oil (organic)

1c Beet (grated)
1c Carrot (grated)
1/2x Green bell pepper (chopped)
1/2x Red bell pepper (chopped)
1/2c Onion (minced)
2tbsp Extra virgin olive oil (organic)
1/4c Parsley (coarsely chopped)
1tsp Rosemary fresh (minced)
1/4tsp Oregano fresh (minced)
1/4tsp Black peppercorn (ground)
1/2tsp Himalayan or Celtic sea salt

8x Cabbage leaves (wrap)
1x Iceberg lettuce head (whole leaves)
2x Tomatoes (sliced)
1x Onion (sliced)
1x Pickle (sliced)

1/2c Special Sauce (recipe on next pg.)
1/4c Real Mayo (recipe on next pg.)

Entrée

SPECIAL SAUCE

Makes Approx. 12 oz
Prep Time: 5 min

1c Real Mayo (recipe on right)
1/2c Sweet Relish (recipe on right)

1/4c Water (filtered)
1x Medjool date (pitted & soaked 15 min.)
1/2x Roma tomato (chopped)
1/4c Sun dried tomatoes (soaked 30 min.)
1/4x Lemon juiced (fresh squeezed)
1/2x Garlic clove (peeled)
1tsp Coconut sugar crystals
1tsp Apple cider vinegar (unfiltered)
1tsp Maple syrup
1/2tsp Himalayan or Celtic sea salt
1/4tsp Paprika
1/4tsp Onion powder
1/4tsp Black peppercorn (fresh ground)

1. Combine in a blender: Real Mayo, water, date, tomato, sun dried tomatoes, lemon juice, garlic, coconut sugar, apple cider vinegar, maple syrup, salt, paprika, onion powder and black peppercorn. Blend into a thick dressing consistency until even in color.

2. Strain ½ cup of sweet relish from its liquid. Stir relish into dressing to create the Special Sauce. Mix the amount of dressing and Sweet Relish that will be consumed within 3 days to extend shelf life.

Note: For the best consistency serve dressing chilled and keep refrigerated.

REAL MAYO

Makes Approx. 16 oz
Prep Time: 5 min

1c Cashews (soaked 4 hrs.)
1/2c Sesame oil (cold pressed)
1/2c Water (filtered)
1x Lemon juiced (fresh squeezed)
1tsp Yellow mustard seeds
1/2tsp Apple cider vinegar
1tsp Himalayan or Celtic sea salt

1. Blend all ingredients until a thick and creamy consistency is reached.

Note: A VitaMix® brand or high speed blender is recommended for the best results.

For the best consistency serve dressing chilled.

SWEET RELISH

Makes Approx. 12 oz
Prep Time: 5 min

1x Cucumber (minced)
1/2c Red bell pepper (minced)
1/2c Sweet onion (minced)
1/3c Coconut sugar
1/4c Apple cider vinegar
1tsp Celery seed
1/4tsp Brown mustard seed

1. Combine all ingredients into a jar. Seal with an airtight lid. Allow to pickle for 30 min or longer.

Note: Lasts in fridge for up to 10 days.

SolFood

Fuel the soul with the sun

The tantalizing world of SolFood (sun food) is fueled with the fiery heat of cooking. The stove light flickers on with a swoosh. The pot sizzles and crackles under the pressure of the flame. The water gods express themselves from soft tender bubbles to a raging boil. To say this food is energizing is an understatement. To make this food one must understand that all fire, heat, electricity, illumination, energy, and dissolution of darkness has its roots in the great sun casting its life-giving glow daily. The making of this food is like a cosmic dance. To dance this cosmic dance of food, one must have sure footing and great faith in what one tastes, ingests, and believes.

This version of vegan food will summon to contest the taste buds of any carnivore or lacto-ovo vegetarian. For one to live life without harmful foods is a vital spark-filled experience. Experience food from the lazy sea sides, to the chilly high elevations of Himalayas, to the Tuscan sunsets, and to the rising sun of the east. International cultures beckon the tongue to dance and sway to their cultural rhythms and pulse. The being who undergoes the experience of SolFood will explore the electrifying macrocosm of the sun and will wander deeper into the culinary terrain than any vegan has ever been before.

ALOO GOBI

"A story of India in every bite." - C

One of our most favorite cuisines to share is Indian food. These recipes we have are a western version of the dishes we learned from a sweet little Indian woman named Urmala. She taught us the "tarka" method. She showed us that making Indian cuisine was a heavenly experience. We learned to bless our meals and offer them to higher powers. So, before you cook say a prayer or two. Light a candle and set the stage for a powerful food experience. - T

COOL AND FRESH

Fresh herbs and cucumber mint tea perfect this English treat.

Years ago in our historic neighborhood there used to be a little English tea shop on the main drive. I had a special gathering of the beautiful women in my life at this tiny tea shop. It was that day I was first introduced to the cucumber tea sandwich. It was unlike anything I ever had, so simple, elegant, and perfect. We now pack coolers filled with these sandwiches on our day trips to the beach. We have also been known to sneak a few into the movies too. They travel well and are welcomed on national flights. - T

CUCUMBER TEA SANDWICH

Ingredients

Serves 4
Prep Time: 5 min

1c Garden herb spread (recipe below)

8x Millet bread slices
1x Cucumber (sliced)
1/4c Mint leaves fresh (whole)

GARDEN HERB SPREAD

Makes Approx. 8 oz
Prep Time: 5 min

1c Cream cheese (recipe on right)

1/3c Onion (minced)
1tbsp Dill sprigs fresh (minced)
1tsp Oregano fresh (minced)
1tsp Rosemary fresh (minced)
1tsp Chives fresh (minced)

1. Remove leaves of herbs from their stems. Mince all herbs and onions in a food processor or by hand with a sharp knife. Then, in a small mixing bowl fold all ingredients into cream cheese to make the Garden Herb Spread.

Note: For the best consistency serve dressing chilled.

If using dried herbs lessen the quantity to 1/3 of the amount listed above. For example, if the recipe calls for 1 tablespoon of fresh herbs, use 1 teaspoon of dried.

Method

1. Generously cover all slices of millet bread with Garden Herb Spread.

2. Then, layer with several mint leaves and sliced cucumbers. Form a sandwich. Then slice diagonally. The Cucumber Tea Sandwich is our favorite on-the-go treat.

CREAM CHEESE

Makes Approx. 20 oz
Prep Time: 5 min

1c Cashews (soaked 4 hrs.)
1c Macadamia nuts (soaked 2 hrs.)
3/4c Water (filtered)
1/2c Lemon juice (fresh squeezed)
1/2x Garlic clove (peeled)
1tsp Himalayan or Celtic sea salt

1. Blend all ingredients on high until a smooth and thick cream cheesy consistency is reached. Use the tamper to frequently move ingredients around during the blending process.

Note: A Vita Mix® brand or high speed blender is recommended for the best results.

For the best consistency serve chilled and keep refrigerated.

CHANA MASALA

Method

1. Soak 2 cups of chana dal in 8 cups of filtered water for 8 hours or overnight. Then drain and add 8 cups of fresh water to pressure cook or slow cook until soft. Slow cooking may take up to 6 hours. Stir occasionally during the slow cooking process. Drain water and set aside for final assembly.

2. In a blender combine: roma tomatoes, cashews, coconut sugar, and ginger. Blend together into a thick tomato sauce.

3. Create Indian masala spice mix. In a small bowl combine following spices: turmeric, cumin, coriander, paprika, fenugreek, salt, black pepper, and cayenne. Set spice mix aside.

4. Set a large size pot on medium-low heat. Heat 2 tablespoons of olive oil. Sauté garlic first. Then ginger and onions. Next, add Indian spices and infuse into oil. Then immediately add tomato sauce. Stir on medium-low heat to create a masala sauce.

5. Then combine chana dal with masala sauce. Simmer covered for 10 minutes.

6. Serve Chana Masala garnished with fresh ginger and cilantro. Chana Masala pairs well with The Perfect Rice (recipe on next page). This traditional Indian style din-din is a pleaser in this household.

Note: Chana Dal (chick peas) can be sprouted before cooking or can be purchased pre-sprouted.

Ingredients

Serves 4-6
Prep Time: 30 min (plus chana dal cook time

2c Chana dal (chick peas)
8c Water (filtered)

4x Roma tomatoes (diced)
1/4c Cashews (soaked 2 hrs.)
1tsp Coconut sugar crystals
1/2tsp Ginger fresh (minced)

Chana Masala Spice Mix
1-1/2tsp Turmeric
1tsp Cumin powder
1tsp Coriander powder
1tsp Paprika
1/2tsp Fenugreek powder
1tsp Himalayan or Celtic sea salt
1/2tsp Black peppercorn (ground)
1/8tsp Cayenne pepper

2tbsp Extra virgin olive oil (organic)
2x Garlic cloves (peeled & minced)
1/2c Onions (diced)

1inch Ginger fresh (julienne)
8x Cilantro sprigs (garnish)

BOMBAY ALOO

Ingredients

Serves 4-6
Prep Time: 45 min

2x Sweet potatoes white (peeled & sliced)
2c The Perfect Rice (recipe below)

Bombay Masala Spice Mix
1tsp Cumin powder
1tsp Coriander powder
1tsp Fenugreek powder
1tsp Coconut sugar crystals
1tsp Paprika
1tsp Himalayan or Celtic sea salt
1/2tsp Onion powder
1/2tsp Garlic powder
1/4tsp Turmeric
1/4tsp Black peppercorn (fresh ground)
1/8tsp Garam masala
1/8tsp Cayenne pepper

2tbsp Extra virgin olive oil (organic)
3x Garlic cloves whole (peeled & minced)
1tsp Ginger fresh (minced)
1/2c Onions (diced)
4x Tomatoes (diced)

1x Carrot medium
4x Cilantro sprigs fresh (garnish)
1inch pc Ginger fresh (julienne)

Method

1. Wash and peel 2 large white sweet potatoes. Cut into ¼ inch slices. In a medium size pot par boil with 4 cups water. Potatoes should be cooked but firm. Drain, rinse, and set aside to cool.

2. Create Indian masala spice mix. In a small bowl combine following spices: cumin, coriander, fenugreek, coconut sugar, paprika, salt, onion powder, garlic powder, turmeric, black pepper, garam masala, and cayenne.

3. In a medium pot heat 2 tablespoons of olive oil on medium-low heat. Sauté garlic first. Then ginger and onions. Add spice mix and infuse into oil. Immediately stir in tomatoes. Place a carrot into sauce to taper the acidity of tomatoes. Stir for 5 to 10 minutes until sauce is reduced to a thick masala.

4. Next, remove carrot. Carefully mix potato slices into masala gravy sauce. Simmer and allow potatoes to absorb the flavors for a few minutes. Then garnish with fresh ginger and cilantro. Serve with The Perfect Rice. This Indian flair will transport you on a one way ticket to India.

THE PERFECT RICE

Serves 4
Prep Time: 35 min

1/3c Sweet brown rice
1/3c Red rice
1/3c Forbidden rice
2c Water

1. In a pot combine rice mix and water, and bring to a boil. Then lower to medium heat. Allow rice to absorb liquid until reduced down just above the surface of rice. Then cover and simmer on low for 20 to 25 minutes until soft.

ALOO GOBI

Method

1. Peel and wash one large sweet potato. Then chop into 1 inch cubes. In a small size pot add 2 cups of filtered water and par boil potatoes. Drain water, remove from pot, and set aside.

2. Cut cauliflower into medium flowerets and then set aside in a large bowl. In a large pan or wok heat 1 tablespoon of olive oil on medium-low (save remaining oil). Sauté cumin seeds. Then lightly brown cauliflower. Stir until fully covered by the toasted seeds. This method is a process known as "tarka" in eastern cuisine. Remove cauliflower from pot and set aside.

3. Create Indian masala spice mix. In a small bowl combine the following spices: cumin, coriander, fenugreek, paprika, turmeric, onion powder, mustard seed, Himalayan sea salt, ground black peppercorn, and cayenne.

4. In a blender combine: tomatoes, cashews, carrots, and coconut sugar. Blend on high into a sauce. Set aside for next step.

5. In a large pan or wok on medium-low, heat 2 tablespoons of olive oil. Sauté garlic first. Then ginger and onions. Next, add Indian spices and infuse into oil. Then immediately add tomato sauce. Stir on medium-low heat to create the masala sauce.

6. Then combine cauliflower and sauce. Allow to simmer for 5 minutes covered. Incorporate parboiled potatoes. Then add green peas. Stir and cover for another 5 min. Garnish with julienne ginger and fresh cilantro. This dish pairs well with The Perfect Rice (recipe on previous page). Ahhh, Aloo Gobi will capture your love every time.

Ingredients

Serves 4-6
Prep Time: 50 min

1x Sweet potato white (chopped)
1x Cauliflower (chopped)
1tsp Cumin seeds (for tarka)

Indian Masala Spice Mix
1tsp Cumin powder
1tsp Coriander powder
1tsp Fenugreek powder
1tsp Paprika
1/2tsp Turmeric
1/2tsp Onion powder
1/2tsp Brown mustard seed (ground)
1-1/2tsp Himalayan or Celtic sea salt
1/2tsp Black peppercorn (ground)
1/8tsp Cayenne pepper

4c Tomatoes (diced)
1/2c Cashews (soaked 2 hrs.)
1x Carrot (sliced)
1tbsp Coconut sugar crystals

2tbsp Extra virgin olive oil (organic)
2x Garlic cloves (peeled & minced)
1tsp Ginger fresh (minced)
1c Onion (chopped large)

1c Green peas (fresh or frozen)

FETTUCCINE ALFREDO

Ingredients

Serves 4
Prep Time: 35min

1x Brown rice fettuccine (12 oz. pkg.)

1c Cashews (soaked 4 hrs.)
1/2c Macadamia nuts
2tbsp Pine nuts (soaked 2 hrs.)
2c Water (filtered)
1x Lemon juiced (fresh squeezed)
1x Garlic clove (peeled)
1-1/2tsp Himalayan or Celtic sea salt
1/4tsp Black peppercorn (whole)

1tbsp Oregano fresh (minced)
1tbsp Chives fresh (minced)
1-1/2tsp Rosemary fresh (minced)
1tsp Dill fresh (minced)

4x Italian parsley sprigs (garnish)
Pinch Red pepper flakes (garnish)

Method

1. Bring 4 quarts of water to a rapid boil. Deposit fettuccine or linguine style brown rice noodles into boiling water and reduce burner to medium-high heat. Boil for approximately 12 minutes and stir frequently to keep noodles from sticking together. Drain, rinse, and set noodles aside.

2. In a blender add: cashews, macadamias, pine nuts, water, lemon juice, garlic, salt, and black peppercorn. Blend into a creamy white sauce.

3. In the same blender add: oregano, chives, rosemary, and dill. Blend until silky smooth.

5. In a pot mix noodles with cream sauce on medium-low heat. Stir frequently until heated. Remove from burner.

6. Garnish with Italian parsley and red pepper flakes. This SolFood version of Fettuccine Alfredo will soon be a classic dish in your household.

Note: A food processor can be used for processing onions and herbs instead of by hand.

For best results serve immediately. If sauce dehydrates, rehydrate with ¼ cup of water on low heat and serve.

If using dried herbs lessen the quantity to 1/3 of the amount listed above. For example, if the recipe calls for 1 tablespoon of fresh herbs, use 1 teaspoon of dried.

PENNE A LA CREMA

"Comfort food of the gods. " - T

PENNE ALLA CREMA

Ingredients

Serves 4
Prep Time: 35 min

1x Brown rice penne (12 oz. package)

1/2c Cashews (soaked 4 hrs.)
1/4c Macadamia nuts (soaked 30 min.)
1tbsp Pine nuts (soaked 2 hrs.)
1/4c Sun dried tomatoes (soaked 10 min.)
1c Water (from sun dried tomatoes)
1/2x Lemon juiced (fresh squeezed)
1x Garlic clove (peeled)
1tbsp Oregano fresh
1/2tbsp Rosemary fresh
1tsp Himalayan or Celtic sea salt
1/4tsp Black peppercorn (whole)
1/4tsp Paprika

2c Tomatoes (chopped)
1/4c Onion (chopped)
1/4c Red bell pepper (chopped)

4x Italian parsley sprigs (garnish)
Pinch Red pepper flakes (garnish)

Method

1. Bring 4 quarts of water to a rapid boil. Deposit penne noodles into boiling water and reduce burner to medium-high heat. Boil for approximately 12 minutes and stir frequently to keep noodles from sticking together. Drain, rinse, and set noodles aside.

2. Soak sun dried tomatoes in 1 cup of filtered water for 15 minutes. Save water for the next step.

3. In a blender add: cashews, macadamias, pine nuts, sun dried tomatoes, water (from sun dried tomatoes), lemon juice, garlic, oregano, rosemary, sea salt, black peppercorn, and paprika. Blend into a creamy consistency.

4. Next, add to blender: tomatoes, onions, red bell peppers. Blend ingredients until combined into a smooth and creamy pink sauce.

5. In a medium pot mix penne pasta into cream sauce. Heat on medium-low and serve garnished with fresh basil leaves. Garnish with Italian parsley and red pepper flakes. This deliciousness satisfies even the most scrupulous.

Note: For best results serve immediately. If sauce dehydrates, rehydrate with ¼ cup of water on low heat and serve.

CREAMY BASIL PESTO

Method

1. Bring 4 quarts of water to a rapid boil. Deposit spaghetti noodles into boiling water and reduce burner to medium-high heat. Boil for approximately 12 minutes and stir frequently to keep noodles from sticking together. Drain, rinse, and set noodles aside.

2. In a blender add: pine nuts, water, olive oil, garlic, black peppercorn, and salt. Blend into a creamy consistency.

3. Next, add the basil leaves. Blend on high until the sauce appearance is light green in color.

4. In a medium pot combine noodles into creamy pesto sauce. Stir noodles on medium-low heat. Then serve garnished with fresh basil leaves. Dish-up this meal hot or chilled. Enjoy this Italian style treat with no remorse.

Ingredients

Serves 4
Prep Time: 20 min

1x Brown rice spaghetti (12 oz. package)

1/2c Pine nuts (soaked 2 hrs.)
1/2c Water (filtered)
4tbsp Extra virgin olive oil
1/2 Garlic clove (peeled)
1/8tsp Black peppercorn
1tsp Himalayan or Celtic sea salt
1-1/2c Basil leaves fresh

4x Basil leaves (garnish)

CHEESE & MACARONI

Ingredients

Serves 4
Prep Time: 30 min

1x Brown rice macaroni (12 oz. pkg.)

3/4c Macadamia nuts
1/4c Nutritional yeast flakes
1x Red bell pepper (chopped)
1x Garlic clove whole (peeled)
1c Water (filtered)
1tsp Himalayan or Celtic sea salt
1/2tsp Paprika
1/2tsp Black peppercorn

1tbsp Extra virgin olive oil (organic)
1x Garlic clove (peeled & minced)
1/2c Onions (chopped)
Pinch Celtic sea salt (fleur de sal)

Pinch Black peppercorn (ground)
Pinch Red pepper flakes (garnish)

Method

1. Bring 4 quarts of water to a rapid boil. Deposit Macaroni noodles into boiling water and reduce burner to medium-high heat. Boil for approximately 12 minutes and stir frequently to keep noodles from sticking together. Drain, rinse, and set noodles aside.

2. In a blender add: macadamia nuts, nutritional yeast, red pepper, garlic clove, water, salt, paprika, and black peppercorn. Blend on high into a thick cheese sauce.

3. In a medium size pot heat olive oil on medium heat. Brown garlic and onions. Then add noodles and stir together for a few minutes. Add a pinch of Celtic sea salt (fleur de sal).

4. Next, pour cheese dressing over warmed noodles and stir frequently. Simmer on low until evenly heated. Remove from burner. Top with fresh black pepper and a pinch of crushed red pepper flakes. Serve immediately and behold the power of Cheese & Macaroni.

Note: For best results serve immediately. If sauce dehydrates, rehydrate with ¼ cup of water on low heat and serve.

GAYO PINTO

Method

1. Soak 2 cups of adzuki beans in 10 cups of filtered water for approximately 4 hours. Then drain. In a pot add 8 cups of fresh water to slow cook beans until soft. This may take up to 4 hours. Remove pot from burner and set aside. Allow beans to remain in water they were cooked in.

2. Create Latin spice mix. In a small bowl combine following spices: salt, cumin, onion powder, black pepper, cayenne pepper, and coriander.

3. In a large pot heat 2 tablespoons of olive oil on medium-low heat. Sauté garlic first. Then add onions. Then add poblano, jalapeño, and bell peppers. Then add Latin spice mix. Immediately stir in chopped tomatoes. Next add cooked Adzuki beans (with the water they were cooked in). Allow Gayo Pinto to simmer on medium-high heat for 10 minutes.

4. Then in a separate pot combine 3 cups of beans from the Gayo Pinto with 4 cups of The Perfect Rice. Stir together until mixed well. Serve garnished with fresh cilantro and Picante Sauce. Enjoy our take on this traditional Costa Rican dish. Pura Vida!

Note: As an option adzuki beans can be sprouted before cooking. They can also can be purchased pre-sprouted. The benefits of sprouting increases nutritional value and also reduces starch levels.

Ingredients

Serves 4
Prep Time: 35 min (plus cook time beans)

2c Adzuki beans (soaked 4 hrs.)
8c Water (filtered)

Latin Spice Mix
1tsp Himalayan or Celtic sea salt
1tsp Cumin powder
1/2tsp Onion powder
1/2tsp Black peppercorn (fresh ground)
1/8tsp Cayenne pepper
1/8tsp Coriander powder

2tbsp Extra virgin olive oil (cold pressed)
1x Garlic clove (minced)
1c Onions (chopped)
1x Poblano pepper (chopped)
1x Jalapeño (chopped)
1/2x Green bell pepper (chopped)
1/2c Tomatoes (chopped)

4c The Perfect Rice (recipe below)
1oz Picante Sauce (next pg.)

THE PERFECT RICE

Serves 4
Prep Time: 35 min

1/3c Sweet brown rice
1/3c Red rice
1/3c Forbidden rice
2c Water

1. In a pot combine rice mix and water, and bring to a boil. Then lower to medium heat. Allow rice to absorb liquid until reduced down just above the surface of rice. Then cover and simmer on low for 20 to 25 minutes until soft.

LIQUID FIRE SAUCES

PICANTE SAUCE

Makes Approx. 12 oz
Prep Time: 5 min

1c Mexican chili peppers (dried)
1/2c Tomatoes (chopped)
2x Medjool dates (pitted)
1x Chipotle pepper
1x Garlic clove
1/2x Lemon juiced (fresh squeezed)
1tsp Apple cider vinegar
1tsp Oregano fresh
1tsp Cumin (ground)
1/2tsp Himalayan or Celtic sea salt
1/8tsp Black pepper

1. Soak Mexican chili peppers and chipotle peppers in water for 15 minutes. Blend all ingredients together on high until liquefied into a sauce.

   Note: Be cautious when blending hot peppers as strong vapors can irritate your eyes. Thoroughly wash hands when handling hot peppers. Avoid contact with eyes for several hours.

PHANTOM FIRE BBQ

Makes Approx. 12 oz
Prep Time: 5 min

1/3c Ghost peppers (dried)
2x Medjool dates (pitted)
2x Carrots small (chopped or grated)
1/2c Pineapple fresh (chopped)
2x Lime juiced (fresh squeezed)
1x Lemon juiced (fresh squeezed)
2tsp Apple cider vinegar
1x Garlic clove (peeled)
1tsp Himalayan or Celtic sea salt

1. Soak ghost peppers in filtered water for 15 minutes. Drain and discard water. Blend all ingredients on high until mixed into a smooth thick sauce that is even in color.

PHILLY-MEXI SUSHI ROLL

Method

1. Make the Cream Cheese recipe (below) and allow to chill in refrigerator for several hours until firm.

2. Slice tomato into thin strips. Then cut sweet onion and yellow bell pepper into thin slices. Thoroughly wash cilantro and spin in salad spinner until completely dry.

3. Place one nori sheet onto a bamboo sushi roller. Cover first half of nori sheet with 1/4 inch thick layer of rice using a sushi paddle or wooden spoon.

4. Spread chilled Cream Cheese across the center of the rice lengthwise from left to right. In the same fashion place a single row of tomato, onion, bell pepper, and cilantro alongside the Cream Cheese filling.

5. Fold bamboo roller over nori sheet while pressing the ingredients firmly into the center of rice. Continue rolling to form a tight sushi roll. Lightly wet edge of nori sheet with water to seal the roll.

6. Slice each roll into 8 pieces with a serrated knife. Serve the Philly-Mexi Sushi Roll with a side of Phantom Fire BBQ Sauce and experience a surge of pleasure. One bite and you will agree this grub is the perfect union of North American flavor.

Note: If using freshly cooked rice, spoon out onto a large plate to cool for a few minutes before assembling sushi roll. It is best to assemble roll when temperature of rice is around 98 degrees.

THE PERFECT RICE

Serves 4
Prep Time: 35 min

1/3c Sweet brown rice
1/3c Red rice
1/3c Forbidden rice
2c Water

1. In a pot combine rice mix and water, and bring to a boil. Then lower to medium heat. Allow rice to absorb liquid until reduced down just above the surface of rice. Then cover and simmer on low for 20 to 25 minutes until soft.

Ingredients

Makes 4 rolls
Prep Time: 15 min

2c The Perfect Rice (recipe below)
4tbsp Cream Cheese (recipe below)

4x Nori seaweed sheets raw
1x Tomato (sliced spears)
1x Yellow bell pepper (sliced)
1x Sweet onion (sliced)
8x Cilantro sprigs

2oz Phantom Fire BBQ Sauce (previous page)

CREAM CHEESE

Makes 8 oz
Prep Time: 5 min

1c Cashews (soaked 4 hrs.)
1c Macadamia nuts (soaked 2 hrs.)
3/4c Water (filtered)
1/2c Lemon juice (fresh squeezed)
1/2x Garlic clove (peeled)
1tsp Himalayan or Celtic sea salt

1. Blend all ingredients on high until a smooth and thick cream cheese consistency is reached. Use tamper to frequently move ingredients around during the blending process.

Note: A Vita Mix® brand or high speed blender is recommended for the best results. Serve chilled.

WILD WASABI SUSHI ROLL

Ingredients

Makes 4 rolls
Prep Time: 15 min.

2c The Perfect Rice (recipe below)

4x Nori seaweed sheets raw
1x Cucumber (sliced spears)
1x Avocado (sliced wedges)
1/4c Carrot (julienne)
1/4c Turnip (julienne)
1/4c Daikon (julienne)
1/4c Chives fresh (whole length)

2oz Wild Wasabi Sauce (recipe below)
2oz Nama shoyu

THE PERFECT RICE

Serves 4
Prep Time: 35 min

1/3c Sweet brown rice
1/3c Red rice
1/3c Forbidden rice
2c Water

1. In a pot combine rice mix and water, and bring to a boil. Then lower to medium heat. Allow rice to absorb liquid until reduced down just above the surface of rice. Then cover and simmer on low for 20 to 25 minutes until soft.

Method

1. Slice cucumbers into long spears. Peel avocado and slice into narrow wedges. Julienne cut carrots, turnips, and daikon radish.

2. Place one nori sheet onto a bamboo sushi roller. Cover first half of nori sheet with 1/4 inch thick layer of rice using a sushi paddle or wooden spoon.

3. Place a single row of cucumber and avocado across the center of the rice lengthwise left to right. Lay several pieces of carrot, turnip, daikon, and chives evenly down the center in the same fashion.

4. Fold bamboo roller over nori sheet while pressing the ingredients firmly into the center of rice. Continue rolling to form a tight sushi roll. Lightly wet edge of nori sheet with water to seal the roll.

5. Slice each roll into 8 pieces with a serrated knife. Serve with Wild Wasabi Sauce. Have a side of nama shoyu as a classic condiment for Wild Wasabi Sushi Roll.

WILD WASABI SAUCE

Makes Approx. 4 oz
Prep Time: 5 min

1/2c Cashews (soaked 4 hrs.)
1tsp Coconut sugar crystals
2tbsp Wasabi powder
2tbsp Nama shoyu
1/4c Water (filtered)
1/8tsp Cayenne pepper

1. Blend all ingredients on high until smooth and creamy.

Note: Organic wasabi powder is available in any health food store in the ethnic food section.

No Philippine meal is complete without exceptional company, an avalanche of hugs, and congenial surroundings. As a foreigner to a Philippine household you will be welcomed, hugged, and fed like you are treasured family. So, draw together extraordinary friends and share the dazzling joys of great comfort foods. Make all the comrades and strangers in your life feel loved & cherished. Like family. A divine family. -T

PANCIT NOODLE DISH

"An Asian affair, never lacking in spirit." - C

PANCIT NOODLE DISH

Ingredients

Serves 4-6
Prep Time: 35 min.

1x Kelp noodles (12 oz. pkg.)
1x Brown rice noodles (12 oz. pkg.)

Asian Spice Mix
1/2tsp Turmeric
1/2tsp Cumin powder
1/2tsp Himalayan or Celtic sea salt
1/4tsp Paprika
1/8tsp Coriander powder
1/8tsp Black peppercorn (ground)
1/8tsp Cayenne pepper (ground)

2tbsp Extra virgin olive oil (organic)
3x Garlic cloves (peeled & minced)
1tsp Ginger fresh (minced)
1/2c Onion (sliced)

2x Celery stalks (sliced diagonally)
2x Bok choy stalks (sliced diagonally)
4x Green onions (sliced diagonally)
1x Carrot (sliced diagonally)
1/2c Yellow bell pepper (sliced)
1/2c Red bell pepper (sliced)

1tbsp Nama shoyu
8x Cilantro sprigs (garnish)

Method

1. Rinse kelp noodles then drain and set aside.

2. Bring 4 quarts of water to a rapid boil. Deposit spaghetti noodles into boiling water and reduce burner to medium-high heat. Boil for approximately 12 minutes and stir frequently to prevent noodles from sticking together. Avoid overcooking noodles to maintain an al dente (which means firm to the bite) characteristic. Drain, rinse, and set spaghetti noodles aside.

3. Combine all following Asian spices into a small bowl: turmeric, cumin, salt, paprika, coriander, peppercorn, and cayenne pepper.

4. Set burner on medium-low heat. In a large pan or wok heat 2 tablespoons of extra virgin olive oil. Sauté minced garlic and ginger. Then stir in sliced onion until browned. Mix in the following vegetables into pot: celery, bok choy, green onion, carrot, and bell pepper. Stir in Asian spice mix and sauté lightly.

6. Immediately add brown rice and kelp noodles into wok. Toss evenly with sautéed vegetables. Mixing the noodles evenly can be accomplished by using two forks. Draw the noodles upward little by little until noodles are completely intertwined.

7. Finally, add nama shoyu and mix into noodles. Keep on low heat. Serve the Pancit Noodle Dish garnished with a few cilantro sprigs. This family favorite has East Asian paradise in every bite!

MODOSCH POTATO SALAD

Method

1. Cut potatoes into medium equal sized cubes. This ensures they cook evenly. Then boil potatoes in a medium pot until a desired softness is attained. Puncture with a fork to check for doneness. When they can be pierced with ease they are ready. Next, drain and rinse with cool water to prevent potatoes from continuing to cook.

2. In a stainless steel mixing bowl combine: celery, onion, dill, salt, paprika, garlic powder, black pepper, and 3/4 cup of Sour Cream. Next, use a wooden spoon to gently stir in cooked potatoes. Serve Modosch Potato Salad chilled.

Ingredients

Serves 4
Prep Time: 30 min.

3/4c Sour cream (recipe below)

2x Japanese sweet potatoes (chopped)

3x Celery stalks (diced)
1/2x Onion red (diced)
1/2c Parsley curly (coarsely chopped)
1tbsp Dill fresh (minced)
1/2tsp Himalayan or Celtic sea salt
1/4tsp Paprika
1/4tsp Garlic powder
1/4tsp Black peppercorn (fresh ground)

SOUR CREAM

Makes Approx. 12 oz
Prep Time: 5 min

3/4c Macadamia nuts (soaked 30 min.)
1/4c Cashews (soaked 2 hrs.)
1/2c Avocado oil (first cold pressed)
1/2c Lemon juice (fresh squeezed)
1/4c Water (filtered)
1tsp Himalayan or Celtic sea salt

1. Soak cashews and macadamia nuts for the suggested amount of time in water then drain. Blend nuts with remaining ingredients into a smooth Sour Cream texture.

Note: A Vita Mix® brand or high speed blender is recommended for the best results.

RASTA PASTA SALAD

Ingredients

Serves 4-6
Prep Time: 30 min.

1x Brown rice spirals (12 oz. package)
1c Nicoise Dressing (recipe below)

1x Broccoli head (chopped)
3x Celery stalks (diced)
2x Carrots (grated)
1/2c Parsley curly (coarsely chopped)
1/2c Onions sweet (diced)
1/2x Red bell pepper (diced)
1/2x Yellow bell pepper (diced)
1/2x Green bell pepper (diced)

1tbsp Green olives (sliced)
1tbsp Black olives (sliced)

Method

1. Bring 4 quarts of water to a rapid boil. Add spiral (fusilli) noodles into boiling water and reduce burner to medium-high heat. Boil for approximately 14 minutes and stir frequently to keep noodles from sticking together. Drain, rinse, and set aside.

2. In a large mixing bowl combine: noodles, broccoli, celery, carrot, parsley, onion, and bell peppers. Stir in Nicoise Dressing into the salad mix.

4. Lastly, toss in black and green olives. Refrigerate the Rasta Pasta Salad for a few hours and serve super chilled. Ire!

NICOISE DRESSING

Makes Approx. 10 oz
Prep Time: 5 min

1c Extra virgin olive oil (first cold pressed)
1x Lemon juiced (fresh squeezed)
3tbsp Dijon mustard (apple cider based)
1tsp Apple cider vinegar (unfiltered)
1/2tsp Himalayan or Celtic sea salt
1/4tsp Paprika
1/2tsp Garlic powder
1/4tsp Onion powder
1/4tsp Black peppercorn (fresh ground)

1. Blend all ingredients together until a thick dressing consistency is reached.

Note: Nicoise is pronounced nee-swahz.

Dessert

Divine love

Love the sensation of guiltless unadulterated joy. These raw desserts will satisfy every whimsical craving from the silky raspberry swirl, vanilla dream, to the divine connection of chocolate and creamy caramel. An ethereal blend of sweet tastes and textures illuminate your entire being. This is not cheating. This is absorption of the worlds finest food, made by the gods.

"Only through coconut can this totally authentic ecstasy be experienced." - T

CHOCOLATE PECAN CARAMEL PIE

Method

1. To make the crust, grind almonds and walnuts in a food processor to create a coarse flour-like consistency. Next, pit dates and process with walnut and almond flour. Then combine with the remaining crust ingredients into a dough in food processor. Then press dough evenly into a 9" deep dish pie pan. Crimp the edge of crust onto the rim of pie pan.

2. To create the pie filling, soak cashews and pecans in filtered water for the suggested amount time. Then drain and discard water. Next, place nuts into a VitaMix® blender with the remaining ingredients for pie filling. Blend on high moving ingredients around frequently with tamper. Use more water if necessary. Continue to blend until a creamy batter is formed.

4. Then pour batter into pie crust. Tap pie pan gently onto countertop to remove air pockets from filling. Place into freezer for several hours until firm.

5. Remove pie from freezer. Then spread an ample amount Creamy Caramel over entire top of frozen pie. Then top with Candied Pecans. Slice pie into 12 servings and keep frozen. Defrost the Chocolate Pecan Caramel Pie for a few minutes before serving. Or enjoy this American classic with a chocolate twist straight from the freezer.

CANDIED PECANS

Makes 2 cup
Prep Time: 5 min (plus dehydration time)

2c Pecans raw (soaked 2 hrs.)
1/4c Maple syrup
3tbsp Maple sugar
1/4tsp Cinnamon
1/8tsp Himalayan salt

1. Soak pecans in filtered water. Drain and discard water. Stir in pecans with all other ingredients into a mixing bowl.

2. Lay nuts flat onto a non-stick dehydrator sheet. Dehydrate at 108 degrees for 12 to 18 hours. Remove from sheet and place onto dehydrator screen. Dehydrate for another 12 to 18 hours until dry and crunchy and a candy shell forms on nuts.

Ingredients

Makes Approx. 12 slices
Prep Time: 35 min (plus freeze time)

Crust

1-1/4c Walnuts raw
1-1/4c Almonds raw
6x Medjool dates (pitted)
1/3c Coconut oil (organic)
2tbsp Coconut sugar crystals
1tbsp Cacao powder raw
1/4tsp Cinnamon powder
1/8tsp Himalayan salt

Filling

2-1/2c Cashews raw (soaked 6 hrs.)
1/2c Pecans raw (soaked 2 hrs.)
2c Water (filtered)
12x Medjool dates (pitted)
1/2c Coconut oil (organic)
1/4c Cacao powder raw
1/3c Maple syrup
2tsp Vanilla extract (non-alcohol)
1/2tsp Himalayan salt

Topping

1/2c Candied Pecans (recipe on left)
1/2c Creamy Caramel (recipe below)

CREAMY CARAMEL

Makes 2 cup
Prep Time: 5 min

8x Medjool dates (pitted & soaked 15 min.)
1/4c Cashews raw (soaked 4 hrs.)
1/4c Pecans raw (soaked 2 hrs.)
1/4c Maple syrup
1/4c Coconut sugar crystals
1/4c Water (filtered)
2tbsp Coconut oil (first cold press)
2tsp Vanilla extract (non-alcohol)
1/2tsp Himalayan salt

1. Blend all ingredients in a high-speed blender until thick and creamy.

CHOCOLATE PECAN CARAMEL PIE

"A mandala of pecans and divine chocolate love." - T

BLUEBERRY CRÈME TART

"A raw vegan dream come true." - C

BLUEBERRY CRÈME TART

Ingredients

Makes 4 tarts
Prep Time: 35 min (plus refrigeration time)

Crust

2c Almonds raw
4x Medjool dates (pitted)
1/4c Coconut shredded raw (dried)
1/3c Coconut oil (organic)
1/3c Coconut sugar crystals
1/4c Maple sugar
1/4tsp Himalayan salt

Filling

1c Cashews raw (soaked 6 hrs.)
5x Medjool dates (pitted & soaked 15 min.)
1c Coconut meat (young Thai)
1/3c Coconut oil (organic)
1/3c Water (filtered)
2tbsp Vanilla extract (non-alcohol)
1/2c Blueberries
1/3c Maple syrup
1/8tsp Himalayan salt

Topping

1c Blueberries

Method

1. To make the crust, grind almonds in a food processor to create a coarse flour-like consistency. Process almonds ½ cup at a time to prevent nuts from turning into a butter. Next, pit dates and process with ¼ cup almond flour until dates are ground into small granular sized pieces. Then combine with remaining crust ingredients: shredded coconut, coconut oil, coconut sugar, maple sugar, and salt. To mix ingredients evenly into a dough use a KitchenAid® mixer or fold together by hand.

2. Press dough into bottom of 4 tart pans and create an ¼ inch thick layer of crust. Crimp edge of crust onto the rim of tart pan. Chill in refrigerator until crust is firm.

3. To create the pie filling, soak cashews and dates in filtered water for the suggested amount time. Then drain and discard water. Next, place nuts and dates into a VitaMix® blender with remaining ingredients from pie filling: coconut meat, coconut oil, water, vanilla, blueberries, maple syrup, and salt. Blend on high moving ingredients around frequently with tamper. Continue to blend until a creamy batter is formed.

4. Pour blueberry filling into 4 separate pie crusts. Cover top of pie entirely with blueberries. Chill in fridge for several hours and enjoy blissfully.   The Blueberry Crème Tart will surely end your blues!

Note: To save surplus blueberries: store fresh unwashed blueberries in a freezer safe container and freeze until ready to use. When ready to use, thaw in a strainer for 15 minutes, rinse and pat dry with a towel.

Remaining pies can be stored in a sealed container in freezer. Defrost in refrigerator before serving.

DOUBLE MINT CHOCOLATE CHIP PIE

Method

1. To make the crust, grind almonds and walnuts in a food processor to create a coarse flour-like consistency. Next, pit dates and process with walnut and almond flour. Then combine with the remaining crust ingredients into a dough in food processor. Press dough flat into the bottom of four 4.5 inch springform pie pans.

2. To create the pie filling, soak cashews in filtered water for the suggested amount time. Next, pit and soak dates in filtered water for 15 minutes. Then drain and discard water. Then in a VitaMix® blender combine all ingredients for pie filling. Blend on high, moving ingredients around frequently with tamper, until a creamy batter is formed.

3. Then pour batter into all four pie pans. Tap pie pans gently onto counter top to remove air pockets from filling. Place into freezer for several hours until firm.

4. Next, create the Mint Chocolate Ganache layer. Fill top of each mini pie with ½ cup of Mint Chocolate Ganache as top layer. Then cover with crushed cacao nibs. Place in freezer again for several hours until firm.

5. Unlock springform pan and allow to defrost until the ring easily detaches from pies. Then decorate with Chocolate Frosting and slice while pies are frozen. Finally, top the Double Mint Chocolate Chip Pie with fresh mint leaves and serve frozen or defrost for a few minutes before serving.

CHOCOLATE FROSTING

Makes 1 cup
Prep Time: 5 min

1/2c Cacao powder raw
6x Medjool dates (pitted & soaked 15 min.)
1/4c Maple sugar
1tbsp Maca powder
2tbsp Coconut oil (first cold press)
1tbsp Vanilla extract (non-alcohol)
1/4c Water (filtered)
1/8tsp Himalayan salt

1. Blend all ingredients in a high-speed blender until smooth. Chill in the refrigerator until mixture becomes a firm frosting-like consistency.

Ingredients

Makes 4 mini pies
Prep Time: 40 min (plus freeze time)

Crust

3/4c Walnuts raw
3/4c Almonds raw
4x Medjool dates (pitted)
3tbsp Cacao powder raw
2tbsp Coconut sugar crystals
2tbsp Coconut oil (organic)
1/8tsp Himalayan salt

Filling

2c Cashews (soaked 6 hrs.)
8x Medjool dates (pitted & soaked)
1/3c Coconut oil (organic)
1/2c Cacao powder raw
1c Water (filtered)
1/3c Maple syrup
2tsp Mint extract (non-alcohol)
1tsp Vanilla extract (non-alcohol)
1/4tsp Himalayan sea salt

Topping

1c Mint Chocolate Ganache (recipe below)
1c Chocolate Frosting (recipe on left)
3tbsp Cacao nibs
8x Mint leaves

MINT CHOCOLATE GANACHE

Makes 2 cup
Prep Time: 5 min

1c Cacao powder raw
1c Maple syrup
3/4c Coconut oil (first cold press)
1tsp Mint extract (non-alcohol)

1. Blend all ingredients together into a thick chocolate sauce. Use as the top layer for the Double Mint Chocolate Chip Pie.

140

DOUBLE MINT CHOCOLATE CHIP PIE

"Pacify every mouth watering desire." - T

GREEN TEA SILK PIE

Method

1. To make the crust, grind macadamia and walnuts in a food processor to create a coarse flour-like consistency. Process nuts ½ cup at a time to prevent nuts from turning into a butter. Next, pit dates and process with ½ cup nut flour until dates are ground into small granular sized pieces. Then combine with remaining crust ingredients: coconut sugar, coconut oil, and salt. To mix ingredients evenly into a dough use a KitchenAid® mixer or fold together by hand.

2. Press dough into bottom of a 9" springform pan, ¼ inch thick. Then place into refrigerator to chill.

3. To create the pie filling, soak cashews and dates in filtered water for the suggested amount time. Then drain and discard water. Next, in a VitaMix® blender combine ingredients from pie filling: cashews, dates, water, lime juice, coconut oil, coconut sugar, maple syrup, matcha green tea, vanilla extract, and salt. Blend on high moving ingredients around frequently with tamper. Continue to blend until a creamy batter is formed.

4. Pour batter into pie pan. Then tap pie pan gently onto countertop to remove bubbles and air pockets from filling. Next, sprinkle coconut flakes and maple sugar on top of pie filling and place into freezer for several hours until firm.

5. Remove pie from freezer then unlock springform pan and allow to defrost until the ring easily detaches from pies. Remove ring carefully from the pie. Slice pie into 12 servings. Keep in the freezer until ready to serve. Take pleasure in the Green Tea Silk Pie, a timeless taste that will merge you softly into bliss.

   Note: For filling, pit and soak dates in filtered water for approximately 15 minutes. Then drain and discard water.

Ingredients

Makes Approx. 12 slices
Prep Time: 30 min (plus freeze time)

Crust
3/4c Macadamia nuts raw
1/2c Walnuts nuts raw
4x Medjool dates (pitted)
1tbsp Coconut sugar crystals
1tbsp Coconut oil (organic)
Pinch Himalayan salt

Filling
4c Cashews (soaked 6 hrs.)
10x Medjool dates (pitted & soaked)
2c Water (filtered)
2x Limes juiced (fresh squeezed)
2/3c Coconut oil (organic)
4tbsp Coconut sugar crystals
6tbsp Maple syrup
2tbsp Matcha green tea
2tbsp Vanilla extract (alcohol-free)
1/8tsp Himalayan salt

Topping
1/4c Coconut shredded raw (dried)
1tsp Maple sugar

COCONUT CREAM PIE

Ingredients

Makes Approx. 4 tarts
Prep Time: 35 min (plus freeze time)

Crust

2c Almond raw
4x Medjool dates (pitted)
1/4c Coconut shredded raw (dried)
1/3c Coconut oil (organic)
1/3c Maple sugar
1/3c Coconut sugar crystals
Pinch Himalayan salt

Filling

1c Cashews (soaked 6 hrs.)
5x Medjool dates (pitted & soaked 15 min.)
1c Coconut meat (young Thai coconut)
1/2c Coconut oil (organic)
1/3c Coconut water
1/4c Maple syrup
1/4c Coconut shredded raw (dried)
3tbsp Coconut sugar crystals
2tbsp Vanilla extract (non-alcohol)
1/8tsp Himalayan sea salt

Topping

1/4c Coconut shredded raw (dried)
1tsp Maple sugar

Method

1. To make the crust, grind almonds in a food processor to create a coarse flour-like consistency. Process nuts ½ cup at a time to prevent nuts from turning into a butter. Next, pit dates and process with ½ cup nut flour until dates are ground into small granular sized pieces. Then combine with remaining crust ingredients: shredded coconut, coconut oil, maple sugar, coconut sugar, and salt. To mix ingredients evenly into a dough use a KitchenAid® mixer or fold together by hand.

2. Divide dough evenly into four sections. Press dough into bottom of 4 tart pans and create an ¼ inch thick layer of crust. Crimp edge of crust onto the rim of tart pan. Chill in refrigerator until dough becomes a firm crust.

3. To create the pie filling, soak cashews and dates in filtered water for the suggested amount time. Then drain and discard water. Next, place nuts and dates into a VitaMix® blender with remaining ingredients from pie filling: coconut meat, coconut oil, coconut water, maple syrup, coconut sugar, vanilla extract, and salt. Blend on high moving ingredients around frequently with tamper. Continue to blend until a creamy batter is formed.

4. Pour coconut cream filling into pie tarts. Cover entire top of pie tarts with organic shredded coconut and maple sugar. Chill in freezer until firm. Allow to defrost for a few minutes before serving Coconut Cream Pie.

RASPBERRY SWIRL LEMON ICE BOX PIE

Method

1. To make the crust, grind macadamia nuts and dates together in a food processor. Process ½ cup at a time to grind into a dough. Then mix in coconut sugar and salt. Fold crust ingredients together by hand to form dough. Press dough into bottom of a 9" springform pan, ¼ inch thick.

2. To create the pie filling, soak cashews and dates in filtered water for the suggested amount time. Then drain and discard water. Next, place nuts and dates into a VitaMix® blender with remaining ingredients from pie filling: water, lemon juice, coconut oil, maple syrup, vanilla extract, and salt. Blend on high moving ingredients around frequently with tamper. Continue to blend until a creamy batter is formed.

3. Pour batter into prepared crust. Tap pie pan gently onto counter to remove bubbles and air pockets from filling. Then follow directions for the Raspberry Sauce and swirl it into top of pie filling. Place in freezer until frozen.

4. Once frozen remove from freezer and unlock latch of springform pan. Allow to defrost a few minutes until springform ring is easy to remove. While pie is still firm, slice frozen pie into 12 servings. Defrost for a few minutes before serving. Serve Raspberry Swirl Lemon Ice Box Pie as a frozen dessert topped with fresh raspberries or as a power packed breakfast to keep yourself truckin' all day long!

RASPBERRY SAUCE

Makes 1 cup
Prep Time: 4 min

1pt Raspberry fresh
2tbsp Maple syrup
1tsp Coconut sugar crystals
2tbsp Water (filtered)

1. In a food processor combine all ingredients for the Raspberry Sauce. Purée to a smooth consistency. Then use a fine wire mesh strainer to strain seeds from sauce. Use an offset rubber spatula to press sauce through stainer. Place strainer over a small bowl to catch Raspberry Sauce.

Ingredients

Makes Approx. 12 slices
Prep Time: 35 min (plus freeze time)

Crust
3/4c Macadamia nuts raw
10x Medjool dates (pitted)
1tbsp Coconut sugar crystals
Pinch Himalayan salt

Filling
4c Cashews raw (soaked 6 hrs.)
8x Medjool dates (pitted)
1-1/2c Water filtered
1c Lemon juice (fresh squeezed)
1/3c Coconut oil (organic, first cold press)
1/2c Maple syrup
2tbsp Vanilla extract (non-alcohol)
1/8tsp Himalayan salt

Topping
1/2c Raspberry Sauce (recipe below)
1/2c Raspberries fresh

CHOCOLATE NUT BUTTER CUPS

Ingredients

Makes Approx. 45 mini-cups
Prep Time: 25 min

1/2c Cacao butter raw
1/2c Cacao powder raw
1c Coconut sugar crystals
1/4c Maple syrup
1/4c Coconut oil
1/8tsp Himalayan salt
1/2tsp Vanilla extract (non-alcohol)

1/2c Almond butter raw

Method

1. In a small sauce pan, melt cacao butter into a liquid using the lowest temperature setting. If available use the warming feature on stove top to slowly melt cacao butter.

2. In a blender combine: melted cacao butter, cacao powder, coconut sugar, maple sugar, coconut oil, salt, and vanilla extract. Blend together well to create a smooth chocolate mixture.

3. Place almond butter in freezer for several hours until nut-butter becomes very firm. Arrange 25 mini fluted paper baking cups on a tray. Then place a small ½ inch scoop of almond butter at the bottom of each cup.

4. Use a disher scoop to spoon chocolate mixture over the almond butter until each cup is filled. Then refrigerate cups until chocolate is firm. Once you taste the Chocolate Nut Butter Cup you will know why this combination is no accident.

Note: For easy clean-up remove any excess chocolate mixture from the blender pitcher. Then rinse out the pitcher with warm soapy water to prevent the chocolate residue from hardening.

MOCKAROONS

BADA BING CHERRY

Ingredients

Makes Approx. 65
Prep Time: 30 min (plus dehydration time)

4c Coconut organic dried (shredded)
2c Almond flour (ground fine)
1c Maple syrup
3/4c Bing cherry (dried, chopped)
1/2c Coconut oil (organic, first cold press)
1/4c Coconut sugar crystals
2tsp Vanilla extract (non-alcohol)
1/2tsp Himalayan salt

1. Mix all ingredients together in a KitchenAid®
   mixer or by hand in a large bowl with a wooden
   spoon. Once developed into a dough, create 1.5
   inch size balls with a disher scoop or by hand.

2. Place onto a dehydrator screen. Set at 108
   degrees for 6 to 10 hours. Dehydrate until a crispy
   coating on the outside appears and the inside
   remains moist.

ALMOND RAISIN BISCOTTI

Ingredients

Makes Approx. 65
Prep Time: 30 min (plus dehydration time)

4c Coconut organic dried (shredded)
2c Almond flour (ground fine)
1c Maple syrup
1/2c Coconut oil (organic, first cold press)
1/2c Thompson raisins
1/4c Hunza raisins
1/4c Almond slivers raw
1/4c Coconut sugar crystals
1tsp Vanilla extract (non-alcohol)
1tsp Almond extract (non-alcohol)
1/2tsp Cinnamon powder
1/2tsp Himalayan salt

Note: To make fine almond flour use a high speed blender
or VitaMix®. Grind almonds ¼ cup at a time. This process
will prevent nuts from turning into a butter and also create
a finer flour. Use a flour sifter or wire mesh strainer to
separate the fine flour from larger granules.

If you do not own a dehydrator, chill in refrigerator to help
mockaroons maintain their shape.

DOUBLE CHOCOLATE

Ingredients

Makes Approx. 65
Prep Time: 30 min (plus dehydration time)

4c Coconut organic dried (shredded)
1-1/2c Almond flour (ground fine)
1-1/2c Maple syrup
3/4c Cacao powder raw
1/2c Coconut oil (organic, first cold press)
1/4c Cacao nibs
1/4c Coconut sugar crystals
2tbsp Maca powder
1tsp Vanilla extract (non-alcohol)
1/2tsp Himalayan salt

1. Mix all ingredients together in a KitchenAid® mixer or by hand in a large bowl with a wooden spoon. Once developed into a dough, create 1.5 inch size balls with a disher scoop or by hand.

2. Place onto a dehydrator screen. Set at 108 degrees for 6 to 10 hours. Dehydrate until a crispy coating on the outside appears and the inside remains moist.

LEMON DROP

Ingredients

Makes Approx. 65
Prep Time: 30 min (plus dehydration time)

4c Coconut organic dried (shredded)
2c Almond flour (ground fine)
1c Maple syrup
1/2c Coconut oil (organic, first cold press)
1/4c Lemon zest
1/4c Coconut sugar crystals
2tsp Vanilla extract (non-alcohol)
1tsp Lemon extract (non-alcohol)
1/2tsp Himalayan salt

Note: To make fine almond flour use a high speed blender or VitaMix®. Grind almonds ¼ cup at a time. This process will prevent nuts from turning into a butter and also create a finer flour. Use a flour sifter or wire mesh strainer to separate the fine flour from larger granules.

If you do not own a dehydrator, chill in refrigerator to help mockaroons maintain their shape.

HOMEMADE PUDDINGS

VANILLA DREAM

Ingredients

Makes Approx. 12 oz
Prep Time: 5 min

1c Cashews (soaked 4 hrs.)
3x Medjool dates (pitted & soaked)
1c Coconut meat (young Thai)
1/3c Maple syrup
1/3c Coconut oil
1/4c Water (filtered)
2tbsp Vanilla extract (non-alcohol)
1/8tsp Himalayan salt

1. Soak dates in filtered water for 15 minutes. Drain water. Then place nuts into a high speed blender.

2. In a blender add: coconut meat, medjool dates, maple syrup, coconut oil, water, vanilla extract, and salt. Blend into a smooth cream.

3. Vanilla Dream is a delicious treat as a topping on your favorite dessert, fruit, or even on it's own.

(To remove meat of a young Thai coconut, refer to instructions in note below.)

CHOCOLATE PUDDING

Ingredients

Makes Approx. 2 cups
Prep Time: 10 min

6x Medjool dates (pitted & soaked 15 min.)
1/4c Coconut meat (young Thai)
1/4c Cacao powder raw
1/4c Water (filtered)
1/4c Coconut sugar crystals
2tbsp Cashews (soaked 2 hrs.)
2tbsp Coconut oil (organic)
2tsp Vanilla extract (alcohol-free)
Pinch Himalayan salt

1. Pit and soak dates in filtered water for 15 minutes. Then drain and discard water.

2. In a high speed blender combine all the ingredients and blend into a smooth pudding consistency.

3. Once mixture is fully blended chill in refrigerator for several hours. Serve chilled. The Chocolate Pudding experience will bring you straight back in time to the simpler things in life . . . easy enjoyment.

Note: The following are two techniques on how to drain water from a young Thai coconut and how to access the coconut meat.

a. Puncture 2 small holes on the top of coconut with a heavy duty sharp knife. Empty liquid from one of the holes into a tall glass. Then to access meat set coconut upright. With a large sharp cleaver, swiftly tap the top of the coconut 4 times. Create a 3x3 inch square notch. Remove the top of the coconut. Remove coconut meat by scooping out with a spoon.

b. Lay coconut on its side. With a sharp heavy duty knife start at the tapered top of coconut and slowly slice through the white husk. You will gradually reach the shell. Continue to cut the shell until it cracks. Then pour out coconut water. Continue to cut around entire top of coconut Then remove the top. Remove coconut meat by scraping out with a spoon.

SALTED CARAMEL BLONDIES

Ingredients

Makes Approx. 9 squares
Prep Time: 35 min (plus freeze time)

2c Almond flour (ground fine)
6x Medjool dates (pitted)
1/3c Coconut oil (organic)
1/4c Maple sugar
1/4c Coconut sugar crystals
2tsp Vanilla extract (non-alcohol)
1/2tsp Himalayan salt

1/4c Creamy caramel (recipe below)
1/8tsp Celtic sea salt (fleur de sel)

CREAMY CARAMEL

Makes 2 cups
Prep Time: 5 min

8x Medjool dates (pitted & soaked)
1/4c Cashews (soaked 4 hrs.)
1/4c Pecans (soaked 2 hrs.)
1/4c Maple syrup
1/4c Coconut sugar crystals
1/4c Water (filtered)
2tbsp Coconut oil (first cold press)
2tsp Vanilla extract (non-alcohol)
1/2tsp Himalayan salt

1. Pit and soak dates in filtered water for approximately 15 minutes. Then drain and discard water. Then blend all ingredients in a high-speed blender into a thick Creamy Caramel.

Method

1. In a food processor grind 1 or 2 dates at a time with ¼ cup almond flour until all dates are ground into small granular sized pieces.

2. Mix all ingredients, except for Creamy Caramel and Celtic sea salt, in a Kitchen Aid® mixer or fold dough together by hand.

3. Divide dough into 2 equal parts. Press one half of dough flat into bottom of a small square pie pan. Then spread ½ cup of Creamy Caramel over first dough layer and top with a sprinkle of Celtic sea salt "flower of the ocean" (fleur de sel). Next, press second half of dough into pan over the top of caramel layer.

4. Set pan into dehydrator at 108 degrees for 8 to 12 hours. Dehydrate until top of dough becomes dry and a crispy texture appears on the surface. Then remove from dehydrator and slice into 3 inch squares. Salted Caramel Blondies can be a dessert on its own or served with your favorite ice cream.

Note: To make fine almond flour grind almonds ¼ cup at a time in a food processor. This process will prevent nuts from turning into a butter and also create a finer flour. Use a flour sifter or wire mesh strainer to separate the fine flour from larger granules.

If you do not own a dehydrator, chill in refrigerator to help Salted Caramel Blondies maintain their shape.

ICE CREAM! WE ALL SCREAM!

FRENCH VANILLA

Ingredients

Makes Approx. 1.5 pint
Prep Time: 15 min (plus freeze time)

2c Cashews (soaked 6 hrs.)
1-1/2c Coconut meat (young Thai)
5x Medjool dates (pitted & soaked)
1c Water (filtered)
1/3c Maple syrup
1/3c Coconut oil
1tbsp Coconut sugar crystals
3tbsp Vanilla extract (non-alcohol)
1inch Vanilla bean
1/4tsp Himalayan salt

1. Soak dates in filtered water for 15 minutes. Then drain and discard water. Remove vanilla beans from shell. Discard shell and save beans for blending.

2. Blend all ingredients in a VitaMix® blender. Blend on high and continuously move ingredients with tamper until mixture becomes smooth.

3. Then follow directions for your ice cream maker. Keep frozen in a freezer safe container.

CHOCOLATE CHOCOLATE

Ingredients

Makes Approx. 1.5 pint
Prep Time: 15 min (plus freeze time)

2c Cashews (soaked 6 hrs.)
1-1/2c Coconut meat (young Thai)
5x Medjool dates (pitted & soaked)
1/3c Maple syrup
1/2c Coconut oil (organic)
1/3c Coconut sugar crystals
1c Water (filtered)
1/2c Cacao powder raw
2tbsp Vanilla extract (non-alcohol)
1inch Vanilla bean
1/4tsp Himalayan salt

2tbsp Cacao nibs

1. Soak medjool dates for 15 minutes. Drain and discard water. Remove vanilla beans from shell. Discard shell and save beans for blending. Place all ingredients, except cacao nibs, into a VitaMix® blender. Blend on high and continuously move ingredients with tamper until smooth.

2. Follow the directions for your ice cream maker. Pour mixture into an ice cream maker container. Sprinkle in cacao nibs during the chilling process. To store ice cream, keep frozen in a freezer safe container. Scoop and dare to share!

CHERRY AMARETTO

Ingredients

Makes Approx. 1.5 pint
Prep Time: 15 min (plus freeze time)

2c Cashews (soak 6 hrs.)
1-1/2c Coconut meat (young Thai)
5x Medjool dates (pitted & soaked)
1c Water (filtered)
1/3c Coconut oil (organic)
1/3c Maple syrup
1tbsp Coconut sugar crystals
1tbsp Vanilla extract (non-alcohol)
1/4c Almond extract (non-alcohol)
1inch Vanilla bean
1/4tsp Himalayan salt

1/2c Cherries fresh (pitted, sliced quarters)
1/4c Almond slivers

1. Soak dates in filtered water for 15 minutes. Then drain and discard water. Remove vanilla beans from shell. Discard shell and save beans for blending. Pit and slice cherries into quarters and set aside.

2. Blend all ingredients, except for cherries, in a VitaMix® blender. Blend on high and continuously move ingredients with tamper until mixture becomes smooth.

3. Follow directions for your ice cream maker. Pour mixture into ice cream maker container and toss in cherries and almonds during this process. Keep frozen.

MINT CHOCOLATE CHIP

Ingredients

Makes Approx. 1.5 pint
Prep Time: 15 min (plus freeze time)

2c Cashews (soak 6 hrs.)
1-1/2c Coconut meat (young Thai)
1/2c Water (filtered)
1/3c Coconut oil (organic)
5x Medjool dates (pitted & soaked)
1/4c Maple syrup
2tbsp Coconut sugar
2tbsp Maple sugar
3/4tsp Green Macha Tea
2tbsp Vanilla extract (alcohol-free)
2tsp Mint extract
1/4tsp Himalayan salt

2tbsp Cacao nibs raw

1. Soak dates in filtered water for 15 minutes. Then drain and discard water.

2. Blend all ingredients, except cacao nibs, in a VitaMix® blender. Blend on high and continuously move ingredients with tamper until mixture becomes smooth.

3. Follow directions for your ice cream maker. Pour mixture into ice cream maker container and toss in cacao nibs during this process. Keep frozen.

SWEET TOPPERS

Use these to top your pies, ice creams, desserts, or any sweet treats you can possibly concoct in your kitchen.
We love to drizzle these all over the pies and share with great company.

CREAMY CARAMEL

Ingredients

Makes Approx. 2 cups
Prep Time: 5 min

8x Medjool dates (pitted & soaked)
1/4c Cashews (soaked 4 hrs.)
1/4c Pecans (soaked 2 hrs.)
1/4c Maple syrup
1/4c Coconut sugar crystals
1/4c Water (filtered)
2tbsp Coconut oil (first cold press)
2tsp Vanilla extract (non-alcohol)
1/2tsp Himalayan salt

1. Blend all ingredients in a high-speed blender until thick and creamy. To ensure Creamy Caramel is fully mixed it should appear even in color. Enjoy this on all sweet treats! You can stir in fresh chopped walnuts and then top the French Vanilla Ice Cream for a dreamy dessert.

   Note: Pit and soak dates in filtered water for approximately 15 minutes. Then drain and discard water.

CHOCOLATE FROSTING

Ingredients

Makes Approx. 2 cups
Prep Time: 5 min

1/2c Cacao powder (raw)
6x Medjool dates (pitted & soaked 15 min.)
1/8c Maple sugar
2tbsp Maca powder
2tbsp Coconut oil (first cold press)
1tbsp Vanilla extract (non-alcohol)
1/4c Water (filtered)
Pinch Himalayan salt

1. Blend all ingredients in a high-speed blender until smooth. Chill in the refrigerator until mixture becomes a firm frosting-like consistency.

FUDGE SAUCE

Ingredients

Makes Approx. 10 oz
Prep Time: 5 min

1/2c Cacao powder raw
1/2c Maple syrup
1/4c Water (filtered)
2tbsp Cashews (soaked 4 hrs.)
2tbsp Pecans (soaked 2 hrs.)
2tbsp Coconut sugar crystals
1/2tsp Vanilla extract (non-alcohol)
1/8tsp Himalayan salt

1. Drain soaked cashews and pecans and discard water. Then blend all ingredients in a high-speed blender until a delicious creamy Fudge Sauce is formed.

PINEAPPLE SAUCE

Ingredients

Makes Approx. 12 oz
Prep Time: 10 min

1-1/2c Pineapple fresh (chopped)
1/2c Pineapple (dried)
1/4c Maple sugar
1tbsp Coconut sugar crystals
1tsp Vanilla extract (non-alcohol)

1. Blend all ingredients in a high-speed blender. Purée to a smooth but slightly chunky Pineapple Sauce.

PART**TWO**

Liquid Fire Yoga® - The Practice

LIQUID FIRE YOGA® THE PRACTICE

The alchemical process of transforming the state of the small self into the state of bliss.

OUT ON A LIMB

When a yogin becomes qualified by practicing moral discipline (yama) and self-restraint (niyama), he can proceed to posture and the other means."
– Yoga-Bhyasa-Vivarana 2.29

The practice of Liquid Fire Yoga® is based on the Yoga Sutras of Patanjali* (threads of knowledge). Through our practice and study, we discovered an effortless way to bridge the gap of the past to the present. Our aim is to help the students of yoga to understand many aspects of yoga that may be confusing or seem unrealistic for today's world. The work of Patanjali's Yoga is still relevant in today's busy and chaotic world.

Patanjali's Yoga is the soul of the Liquid Fire Yoga® System. The Yoga Sutras of Patanjali is a clear set of universal and timeless instructions listed as threads of profound teachings. While there are historical references of yoga long before Patanjali's treatise on yoga, many schools of yoga continue to regard Patanjali as one of the supreme gurus of yoga.

The Yoga Sutras of Patanjali consist of four padas or books and begin with what the student needs to do to achieve the state of yoga. Then they outline the work one needs to do on oneself to settle the mind into stillness. Next, the yoga sutras illustrate the benefits that occur from the practice of stilling the mind. They conclude by describing the profound effect of attaining the space of samadhi (unending bliss or oneness with divinity). Patanjali illustrates the common challenges a student may face on their path of yoga. He sheds light on the inner workings of human nature and instructs the practices one may use to overcome these tendencies. To gain a clear perception of the teaching from the sutras, take the time to study all four sections as a whole.

The yoga method of Patanjali is most commonly referred to as Astanga Yoga. Ashto is the number eight, and anga is a limb. In book two of the sutras, the eight-limbs are instructions on how to begin the work of yoga practice. These eight limbs are practical and can be utilized every day. In this chapter Out On A Limb, its focus is on the eight-limbed system outlined in book two of Patanjali's Yoga text.

Patanjali's method is also referred to as Raja Yoga and Kriya Yoga. The sutras of Patanjali are described and referenced by many names and aspects of practice. The sutras appeal to all sorts of yoga students, from the physical student to the meditative student to the spiritually devout student. Depending on where you are in your life, you may perceive the lessons in a new light every time you study them. You may be drawn toward the action of the practice, the knowledge of practice, or the devotion of practice. No matter the method or how you describe it, the goal remains the same: to experience blissful meditation.

Raja translates to illuminated or royal. It is the path of yoga where the yoga student does the internal work to conquer their mind. This ability to gain control over the mind allows space for meditation to occur.

Kriya Yoga is another term used to describe the method of Patanjali. Below we illustrate the work of Kriya Yoga. The heart of Kriya Yoga is found in the niyamas (the self-restraints). The niyamas are the second limb of the Astanga sutra in Patanjali's Yoga text. Kriya Yoga integrates the following work of yoga:

Karma Yoga - Path of action and selfless service (third niyama, tapas)

Jnana Yoga - Path of knowledge or wisdom (fourth niyama, svadyaya)

Bhakti Yoga - Path of devotional practice (fifth niyama, Ishvara pranidhana)

Patanjali's Yoga shifts the mind-set of the student to see yoga beyond the physical exercise. They will begin to see that yoga is a divinely devotional discipline.

THE EIGHT LIMBS - ASTANGA YOGA

1. Yamas - Ethics (moral discipline)

2. Niyamas - Self-restraint (internal renunciation)

3. Asana - Postures (sacred movement)

4. Pranayama - Controlled movement of energy (deep and intentional breathing)

5. Pratyahara - Withdrawal from the senses (having no reaction to the data of the senses)

6. Dharana - Concentration (learning to meditate)

7. Dhyana - Deep meditation (steady unbroken focus)

8. Samadhi - Euphoria (complete immersion with the divine Self)

*Please make sure you find a copy of The Yoga Sutras to help you learn more about the practice. (See our Yoga Sutra study recommendations in the back of this book).

INWARD GAZING

Infinite bliss is attainable.

Developing a sense of harmony starts from looking at the foundation of the yamas (ethics) and niyamas (self-restraint). This understanding begins with the fifth niyama, divine love - Ishvara pranidhana (surrendering to the compassionate force within you).

When your entire being can cultivate genuine care for others, and the world, the development of yoga practice will unfold safely and peacefully. Developing compassion with no desire for reciprocation is the divine compassion yoga asks the student to partake in.

This initiation of love and compassion (Ishvara pranidhana) is a significant building block to understanding not only your purpose in this world but to recognize the purpose of all beings in this world. The balance of the world's ecological systems immeasurably depend on your compassionate nature. Compassion increases the desire to make a tremendous inward change. This profound inner change sparks focus and dedication and eliminates doubt. Doubt holds a practitioner back from the aim of yoga.

In yoga, the symbology of an arrow is quite powerful. The bow is light, energy, or prana. The arrow is the intense focus (tapas) of the yoga practitioner. The holder of the bow must be calm, balanced, and confident. When the arrow is drawn and released, it is symbolic of one who is on their way to experience infinite bliss. Any doubt or insecurity in the one who releases the arrow will cause the arrow to miss the goal. A practitioner who is grounded in yamas (ethics) and niyamas (self-restraint) can aim with confidence. Even if they miss the bull's-eye, they come closer to infinite bliss. That closeness to infinite peace is enough to inspire you to continue practicing.

Yoga practice triggers self-reflection and compassion and inspires one to adjust their behaviors and perceptions in accordance with the yamas and niyamas. The next time one sets their sight on the target, infinite bliss is attainable.

THE YAMAS - The Ethics (moral discipline)
1. **Ahimsa -** Non-violent or non-harming.
2. **Asteya-** Non-stealing.
3. **Satya -** Truthfulness.
4. **Bramacharya -** Self-control.
5. **Aparigraha -** Non-greediness.

THE NIYAMAS - The Self-Restraint (internal renunciation)
1. **Saucha -** Purification and cleanliness.
2. **Santosha -** Contentment.
3. **Tapas -** Desire for practice.
4. **Svadyaya -** Self inquiry.
5. **Ishvara Pranidhana -** Divine Love.

When you are inspired by some great purpose, some extraordinary project, all your thoughts break their bonds: your mind transcends limitations, your consciousness expands in every direction, and you find yourself in a new, great and wonderful world. Dormant forces, faculties and talents become alive, and you discover yourself to be a greater person by far than you ever dreamed yourself to be." -Patanjali

PRACTICE OF PERCEPTION

THE YAMAS

The Ethics (moral discipline)

1. AHIMSA - Non-violent or non-harming.
Compassion towards the sentient and non-sentient.

2. ASTEYA - Non-stealing.
Attaining a state free from selfish desires.

3. SATYA - Truthfulness.
Honesty and recognition of the world without illusions.

4. BRAHMACHARYA - Self-control.
Goodwill and moderation of food, thoughts, and indulgent desires.

5. APARIGRAHA - Non-greediness.
Only acquiring what one truly needs to live.

THE NIYAMAS

The Self-Restraint (internal renunciation)

1. SAUCHA - Purification and cleanliness.
Referring to both outer surroundings and inner body.

2. SANTOSHA - Contentment.
Constant connection to joyous nature.

3. TAPAS - Desire for practice.
Burning impurities. Zealous learning of Self. Intensity for deep practice. Prayerful discipline.

4. SVADYAYA - Self inquiry.
Study of the inner self and sacred scriptures.

5. ISHVARA PRANIDHANA - Divine Love.
Surrender to the compassionate force within you.

KINDNESS DEVELOPS FROM STUDY

To look in, that's fearlessness.

The science of yoga is the study (svadyaya) of many facets of life. Studying the body, the breath, and the mind, we begin to understand these aspects of life through the experience of practice. The study of yoga allows the student to comprehend consciousness and learn how to calm it during practice. The yoga student takes the time to learn how foods affect their mind and how healthy food supports their meditation practice. Yoga study is designed to raise questions. Answers to the questions are found through the practice and the application of what was studied. Most of what is learned in yoga is learned through experience. The focus of yoga study is to inspire you to continue practicing.

Through the study of yoga texts, the effect of asanas on the body, and how breathing stabilizes the physiological and mental states of being (svadyaya), profound learning gradually takes place. This education is not something one can be graded on, but something one learns firsthand. Self-study leads to the space of presence and the spiritual practice.

Clearing the mind and understanding consciousness (chitta) takes a little practice and time. You can easily accomplish it through the practice of breathing, mindful eating, and redirecting negative thoughts toward thoughts of compassion and kindness (pratipaksha bhavanam). Taking a few moments to self-reflect on what caused the negative thoughts to rise in the first place will help you clear the residue of the misunderstanding. Through daily practice, you will feel the power of learning about yourself, your actions, and you will have the ability to change what needs to be changed to maintain clarity.

Although the mind is a subtle part of our being, it is commonly accepted to be the brain itself. In actuality, the mind is experienced throughout the entire body, and its presence is deeply seated in the cellular being. Perceptions of ourselves develop from memories of sensory data coming through the body's cells and the five senses.

Clean thoughts are just as important as fresh provisions. What is absorbed in the intestines affects the mind, and if the food is clean, the mind will be clean, and the thoughts will be easy and pleasant. Eating fresh food, hydration, deep breathing, sacred movement, and wisdom are essential for creating the space for meditation. The daily work of these practices contributes to creating positive memories. This new memory bank of feeling excellent and vibrant will continue to grow. As it magnifies, you will feel inspired to create more time for practice. With continued practice, you will naturally begin to understand mind and consciousness (chitta) and how to direct them. When consciousness and mind connect to the rhythm of the breath, you will find yourself gliding right into the space of meditation with ease.

The power of consciousness cannot be schooled. It is already within; an essential comprehension. It is the same force that creates the blueprint for a seed to grow into a tree. Consciousness is a principle of nature; one cannot touch it but can experience its existence. Consciousness is like the body, and it, too, needs the continuous practice of alignment. Alignment for the yoga practitioner is a constant endeavor. It seems that every day there is something new to align and shift in the body.

The inner renunciation (niyama) is the yoga practice of restraining the uncontrolled behavior of yourself. Some days you may feel as if the five senses are impulsive and desirous. When you experience this, it is because your senses, consciousness, and breath are out of alignment. To bring them back into a space where you feel blissful and calm, start with the yamas (ethics) and niyamas (self-restraint). Then the practice of hydrating the system and fueling it with healthy food will be effortless. Once the body is hydrated and well-fed deep breathing is natural and comfortable. Movements in the yoga postures feel controlled and steady. Through continuing these practices naturally, you will find mental and physical calmness returning.

THE SIX AVARICES

Passion, Anger, Greed, Infatuation, Envy & Malice

The work one does on themselves affects the ability to become an outward renunciate, renouncing the actions that adversely affect others and the self. The practice of ethics (yama) and self-restraint (niyama) clear the path to remove the six avarices. Passion, anger, greed, infatuation, pride, malice & envy. Yoga meditation creates light where there once was darkness. Working to remove avarice from the mind opens the space for you to have clarity, reason, and contentment without any interruption.

Yoga practice reinforces good habits that benefit the body and the mind. It continually asks you to look inward. Are you forcing this stretch, is the breathing labored, are you present with the experience right now? Why are you doing this work today? It makes you look inside. It's so easy to look out, to see others. But to look in, that's fearlessness. To be unafraid of what you will find.

When you find the actions and thoughts that cause you suffering, you can weed them out. Removing old habits that cause pain is like weeding a garden. One weed at a time you pull, tug, and get to the root. Sometimes, you might pull little too hard (force) and break the weed at the stem, which will cause the weed to grow back stronger. When the weed grows back, you know now from experience force isn't the route to go. So through changing your course of action, you gently move the dirt surrounding the base of the weed looking for the most substantial part of the stem. And tug, with steady concentration.

Weeds are self-growing. So you can't just pick it and be prideful of the work you accomplished. Focus. Be vigilant and continue working. We need to burn the avarice out of the mind. How does one burn a weed of avarice? Through intense focus (tapas, the third niyama). Keep practicing. Yoga practice is what burns the harmful weeds out of your mind.

SVADYAYA

Self-study challenges personal beliefs, creating friction to BURN what needs to change.

Yoga study is two-fold. First, there is the study of sacred texts or scriptures. Inspiring books like The Yoga Sutras of Patanjali, The Hatha Yoga Pradipika, The Upanishads, and The Bible all guide the student to look inside at their thoughts and actions. They remind us of the good in the world. And while yoga itself is not a religion, it is helpful to know whatever your faith is; yoga makes faith stronger and unbreakable. That is the power of study. It supports your current beliefs and faith and guides you diligently on the path of well-being, kindness, and compassion.

The other aspect of study is looking inward at yourself. Previously in the last section, we discussed about burning the weeds of avarice from the mind. Self-Study supports the work of looking at your entire self and watching the body, how it moves in yoga postures. The mind and what it's focused upon. The food you eat and how it's affecting your mind, your body, and your weight. Watching your actions (yamas and niyamas) and discovering how you react and whether or not you want to repeat that reaction. Looking in is the most challenging aspect of self-study.

Yoga practice is meditation practice. It makes us look inwards, slow thoughts down, and feel our body. It lets us connect with and experience the moment. It supports feeling content and clear. Without the aspect of focus, yoga postures are gymnastic tricks. The ability to control the breath, align the mind and consciousness to the breath and move the body with the breath, you have positively shifted the posture into a moving meditation experience.

In yoga practice, intellect allows us to reason. It's the voice that says you shouldn't eat pizza before yoga class. Mind is what wants you to eat the pizza anyway because it is craving it. Intellect will retreat because it has been trained; the mind is in control. Self-study allows us to shift this imbalance. Slowly we encourage the intellect, give it strength. We enable it to observe our postures and alignment. It counts our breaths, and the space from the inhale to the exhale. Intellect allows us to deepen our practice.

As the intellect gains strength, we can apply the knowledge gained from the study of the texts and self-study during the action of practice. When this happens, wisdom flourishes. And when you are filled with wisdom, going back to old habits doesn't look rewarding nor as fun as they once did. You find yourself enjoying the healthy foods, savoring the breath, and present every minute of your practice. Study. It moves you into meditation.

HUMANTENDENCIES

The practice of yoga can eliminate the tendencies of depression, doubt, insecurity and anxiety.

You've heard the phrase, "I'm only human!" It's common to use this expression to explain we're not perfect. It's also interpreted it to mean that shortcomings, laziness, and forgetfulness should be accepted, which to some degree, makes perfect sense. Sometimes we might find that being human also creates blame for others when things go wrong or holding too high of an expectation of another person. These tendencies cause an imbalance because these actions are, in fact, human. Yoga practice aims to change this imbalance and to create a natural state of peace.

Yoga practice inspires us to aim for change and to change the influence human tendencies have on us. It allows us to be in control of being human. Yoga indeed explains what it is to be human and precisely what human nature is and how we can change it. That's the part of yoga that is powerful; you can make a change because you are educated on how to make the change happen.

Through consistent practice (abhyasa) and looking inwards, you will see that are three modes your mind fluctuates between. On the next page is a quick breakdown of these human tendencies. We will explain further what they mean and how you can make shift happen.

In the Yoga Sutras of Patanjali, the word for nature is prakriti. This word shows up many times in the text and is in relationship to the following three modes of nature called - the gunas. The gunas are inherent qualities found in all aspects of nature from humans, to plants.

Learning about the gunas is like discovering you have three different minds. Some days you feel like your body is seized by laziness, but the mind is vibrant, and it's thinking about traveling and creating. You are, at that moment, experiencing the pull of tamasic (inactive) and rajasic (active) natures. These fluctuations in your mind and body can make you feel out of sorts. Yoga teaches us to balance these qualities of nature, we should take action, but to take action calmly (sattvic).

The practice of yoga can eliminate the tendencies of depression, doubt, insecurity, and anxiety. From learning to study, breathe, and move calmly in yoga postures, we create an atmosphere of balance and harmony.

The approach one has towards yoga is so important. When the poses are practiced with a lot of stimulation and intensity, it will increase the state of rajas. The student may feel high while doing the poses, but after the postures conclude, they feel exhausted and unable to think clearly. This example demonstrates a massive swing from rajasic to tamasic nature.

On the other hand, when one is too depressed, unmotivated to practice, or is lackadaisically stretching without attention to alignment, this further pushes one into a lethargic nature (tamasic).

If one approaches the postures mindfully and steadily, the rewards are tremendous. The student is in a state of meditative focus, rather than being pulled toward sleep and laziness. They are listening to the breath and are aware of the entire body from head to toe. Complete and total presence with the moment. Grateful. Uplifted. Content.

The practice of yoga has highs and lows, too. Since the student is still working on gaining control of their human tendencies, the desire to fall back into laziness and say, "I am only human" will slow the process and create excuses for not working diligently.

The practice is not of perfection to satisfy the ego or to even tell others that you are perfect. The aim toward yoga perfection and gaining control of the gunas will intensify your confidence, and it will help pull you up from the plateaus and remove the boredom of repetition. It generates interest, and it allows you to look inside and realize how strong human tendencies are. This recognition can be used as an inspiration to keep practicing.

The Three Gunas

Rajasic

Color: red

Relation to nature: sun, fire

Positive qualities: inspiration, energy, vibrant, action

Negative qualities: erratic, chaotic, uncontrolled, volatile, angry

Tamasic

Color: black

Relation to nature: murky black water, earth

Positive qualities: slowing down, rest

Negative qualities: lazy, vindictive, bored, depressed, inaction

Sattvic

Color: white

Relation to nature: the aspect of light that brightens a room, rays of the sun. The balanced feeling you get when walking through the woods or when at the beach.

Positive qualities: balanced, right action, vibrant meditative space, tranquil, peaceful

Negative qualities: none

When one eats food
it breaks down into 3 parts.
The densest becomes feces
The medium becomes flesh
The finest becomes the mind.

When one drinks water
it breaks down in 3 parts.
The densest becomes urine
The medium becomes blood
The finest becomes the breath.

When one eats heat {prana}
it breaks down in 3 parts.
The densest becomes bone
The medium becomes marrow
The finest becomes the speech

-The Upanishads

EXTRACT THE POISON

The practice of yoga is not meant to feed our human nature, it is meant to fuel our Divine nature.

THE NINE OBSTACLES

1. **Illness, disease** (Vyadhi)
2. **Mental stagnation, dullness** (Styana)
3. **Doubt, insecurity** (Samsaya)
4. **Lack of foresight, carelessness** (Pramada)
5. **Fatigue, laziness** (Alasya)
6. **Overindulgence** (Avirati)
7. **Illusions about one's true state of mind, false perceptions** (Bharantidarsana)
8. **Lack of perseverance, failure to reach firm ground** (Alabdhabhumikatva)
9. **Regression, slipping from ground gained** (Anavasthitatvani)

Poison. It's tenacious, like water. It moves through crevices and absorbs into the depths of the body. It can flood into the memory bank of the mind. It's a powerful substance. We can recognize this poisonous substance by the skull and cross bone warning label. So, we won't consume it. But, what do we do when the poison isn't labeled? We look at it. We smell it. If it seems innocent enough, we ingest it. It alters our actions and how we move. It harms us. The nine obstacles and the five afflictions are the unlabeled poisons that surge through body and mind. Patanjali gives the obstacles (and afflictions) a label so that we can recognize the obstacle (and affliction), and you can make a conscious choice to consume it, or to burn it. For the most part, the limitations of the nine obstacles are self-explanatory. But, when we look at the obstacles and how they affect our ability to live and practice, they take on a new meaning. They work as a force together, one obstacle causing another obstacle to rise.

Patanjali's Yoga Sutras start with the goal of yoga practice to still the mind into silence. Further, in the sutras, he dissects the nature of the human mind and teaches us to recognize the bite-sized morsels of poison (nine obstacles) we innocently swallow. He's asking us to watch for the nine obstacles surging through our thoughts and our actions. And then apply the yoga practice to help to shift them and eventually burn them (tapas). Once we burn these obstacles from our character, we see that our natural, peaceful nature is a real treat.

This serene and joyful mental space floods our life with positive memories and the ability to be courageous in the face of challenges. One of the most significant challenges every human being faces is the challenge of learning about themselves. Overcoming the little obstacles that arise daily will slowly amount to a very sound foundation from which to grow into the courageous and kind person you are meant to be. Yoga provides us with the energy and encouragement we need to maintain the peace we worked for.

Patanjali reminds us the work of yoga is continuous. It is ever-evolving. It's also about having the foresight of future obstacles that may begin to grow. Similar to a weed dropping its seeds. As more weeds grow, more obstacles arise. They will keep feeding each other until the entire forest of your being is covered in toxic weeds and invasive vines. We need to cut these vines down and pull the weeds from the root and then burn the whole stack of poisonous material in a nice warm fire. Patanjali says we need to continue to have a strong desire for yoga practice, so that we can also burn the seeds of future obstacles, too.

HALLUCINATION

Mental distractions

The FIVE Kleshas - AFFLICTIONS

1. Ignorance, not knowing the self (Avidya)
2. Egoism, self-forgetting, misunderstanding (Asmita)
3. Attachment, desire, jealousy (Raga)
4. Aversion, hatred (Dvesha)
5. Clinging to bodily life, fear of death, fearfulness (Abhinivesa)

The five afflictions and nine obstacles are crucial topics often avoided because they make us look at the challenges of being human. The nine obstacles are related to the inactive nature (tamasic), the five afflictions are related to the active nature (rajasic), and the practice of yoga is related to the nature of right action (sattvic). If you look at the obstacles, you will see that many of them prevent us from taking any action, while the afflictions cause us to take negative actions. The practice of yoga is to create inspiration to take right action. It's less about just writing down the intention "make it a great day" and more about taking action through yoga practice so we can actually make today a great day!

The five afflictions (the kleshas) cause us to see things that are not there. They make us look at life and ourselves through smoke-filled lenses. The kleshas are the emotions you are faced with, like your desires and fears. Emotions are necessary. Yoga practice is not asking us to be rid of all feelings and become stoic and cold. It's asking us to look inside and see when we are letting the afflictions grip us. And to decide to use the emotions to motivate us into right action or to let them go. The practice of yoga is like the voice of reason. Sometimes the

desire or anger is so strong the voice of reason sounds insignificant. If our focus is on the emotions, and we continue to disregard the voice of reason, it will fade completely. Anger will take hold.

Take the time to stop and practice self-reflection. This allows reason to have a voice in your mind. Taking time to practice can change the course of your emotions and give you a moment to decide if this emotion necessary right now. Will it cause you agitation, or will it help and inspire you to move into an uplifting action?

At the moment when the emotion strikes, it is challenging to be self-reflective. The troublesome emotion usually happens when it's impossible to escape to a quiet place and reflect. There is a way out. Swiftly flip the thoughts causing the emotion. This work is the first stage of the practice of thought reversal (pratipaksha bhavanam).

For example, when fearful, change the course of your thoughts one hundred eighty degrees to a thought unrelated to what's causing the negative emotion. When you have quiet time, reflect to the moment you had to flip the thought. What caused the emotion to develop? Then, understand it. From understanding the cause, you will be wise. The next time this emotion pulls at you, you will see it and recognize it before it intensifies. This recognition will grant you an opportunity to make a choice. Do you want to feel that agitation from the emotion again, or do you want to feel free of it? You have a choice. You are now in control of being human.

Care of the mobile temple (the body) is of utmost importance
as it is the vehicle of our journey through life.

PANCHAVAHANAS

The five vehicles that move your practice.

1. Food - Consuming fresh food
2. Hydration - Liquid cleansing
3. Asana - Mindful movement
4. Pranayama - Controlled movement of breath/energy
5. Wisdom - Application of studies and practice

The Pancha Vahanas (five vehicles) help with the effortless action of taking care of oneself without intricate formulas to memorize. These five vehicles are daily actions needed to have a body and mind fit for the work of yoga. Vahanas in Sanskrit mean vehicles and that which carries. They are vehicles that offer guidance on the practice of right-action for the yoga student. Vahanas can also translate to mean having power over vices. Yoga students can practice overcoming the influence of their vices and human tendencies to create an upward movement of energy.

Movement. Flow. Rhythm. The easiest way to create flow is through the Pancha Vahanas. Learning to flow takes a little effort — it' not a space of doing whatever one wants whenever they want. Many of the choices you make throughout the day can cause you to fall out of sync with nature's cycles, and when you feel out of sync, it's challenging to get back into the rhythm you once had. To learn to flow is to train the body and mind to get back into sync. To create a cohesive space where creativity and energy can flow abundantly.

Creating home-made meals is a vital part of your mood enhancement. Exploring a variety of food, taking cooking classes, and using the recipes in this book gives you the confidence and the skill to make meals quickly and easily. When was the last time you were invited to have a home-cooked meal at a friend's house? On special occasions, perhaps, but daily home-cooked meals are not a regular feature in most households. It's surprising because the very act of creating a home-cooked meal in itself is a stress reliever and mood enhancer. It's a beautiful way to shift from the negative aspects of the day and to refocus the energy into something great, a wonderful home-cooked meal filled with plentiful nutrients and fresh ingredients. Just knowing that you took action and made something good for your body and mind, a natural and easy-going joy rises inside your being. The mind and body become filled with clean fuel, steady energy, and power for profound meditative living. Cooking is a form a meditation practice, and it can become a part of your daily life. Your daily meditation and cooking can become as one.

Focused meditation relies on being well hydrated. When the system is dry and dehydrated, this causes the breath to become inconsistent, and it interrupts the body's ability to attain natural movement. Irregular breathing leads to disturbance in the body and mind. It causes agitation. To remove this arid layer, drink plenty of clean water. Water is a natural cleansing agent. Clean, purified water supports a healthy vital system which is necessary for the advancement of the yoga practice. It is also essential to consume beverages that are natural and made from pure ingredients. However, nothing replaces water for proper hydration. Instead of reaching for the coffee pot in the morning, reach for a tall glass of water. And start the day in a genuinely good mood.

Getting to the yoga mat to move and breathe deep into the body is a gift and puts you in a good mood. The joyful meditation that rises from the focus and concentration of feeling the body move and breathe is extraordinary. As you practice the postures (asanas), you discover the breath moves from your head to your toes. Eventually, a feeling every yoga student delights in. Controlled breathing (pranayama) is most beneficial practiced in asanas (posture practice) as well as seated in a meditation pose. Controlled breathing and mindful movement are vital contributors to complete health and well-being, and they should most definitely become a part of the wellness system you are developing for yourself. Slowing down the breath calms down the mind, so it is open for learning. When the mind is open to learning, it is free to look deep inside.

Watch. Listen. Witness. The mind observes how the delicious lunch and proper hydration of the body led up to a positive posture experience on the mat. The controlled breath becomes second nature and is smooth and steady. Taking all that you have studied about yoga and yourself and applying the lessons learned, creates wisdom. Wisdom is awareness to practice the actions that are right for your well-being.

The Pancha Vahanas (the five vehicles) are the vehicles that get your practice moving!

"I believe in the absolute oneness of God, and therefore, humanity. What though we have many bodies? We have but one soul. The rays of sun are many through refraction. But they have the same source. I cannot, therefore, detach myself from the wickedest soul nor may I be denied identity with the most virtuous." - Mahatma Gandhi

PRIMORDIALWISDOM

Constantly united with the godhead, this yogi's bliss is eternal.
Touched in this way this yogi sees unity and divinity everywhere in every creature, in all creation.
Bhagavad Gita 6.28-29.

Yoga looks at the body as layers, layers that interact, and influence each other all day long with or without our knowledge. The layers of the body are called sheaths and are also known as koshas in Sanskrit. Each sheath encases a single layer or multiple layers of our body and mind. In yoga, the mind is not separate from the rest of the body. Meditation in yoga helps one to develop an understanding of these layers and acknowledgment of their existence.

These layers in the body are invisible, and because we cannot see them with the eyes, there is speculation that they may not exist. Yoga teaches you to become aware of the layers of the body and mind, to observe, and to gather your truth about what you see inside. It's an honest perception of the emotions and cognizance of where they spring from. It's a realistic sensation of reasoning and using the voice of reason to make decisions. The experience of the sheaths is an understanding of where the blissful and joyful modes of living exist.

The mind is in the muscles, the organs, and the bones. Because the mind dwells in every part of the body, memories also exist throughout the body. This is why when we are touched a certain way, breathe in a scent, or move a certain way, a memory or emotion may be triggered. Understanding the layers of the body will help you learn about yourself and your actions, more in-depth.

The layers move from what you can see and feel to the most subtle layer, the layer that meditation originates. It is an inward layer that affects how we speak and grow as a person. Learning about the layers of the body comes from watching, listening, and witnessing.

The koshas interweave everything we have been learning about food, hydration, movement, breathing, and wisdom into a beautiful web of knowledge. Like a spider weaves its web, we too are weaving a web to live on. When a part of the web becomes compromised, the spider, without hesitation, moves quickly to repair the damaged web. When we destroy our web through food or beverages that create imbalance, we can promptly move to that area of our life and begin to repair it. Simply by making different choices. Yoga gives us opportunities to lean into a lesson plan. It guides you and moves you into living your best life.

PHYSICAL BODY (sarira) - The Outer Layer
    Annamaya kosha - The Food Body (muscular structure)
    Cared for through postures of yoga and food choices.

THE SUBTLE BODY (sarira) - The Internal Layers
    Pranamaya kosha - The Physiological Body (organs)
    Cared for through proper hydration and breath control

    Manomaya kosha - The Psychological Body (mind)
    Cared for through studying texts and focusing the mind on the present.

    Vijnamaya kosha - The Wisdom/Intellectual Body (reasoning/intellect) Using the lessons learned and applying them daily.

THE BLISSFUL BODY (sarira) - The Innermost Layer
    Anandamaya kosha - The Blissful Body (peace)
    Where the experience of presence and meditation exists. The body of constant peace.

PARTTHREE

Sacred Practice Of Divine Placement

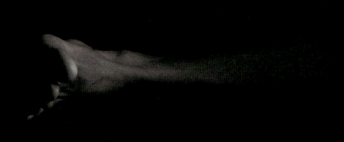

THE LIVING ESSENCE

Witness the body become exactly the essence divinity intended it to be powerful, strong, and beautiful.

Inhale, and God approaches you. Hold the inhalation, and God remains with you. Exhale,

and you approach God. Hold the exhalation, and surrender to God.   -Krishnamacharya

Raja yoga means to conquer the mind and the word ujjayi also means to conquer. To conquer something we must arrive prepared.

Instead of arriving to battle with weapons drawn, we arrive with an impenetrable shield created by ujjayi pranayama.

PRANA**YAMA**

Don't Forget To Breathe

What you breathe in is what you become.

Breathe in...Breathe out...Expand your energy up.

The breath of Liquid Fire Yoga® practice is called the wave breath. In Sanskrit, it's ujjayi pranayama. Just as the ocean is expansive and powerful, the breathing practice of ujjayi pranayama expands the body's and mind's ability to sustain focus, concentration, and, eventually, long-lasting meditation. When there is breath, there is light energy — prana. Prana is an upward movement of breath and energy. A natural force that motivates and inspires. Pranayama sheds light where there is darkness — brightening your mind, body, and intelligence. It is an internal aspect of the breath-work practiced in yoga postures, whether the position is a standing pose, seated pose, or a moving pose. When the breath is controlled, it moves up in the system. You can feel the mood of your mind and body change. Pranayama is a potent element essential for yoga practice.

Pranayama is two-fold. There is the prana (light, energy), and there is the yama. Yama literally is "to restrain." It's the stimulus that expands the element of freedom in your life. Without restraints, there is chaos and distraction. Restraint alters the state of mind in such profound ways that it expands meditation into every facet of your life. From cooking dinner to washing the dishes, the meditative experience of bliss is readily attainable.

The breath is the master teacher. It educates you when you are stressed. It lets you know that something good is about to happen.
The breath is the greatest gift of yoga practice. It is the mind-altering, body-shifting ultimate experience of freedom. This freedom the breath gives is from the restraint we have to focus on nothing else but - the breath. The breath, prana, and mind are all linked. When the breath is controlled, the body feels light, and the mind has clarity and calmness. Just as proper and controlled breathing can bring lightness, an uncontrolled and improper breath can cascade one into anxiety and depression within a single moment. The breath is like a diamond that glistens in the sunlight casting light where there was once darkness. When it comes to the breath, there is no need for positive thoughts or forcing a positive will. The breath creates positivity naturally.

Ujjayi is the expansion; prana is the light; yama is the control. Ujjayi pranayama expands the light in a controlled way. Its goal is not to throw light everywhere, but be the light, where you stand. An internal sensation of confidence wells up inside. This is not the confidence of false ego and faking; this is a calm, quiet radiant confidence, and assurance that your existence is purposeful and mindful.

You have the power to brighten your life. Just don't forget to breathe.

The technical side of breathing

The most effective way to learn ujjayi pranayama is through a teacher's guidance. A skilled teacher understands the breaths rhythm and its sound. Each person's breath is slightly different. Its unique qualities are so subtle, and a live teacher can remind you to soften it or intensify it. They can offer guidance on how to regulate it—giving you the ability to have direct experience with the breath. This connection is all-encompassing and life-changing. You will never forget about the breath after having a moment of what it feels like to be in total control of your breath, mind, and body all at once. This elevated state gives you the ability to remove the suffering of an entire day in a single breath. It is that powerful.

THE SOUND OF THE SEA

Our society's instinct is to learn everything from books and videos; learning about yoga is not like learning how to change a tire on your car. The description below is for informational purposes only.

Sitting near the ocean calms the vacillations of the mind because the sound of the waves is very consistent. The waves never cease. They get stronger, and sometimes they soften. The sound of a wave hitting the shore and then drawn back into the sea is constant. The sound of the ocean is exactly like the sound of ujjayi pranayama. This breath is also called the wave breath because it slows down the waves of the mind.

The sound on the exhale is like a soft h as if you are whispering in a library. The inhale is a soft s sound. Breathing practice is through the nostrils, with the mouth closed. The sound of the breath is in the throat. It takes mental concentration to apply this whispering sound, but the moment you move the breath sound away from the nostrils, and into the throat, it will be a lesson that says with you forever.

ONCE YOU BUILD PRANA, LOCK IT IN.

The breath starts with how the body is aligned. Without alignment, the control of the breath is next to impossible. And while we are a society of breaking the bounds of impossible, why struggle against something when it can be practiced with such ease and a little training to get it comfortable and strong?

There are three locks in the body. The Sanskrit word bandha is to lock.

THE THREE BANDHAS
Jalandhara Bandha

Uddyana bandha

Mula Bandha

The first lock is the mula bandha. In Sanskrit, mula is root. It is the root lock in the body — part of the root system to the tree of yoga practice. To practice the root lock of mula bandha is to ensure the healthy development of yoga practice. This lock will ensure that the excellent work of controlling prana stays inside. It's definitely worth the energy and effort to explore locking mula bandha. It makes the good vibes you created through movement and breathing remain with you for days and weeks. Many students sleep better after learning this controlled practice of moving the breath through the system.

The second lock is the uddyana bandha. Uddyana is to fly upward. It is the lock that moves the breath up in the system, causing the rib cage to expand, increasing the lungs capacity to take in more oxygen. The better the control is of uddyana bandha, the easier it is to remove stress from the body. Students that become masterful at controlling this bandha can stop stress from rising in a single breath.

The third lock is the jalandhara bandha. It is the throat lock and one of the most subtle of locks. This lock prevents the need to express emotions and thoughts during meditation. It's not a suppression of ideas, but its job is to ensure the prana circulates the system and doesn't get lost in the head and the world of thought, desire, and memory.

The breath alignment for the body is very subtle. The actions to engage these locks are gentle but firm. The first movement is a slight tuck in the pelvis. The slight tuck in the pelvis engages the two lower locks (mula bandha and uddyana bandha) naturally and simultaneously, and it realigns the tailbone setting it in the correct placement for breathing. This slight tuck of the pelvis also engages the abdominal muscles and provides a subtle lift in the perineum. Sometimes the tuck in the pelvis is too extreme, and the students upper back rounds or they feel pressure in the lower back. If either of these sensations persists, the effort on the locks is too intense. Softening it a little bit will earn you success.

The throat lock (jalandhara bandha) is a slight downward movement of the chin and little pulling in toward the throat. This movement is easy to attain in the downward-facing dog, for example. Turning the eyes toward the navel center helps the chin naturally pull down and in.

No matter what the level of practice your mind places you, the work of alignment is practical and necessary and beyond the scope of advancement. Once these three locks are engaged, the sound of the breath will move effortlessly. Soothing the mind and inspiring the body into movement.

LIQUID FIRE YOGA® PRACTICE is a poetic pulse of rhythms and devotional gestures linked through the self-conquering whispers of ujjayi pranayama. This profound yoga discipline summons the aspirant to develop exalted states of sentience.

LIQUIDFIREYOGA®

Asana Practice - Take it easy

Submit to the light as the shadows of affliction fade.
Exalt in reverence as the sun instructs the indwelling presence.

Asana extends beyond physically stretching the body. The word asana translates to the practice of sacred movement. But many of the commercialized yoga classes today are removed from the benefits of the ancient teachings of yoga and the yoga practice is often referred to as merely postures. Therefore, the practice of yoga asana is frequently misunderstood. Change your perspective. Asana practice is sacred and self-reflective work. In this section, explore an effortless approach toward asana practice.

When one embarks on learning asana, it is essential they have the foundation of mental control (the yamas and niyamas) already established. The mind-set of Liquid Fire Yoga® is to approach the asana less mechanically and more creatively. Creative alignment is the key to effortless yoga asana practice. Imagine the postures as lines. The lines and shapes of the postures when properly aligned create passageways for the breath to travel through the body with the least amount of resistance. This process of steady, uninterrupted breathing applied to yoga asana is known as sthithi krama. To create easy passages for the breath may mean you will feel less of a stretch. However, you will be aligned properly and comfortable in the positions. Properly aligned postures help free the body from tension and illness. However, forcing the stretch in a posture creates tension and

prohibits the benefits of the conscious breath-work (pranayama). The practice of linking of the conscious breath-work to asana is not an overnight event. It is something that takes continuous practice and effort. There is no need to place pressure on yourself to achieve postures or flexibility. Instead, explore the natural mobility of your body.

Create a suitable setting for your asana practice. Set your yoga mat in a clean room free from distractions and clutter. Light a candle to set an intention for practice. When setting an intention go beyond your physical expectations and goals. Begin the session with the sound of OM. Use this sound to create a pleasant space for this energetic work.

OM (infinite bliss) is pronounced with the three sounds of A-U-M. This sound is called the pranava. Pranava is the all pervading sound. Create the intention of blissful space and gratitude when chanting OM. Hold this space of heartfelt gratitude throughout the duration of your asana practice. The mind cannot experience anything negative when it is filled with the space of gratitude.

With consistent practice (abhyasa), the mind will become still and tranquility will become a way of life. Apply this mindful approach toward asana and allow yourself to discover the experience of yoga.

SURYA NAMASKARA

Sun Salutations; Blazing devotion of joyful space

Incline with quiet composure as the lumbar spine ushers in a deep bow steering the eyes of the soul inward. Vitality and willpower shower down from the highest altitude of space in the heavens, shining phosphorescent adoration into the heart.

As one moves with the sun's rhythms, the body illuminates in total pleasure. No longer seeking bliss outwardly, but discovering its location deep inside the heart. When we can see the self in the sun and the sun inside the self (the Upanishads), all knowledge of yoga, the body and the world will be known on profound levels. When sun salutations are practiced with mental grace and humbleness they are the gateway to samadhi (the conscious bliss of connecting with the great divine).

Surya Namaskara (sun salutations) deliberately pulses the beat of the heart into a great vital space. This gives the aspirant of yoga an opportunity to connect with the source of self-illumination. Eliminate the darkness within and prepare the body for further and deeper Self-recognition. Warming the body naturally through the rhythmic pulses of sun salutations is timed like the rising and setting of the sun. Just like the sun does not rush to rise or set neither does one hurry to practice these divine movements. Each motion of the body is directly connected to the length and strength of breath. Only at the completion of the inhale or the exhale does the body finish its motions. There is no separation between body, mind, and breath. The following is an abridged description of common Sanskrit language used to describe the stirring movements of Surya Namaskara.

Vinyasa - To place down mindfully, to move and to think with conscious bhodhicitta (action performed for the benefit of all sentient beings).

Krama - Step by step. To execute steady movement with the count of the breath. Uninterrupted rhythm.

Sthithi Krama - To place, align, and set oneself in an asana with the intent to move the conscious breath in an uninterrupted rhythm deeper into the body.

To maintain complete focus utilize the drishti as suggested in the following postures. Drishti is the gazing point for the eyes while moving the attention of the mind inward. Begin your asana practice with five Surya Namaskara A and five Surya Namaskara B. If it is too intense to start with 10 sun salutations, then begin with three each. Build up your endurance with time.

Be loose, be natural and let the process unfold. See yourself with a gleam of confidence. You are a divine being practicing sublime motions. This is a beautiful moment to dwell on the sun that lies within the center of your heart.

Liquid Fire Yoga® - Asana Practice

SUNSALUTATIONS

Soft Compositions of Sun Salutations
Modifications for the Surya Namaskaras are necessary for the fledglings of yoga.

Sharpen your skillfulness with the dynamics of your light self.

You are truly as light as air, as fluid as the sea, and as bright as the sun. Move yourself serenely and gently. It takes years for students to master the physics of yoga asana. Work on breathing deeply and perform the modifications for at least a few months. Modifications are crucial for your safety. Practice them if you are having distress from injuries, arthritis, soreness, and overall tenseness in the body.

Look at the description of each asana and assign yourself to a modification that works for your body. Make sure the modification you choose allows you to maintain the integrity of sthithi krama (aligning the body for the deepest breath possible).

SAMASTHITHI

Equal distance from extremes

Persevere with total intent upon honesty. Balance equally on both feet and abide in the ecstasy of divine being. Stand tall at the intersection of the horizon and the meridians of the soul. Allow the center of the universe to breathe into the palms of your hands.

This posture sets the stage for the intentional work of the yoga asana practice. While in this pose, begin to focus on why you are practicing today. Devote your practice to something greater than yourself. This devotional act can be for a person, divinity, an event, or any good intentions. This posture is grounding as much as it is invigorating.

Be mindful of the placement of the feet. They are the physical foundation that builds the remaining alignment of the body. They should be thoughtfully placed, even if they are slightly apart as shown in the modifications. Begin to practice the ujjayi pranayama breath-work while standing firmly.

Take the time to soften the face and to relax into the sacred work. Abstain from the idea or the thought of being tired and make a conscious shift of your energy. Be energized by standing tall and practice exploring the present moment with your breath. This will allow your practice to unfold without expectations.

Honor where you stand. Honor your body and how it feels. Make a commitment to yourself that you will not force the body through any of the coming work. This mindset will help support a pleasant space and the body will ease into the asanas freely without struggle.

English translation Balanced Standing Pose

SAMASTHITHI
(BALANCED STANDING POSE)
FEET: Together. Equally balanced into 4 corners of both feet.
HANDS: Anjali Mudra (palm to palm), heart center.
DRISHTI: Nose (nasagrai) or straight ahead.
BREATH: Focus and set an intention for the practice for 5 to 10 cycles of ujjayi breathing.

DO: Become equally balanced into both feet. Avoid falling too far backward onto the heels or forward onto toes. Relax the facial muscles and calm the mind. Breathe and softly smile as you connect deeply with the earth.
DON'T: Slump forward or shift your weight onto a single foot.

VARIATION 1:
FEET: Together. Equally balanced into 4 corners of both feet.
HANDS: Down to the sides.
DRISHTI: Nose (nasagrai) or straight ahead.

VARIATION 2:
FEET: Hip width apart. Equally balanced into 4 corners of both feet.
HANDS: Down to the sides or anjali mudra (palm to palm), heart center.
DRISHTI: Nose (nasa-grai) or straight ahead.

URDHVA VRKSASANA

Upward movement away from ego

Regenerate the space of the Divine inside of you as your ego yields from intention. The lifting of anjali mudra supports alchemical change in your body. Purposeful energetic alignment increases the intensity of the cosmic light at your sacral space.

The palms reach up above the head in an exalted anjali mudra (seal of honor) as a form of respect for your higher self. Touching your hands together seals in this space of honor. Settle in each time you feel this pose as a reminder that there is a greater purpose propelling this divine movement.

Raising the hands above the head is symbolic of trust, as the heart is completely open and unprotected. You are physically expressing the internal trust of presence and allowing it entry into your heart.

The slight tuck in the pelvis awakens the fire located at the base of the spine and creates a powerful alignment for deep breathing. The feet should be firmly rooted in this pose. Maintain the experience created in Samasthithi. Settle with balance, composure, and a gentle attitude towards the work ahead. As you open your heart in this pose, hear the breath flow deeply inward.

English translation Ascending Tree Pose

URDHVA VRKSASANA
(ASCENDING TREE POSE)
FEET: Together. Equally balanced into 4 corners of both feet.
HANDS: Pressed together, exalted anjali mudra (palm to palm).
DRISHTI: Third eye (ajna chakra).
BREATH: Inhale (see gallery for connecting postures of sun salutation sequence).

DO: Reach arms up with shoulders moving back and down. Keep spine as straight and long as possible. Tuck the pelvis slightly to level the pelvic floor. Honor a higher presence.
DON'T: Arch the back.

VARIATION 1:
FEET: Hip width apart.
HANDS: Pressed together, exalted anjal mudra (palm to palm).
DRISHTI: Third eye (ajna chakra).

VARIATION 2:
FEET: Hip width apart.
HANDS: Shoulder width apart.
DRISHTI: Third eye (ajna chakra).

UTTANASANA

Bow of humility

Form a physical symbol in recognition of the release of moksha (freedom) into the crown.
Illuminate the internal landscape.

To bow in surrender is the greatest act of humility. This third sun salutation posture gives the practitioner a deep opening of great gratitude. The experience of the posture is to bow to your intention.

Be mindful of not overdoing it. Many students mistake over-stretching for a more advanced posture. Yoga asana is not about the stretch so much as it is about moving the breath. A gentle approach allows the breath to move deeper into the body and promotes healing. Even if your bow is only partway it is better to feel soft than to feel distressed.

You are a beautiful and resilient being. The movements of yoga are completely natural for the body and there is nothing you need to force. Bow deeply to the highest state of being. Let yourself exhale fully and surrender.

English translation **Reverant Bow Forward Pose**

UTTANASANA

(REVERENT BOW FORWARD POSE)

FEET: Together, equally balanced.

HANDS: Flat to the mat on either side of feet with fingers in line with toes.

DRISHTI: Nose (nasagrai).

BREATH: Exhale (see gallery for connecting postures of sun salutation sequence).

DO: Bring the nose towards the knees and fold deeply while pressing the navel to the thighs. Bend the knees to avoid back strain or overstretching the hamstrings. Bend the knees and lift the chest to avoid hyperextension of the back as suggested in the variations.

DON'T: Slump into a rounded back or lift the head.

VARIATION 1:

FEET: Together. Equally balanced into 4 corners of both feet.

HANDS: Tips of fingers on the floor on either side of feet.

DRISHTI: Nose (nasagrai).

VARIATION 2:

FEET: Hip width apart. Equally balanced into 4 corners of both feet.

HANDS: Lightly on shins.

DRISHTI: Nose (nasagrai).

VARIATION 3:

FEET: Hip width apart. Knees bent.

HANDS: Resting on thighs.

DRISHTI: Nose (nasagrai).

ARDHA UTTANASANA

Heart-lifting half-lift

Awareness of the core increases the love flooding the anahata (heart) chakra.
The heart-lifting shape allows discernment of real from unreal.

Half does not mean less than whole but rather a lifting up of the upper half of the body. This lift creates the experience of internal alertness, presence, and acute awareness of self. Settle into the core as your being prepares to move deeper into the greeting of the sun. This posture honors the life-giving force of the sun as well as the internal cosmic light. The backbone lengthens, the base of the spine uncoils, and your body brightens with unadulterated joy.

Give yourself expansion in the rib cage as the inhalation runs deep to the toes. The inhale should be powerful with the core completely lifted. Feel the lower abdominal region secure the body prior to taking flight.

English translation **Reverent Half Lift Pose**

**ARDHA UTTANASANA
(REVERENT HALF LIFT POSE)**

FEET: Together, equally balanced.

HANDS: Fingertips on either side of feet with fingers in line with toes.

DRISHTI: Third eye (ajna chakra).

BREATH: Inhale (see gallery for connecting postures of sun salutation sequence).

DO: Lift heart center and extend through the entire spine. Engage quadriceps and maintain grounded support from both feet. Find the variation that is comfortable for your body.

DON'T: Slump into a rounded back or force hands to reach the floor.

VARIATION 1:

FEET: Hip width apart.

HANDS: To shins.

DRISHTI: Third eye (ajna chakra).

VARIATION 2:

FEET: Together, equally balanced.

HANDS: To knees or thighs.

DRISHTI: Third eye (ajna chakra).

VARIATION 3:

FEET: Together. Knees bent.

HANDS: To knees or thighs.

DRISHTI: Third eye (ajna chakra).

CHATURANGA DANDASANA

Offering of the four roots

The extremities hold horizontal endurance.
In the pause find protection and equanimity.

Chaturanga dandasana is not merely a low push-up. It is a posture of great endurance. Students of yoga cannot practice this posture without recognizing a personal challenge. It is not a matter of physical strength but internal will.

At times a yoga practitioner stands on the edge of a cliff in life. Chaturanga Dandasana gives you the confidence to float right off the edge and trust that the world will support you. New students and those with shoulder issues should practice the modified versions until finding a trusted teacher that can offer safe guidance. The shoulders and elbows should be close to the same height for safety and proper alignment. Advanced students should land soundlessly into Chaturanga Dandasana while floating back from Ardha Uttanasana. When in transition to this posture avoid creating a jerking motion with the legs (donkey kick). Also avoid jumping back into high plank. These movements cause unnecessary strain on the joints. New students and those with knee and hip issues should step back one foot at a time.

English translation   Four Limbed Low Staff Pose

CHATURANGA DANDASANA (FOUR LIMBED LOW STAFF POSE)

FEET: Hip width apart on ball of feet for balance. Draw heels back.

HANDS: Shoulder width apart pressed firmly onto mat. Bend elbows to 90 degrees. Elbows towards ribcage.

DRISHTI: Nose (nasagrai).

BREATH: Exhale (see gallery for connecting postures of sun salutation sequence).

DO: Keep shoulders, hips, and heels in a straight line. Palms flat with forefingers and thumbs firmly into mat spreading wide through all fingers. Maintain integrity of the pose by engaging quadricep muscles and lifting abdominals upward.

DON'T: Dip shoulders down below height of elbows. Don't sacrifice good alignment by forcing or moving too quickly.

VARIATION 1:

FEET: Hip width apart and on ball of feet. Draw heels back. Knees grounded to mat.

HANDS: Shoulder width apart. Bend elbows to a 90 degree angle.

DRISHTI: Nose (nasagrai).

VARIATION 2:

FEET: Hip width apart and on ball of feet. Draw heels back. Knees grounded to mat for extra support.

HANDS: Shoulder width apart. Keep arms straight for this modification but avoid hyperextending the elbows.

DRISHTI: Nose (nasagrai).

VARIATION 3:

FEET: Hip width apart and on ball of feet. Draw heels back. Keep legs straight.

HANDS: Shoulder width apart. Keep arms straight but avoid hyperextending the elbows.

DRISHTI: Nose (nasagrai).

URDHVA MUKHA SVANASANA

Shining Upward

Sacred expressions from the recesses of the heart burst forth.

There is a serenity that comes from understanding oneself. When you can find the answers hidden in the caves of your own body you become filled with courage. This is what true confidence is.

Curving the spine awakens the central nervous system. When the nervous system opens up the awareness dawns that we are liquid instead of solid. It is important for the yoga student to see the material world as a moldable substance. The upward motion of this pose causes the heart to open and the body to release inner turmoil. A student may experience an emotion that has been buried for quite some time.

As the heart lifts, take caution in the movement of the neck. The movement originates in the heart followed by a slight lift in the chin. The curve in the neck should be gentle to protect the spine.

English translation Upward Facing Dog Pose

URDHVA MUKHA SVANASANA
(UPWARD FACING DOG POSE)

FEET: Hip width apart with toes pointed. Press tops of both feet onto mat and keep quadriceps contracted and off the mat.
HANDS: Press firmly onto mat shoulder width apart. Keep arms straight and engage triceps.
DRISHTI: Third eye (ajna chakra).
BREATH: Inhale (see gallery for connecting postures of sun salutation sequence).

DO: Feel a pleasant upward opening in the chest through the heart center. Keep uddyana bandha engaged and quadriceps uplifted to prevent hips from dropping down. Prevent strain in the lumbar region (lower spine) of the back. Avoid throwing the head too far back towards the tailbone. Perform a natural backbend for your range of movement.
DON'T: Hyperextend the elbows or hang torso from shoulders.

VARIATION 1:
FEET: Hip width, toes pointed and press tops of both feet onto mat.
HANDS: Shoulder width apart. Keep arms straight.
DRISHTI: Third eye (ajna chakra).

VARIATION 2:
FEET: Hip width, toes pointed. Rest hips down onto mat.
HANDS: Shoulder width apart with fore-arms onto mat.
DRISHTI: Third eye (ajna chakra).

ADHO MUKHA SVANASANA

Face shining downward

Inverting expressions of the face guide the spirit upwards.

Tuned inwardly, the student of tradition discovers an entrance to the soul.

Downward facing dog is one of the most underrated postures of yoga yet one of the most transformative. Breathing into this inversion affects the physiology of the body by reducing blood pressure which then reduces stress. Stress reduction puts the ego to rest. When the ego is at rest then life becomes effortless.

Honor this pose as an opportunity to disconnect from distractions. The inverted lines of downward facing dog allow a heightened level of awareness to occur. Tranquil thoughts then flow and deepen the dedication to practice.

Remain calm and breathe deep. Mindful placement allows natural micro-movements to occur in the joints. Hold this pose without any rigidity.

English translation Downward Facing Dog Pose

**ADHO MUKHA SVANASANA
(DOWNWARD FACING DOG POSE)**

FEET: Hip width apart. Press heels down towards mat.

HANDS: Slightly wider than shoulder distance apart. Palms flat. Firmly press forefingers and thumbs onto mat. Spread wide through all fingers.

DRISHTI: Nose (nasagrai).

BREATH: Exhale (see gallery for connecting postures of sun salutations sequence).

DO: Allow head to comfortably be suspended from the neck. Pull the hips up using the abdominal muscles. Abstain from frustration at the inability to hold the pose for a long duration. To be steady and comfortable in this position requires consistent practice and dedication.

DON'T: Become forceful by pushing bottom of heels down to the mat.

VARIATION 1:

FEET: Hip width, toes spread apart. Knees bent.

HANDS: Slightly wider than shoulder distance apart.

DRISHTI: Nose (nasagrai)

VARIATION 2:

FEET: Hip width, toes spread apart. Knees directly below hips.

HANDS: Shoulder width apart. Elbows to the floor.

DRISHTI: Nose (nasagrai)

UTKATASANA

Throne of peace

A bolt of strength tremors up the back.

Connect with the upward moving prana you are expanding and watch it intensify.

How fierce is the desire to know yourself?

Energy surfs through the spine as your body creates the shape of a lion's salient. The power of this pose lies in prana simultaneously flowing up and down. Exalted anjali mudra and ujjayi pranayama increase the digestive fire thus cleansing the practitioner of impurities. Bear witness to the powerful shifts that occur without distraction from the intense sensation rising in the core.

There is a sense of striking the floor like a bolt of lightening. The body is growing in vigor; lit up with gratitude for the ability to feel the self in such an enormous way. Tap into the bolts of light radiating outward from within. This is an energetic approach to witnessing the inner spirit. It is a flash of lightening striking quickly and leaving as fast as it came. Be zealous in obtaining peace right now.

English translation Fierce Pose

UTKATASANA (FIERCE POSE)

FEET: Together, spread toes wide apart. Ground into heels. Knees bend.

HANDS: Pressed together in exalted Anjali mudra (palm to palm).

DRISHTI: Third eye (ajna chakra).

BREATH: Inhale (see gallery for connecting postures of sun salutation sequence).

DO: Bend deep into knees at a comfortable range of motion. Remain with heels grounded and all ten toes on the mat. Extend arms up energetically. Hold a light composure with consistent ujjayi pranayama (breath work).

DON'T: Become discouraged or agitated from the burn in the quadriceps.

VARIATION 1:

FEET: Together, spread toes wide apart. Ground into heels.

HANDS: Anjali mudra (palm to palm) heart center.

DRISHTI: Third eye (ajna chakra).

VARIATION 2:

FEET: Together, spread toes wide apart. Ground into heels.

HANDS: Shoulder width apart. Palms face in with arms lifting overhead.

DRISHTI: Third eye (ajna chakra).

VIRABHADRASANA I

Fearless love

The warrior Virabhadra stormed through the three worlds due to his unquenchable passion for his love.

A great battle began over his power of undying love. Virabhadrasana will quell any desires for war other than the one of

pure love, and in its place leave you feeling larger than life and utterly fearless.

The story of Virabhadra is one of deep love. Virabhadra was one of the world's greatest renunciates, a yoga practitioner who renounces all worldly things. We can ourselves glimpse the practice of a renunciate through Virabhadrasana. Allow the power of Virabhadrasana to settle deep into your heart (anahata) chakra, let yourself truly open up with faithful trust. Through the posture of Virabhadrasana this deep inner love gives one the ability to eliminate all inner demons. In exalted anjali mudra, the hands held high above the head, the heavens are invited to descend down straight into the heart. Reverently gaze upwards towards the sun. Allow yourself to reset your life into one of radiance. Choose to love unconditionally.

Never underestimate the power of true love.

English translation   Warrior One Pose

VIRABHADRASANA I (WARRIOR ONE POSE)

FEET: Set 3 to 4 feet apart. Back foot angled at 45 to 60 degrees, keep leg straight.

HANDS: Pressed together in exalted anjali mudra (palm to palm).

DRISHTI: Third eye (ajna chakra) or hand (hastagrai) when holding pose.

BREATH: Inhale (see gallery for connecting postures of sun salutation sequence).

DO: Bend front knee towards a 90 degree angle with front foot pointing forward. Keep the back leg straight and active with the heel grounded. If bending the back leg, modify by pivoting weight solely onto ball of foot. This prevents strain and injury to the knee joint. Use ajna chakra drishti (third eye) when performing sun salutations.

DON'T: Arch the back or bend the back leg.

VARIATION 1:

FEET: Set 3 to 4 feet apart.

HANDS: Shoulder width apart. Palms face in with arms lifting overhead.

DRISHTI: Third eye (ajna chakra).

VARIATION 2:

FEET: Set 2 to 3 feet apart. Front knee is slightly bent.

HANDS: Anjali mudra (palm to palm) heart center.

DRISHTI: Upward (urdhva).

VIRABHADRASANA II

Tenacity to quell inner turmoil

gnite the ego-burning energy of agni and light up the center of the spine. Shift perspective as the heart is opened to deep reverence. Eliminate forceful nature here, as Virabhadra used burning intensity to develop his meditative state. Feel the intensity of the pose and breathe through it.

Alignment fueled with enthusiasm is the great teaching. Allow the energy to have buoyancy as it runs through the length of the back leg. Keep the front leg bent to hold prana in the quadriceps. The body can effortlessly implement this magnitude of energy, it is only the mind that struggles.

English translation Warrior Two Pose

VARIATION 1:

FEET: Set 2 to 3 feet apart in a shorter stance. Front knee slightly bent.

HANDS: Reach apart with arms expanded and palms facing down.

DRISHTI: Hand (hastagrai).

VIRABHADRASANA II (WARRIOR TWO POSE)

FEET: Set 3 to 4 feet apart. Front foot points forward. Front knee bends toward a 90 degree angle. Back foot parallel to back edge of mat.

HANDS: Reach apart with arms expanded and palms facing down.

DRISHTI: Hand (hastagrai).

BREATH: Hold for 5 to 10 cycles of ujjayi breathing.

DO: Expand the arms apart energetically with shoulders back and down. Bend front knee toward 90 degree angle. Keep back leg straight and strong. Drive pressure down equally through bottoms of both feet. Avoid leaning over front or back leg to help maintain an upright spine. To prevent a bent back leg, shorten stance.

DON'T: Arch the back or lean forward.

VARIATION 2:

FEET: Front foot: points forward Back foot: parallel to back edge of mat.

HANDS: Akimbo or Anjali mudra (palm to palm) heart center.

DRISHTI: Side (parsva).

VIPARITA VIRABHADRASANA

Invert sorrow into gratitude

Great heroes among us convert pain into a powerful life-giving nectar. Drink the joy of a warrior king forever free

from battle. Witness yourself light an internal fire that Illuminates the darkness within.

Viparita Virabhadrasana illuminates darkness, causing the yoga student to shift perspective. Dive into ideas and creative movements as the body expands into sublime peace. Even erupting volcanoes did not distract Virabhadra, the warrior king, from his practice. Move past the look of the pose and make prayerful discipline (tapas) the focus.

The arch of the back is energetic yet subtle as it rises from the hips. One should experience comfort in the lumbar spine as each vertebra is evenly spaced. The front thigh should be strong and powerful. This alignment allows the heart to find its calming center in the world.

English translation Inverted Warrior Pose

VIPARITA VIRABHADRASANA (INVERTED WARRIOR POSE)

FEET: Set 3 to 4 feet apart. Front foot points forward. Bend front knee towards 90 degrees. Back foot parallel to back edge of mat.

HANDS: Lead arm extends straight up with palm facing in towards back wall. Opposite arm behind lower back reaching for inner thigh.

DRISHTI: Hand (hastagrai).

BREATH: Hold for 5 to 10 cycles of Ujjayi breathing.

DO: Bend front leg towards 90 degree angle and keep back leg straight and strong. Drive pressure down equally through bottoms of both feet. Prevent a bent back leg by shortening stance. This limits strain on the back knee joint.

DON'T: Bend back leg.

VARIATION 1:

FEET: Set 3 to 4 feet apart. Front knee bent towards a 90 degrees.

HANDS: Lead arm reaches up. Back hand rests lightly on back leg.

DRISHTI: Hand (hastagrai).

VARIATION 2:

FEET: Set 2 to 3 feet apart. Slight bend in front knee.

HANDS: Lead arm reaches up. Back hand rests lightly on back leg.

DRISHTI: Hand (hastagrai).

VARIATION 3:

FEET: Set 2 to 3 feet apart. Slight bend in front knee.

HANDS: Lead arm reaches forward. Back hand rests lightly on back leg.

DRISHTI: Upward (urdhva).

ANJENAYASANA

The crescent moon of perfected mind

The crescent shaped moon rises as the body bends. The masculine and feminine energies are consummated creating a line of concentrated potential. Adore the power as the spinal flexure oscillates towards the crescent present at the ajna chakra (third eye). Expand freedom and let heartfelt devotion flood the moonlit sky from the deep epicenter.

The moon at its final stage before sinking into nothingness initiates self reflection. As it slowly returns to its full luminescence, the curve of the moon creates a channel of prana to revitalize the spirit. A calm mind is not a luxury here, it is a necessity.

The root of power lies in the thighs. Celebrate the hips, the center, the core. Spread the chest open to the heavens and let its power descend upon you. Hear the rhythm of ujjayi pranayama increase as the physiological body dances to the beat of the heart. Make the necessary modifications in order to explore the lunar qualities of deep devotion.

English translation Cresent Lunge Pose

VARIATION 1:

FEET: Front foot firmly grounded. Balance on ball of back foot.

HANDS: Anjali mudra (palm to palm) heart center.

DRISHTI: Upward (urdhva).

VARIATION 2:

FEET: Front foot grounded. Back knee on mat. Toes of back foot pointed or tucked.

HANDS: Resting on thigh.

DRISHTI: Upward (urdhva).

VARIATION 3:

FEET: Front foot planted flat. Ground top of back foot and back knee down to mat.

HANDS: Shoulder width apart and extended straight up. Palms face in.

DRISHTI: Upward (urdhva).

ANJENAYASANA (CRESCENT LUNGE POSE)

FEET: Front foot firmly grounded. Balance on ball of back foot. Press back through the heel.

HANDS: Shoulder width apart. Palms face in. Arms extend straight up.

DRISHTI: Upward (urdhva).

BREATH: Hold for 5 to 10 cycles of ujjayi breathing.

DO: Bend deep into front knee and move forward through hips. Stay strong and active in the quadriceps. Keep heart center (anahata chakra) open and upward. Avoid back and shoulder strain. Follow modified expression of postures and find your natural range of movement.

DON'T: Force the knee or hip joints into a deep lunge.

UTTHITA PARSVAKONASANA

The side of lustrous wisdom

The internal sky is activated by the power of the lateral body expanding. Once the center star of the

compass has been recognized, no recurrence of fear emanates from an unanticipated direction.

Open through the vibrant heart center; let the lungs fill. As the arm extends, the entire being is filled with illumination. Prana vayu, the upward moving life-force breath, has a purpose in the body. Direct the prana vayu up through the channel of the digestion and move prana through the spine to the brain. This work diminishes ego and encourages the space of lustrous wisdom (prajnalokah). The central channel is illuminated and firmness and flexibility is enhanced. From heel to fingertips this lengthened pose directs the fiery breath. In order to move freely in the asana one must breath deeply. When the prana of the body is regulated, the waist slims, the body tones, and arthritis subsides. This deep breath contributes to a calm mind and a joyful demeanor. Allow calmness to enter as you move into this space. A well-practiced body and a settled spirit are necessary in order to experience the intensity of this posture with a soft mind. Start slow. Utilise the modifications.

English translation Extended Side Angle Pose

VARIATION 1:
FEET: Set 3 to 4 feet apart. Front knee bends towards 90 degrees.
HANDS: Lower forearm rests on thigh. Upper arm extends over ear.
DRISHTI: Hand (hastagrai).

VARIATION 2:
FEET: Set 2 to 3 feet apart. A closer stance with less bend in knee.
HANDS: Upper arm extends upward above shoulder. Opposite arm on thigh.
DRISHTI: Hand (hastagrai).

UTTHITA PARSVAKONASANA (EXTENDED SIDE ANGLE POSE)

FEET: Set 3 to 4 feet apart. Front foot points forward. Front knee bends towards 90 degrees. Back foot parallel to back edge of mat.

HANDS: Lower palm is flat to mat. Upper arm extends energetically over ear with palm facing down.

DRISHTI: Hand (hastagrai).

BREATH: Hold for 5 to 10 cycles of ujjayi breathing.

DO: Feel the equal balance and support from the feet and the legs. The back leg should be extended straight. Move upward with a lift from the torso. Feel the full extension through both arms. To maintain a safe and stable pose follow modifications with a closer stance between both feet.

DON'T: Drop head into bottom shoulder or bend the back knee.

PARVRITTA PARSVAKONASANA

Intertwined with the unoccupied ground between the angles

Devotion to inward beams of existence illuminates the side of the body.

A phosphorescent compass raises the path of excellence.

This asana is not a twist, it is a revolution. The hips reset themselves and open the lateral body to move and revolve from the navel. The bending of the front knee should never steal the energy from the rear leg. The back leg should hold its own power.

When working on this position it is important to move into it slowly if you are new to it. Take your time and set the feet as we have shown in one of the modifications. Avoid the confusion of twisting the lower back in this posture. Your back should have length and feel supple. Feel a gentle lift in the center of the body at your navel. This lifting removes spinal compression and increases the healing heat of this posture.

Permeating through the body is a liquid fire that melts away dukha (suffering). This liquid heat activates the joyful state of sukha (effortless existence).

English translation Revolved Side Angle Pose

PARVRITTA PARSVAKONASANA (REVOLVED SIDE ANGLE POSE)

FEET: Front foot firmly grounded. Back foot angled at 45 to 60 degrees.
HANDS: Lower arm crosses outside knee with palm flat to mat. Upper arm extends energetically over ear with palm facing down.
DRISHTI: Hand (hastagrai).
BREATH: Hold for 5 to 10 cycles of ujjayi breathing.

DO: Stay strong and active in the quadriceps. This prevents stress on back, knee, and hip joints. Use the lower arm against leg as leverage for proper rotation. Follow the modified expressions of pose until the body becomes more adept with the asana.
DON'T: Force the back into rotation.

VARIATION 1:
FEET: Front foot firmly grounded. Balance on ball of back foot.
HANDS: Anjali mudra (palm to palm) while crossing elbow outside of knee.
DRISHTI: Upward (urdhva).

VARIATION 2:
FEET: Front foot firmly grounded. Balance on ball of back foot.
HANDS: Resting on front thigh with fingers interlaced.
DRISHTI: Side (parsva).

UTTHITA TRIKONASANA

Sublime space of a brilliant trinity

The holy triangle. To align oneself properly is to gain the knowledge of the universe. Set up softly with a mysterious strength that is totally unmoving. Recognize this effort is all powered by a single source of prana.

In this posture energy is located in the epicenter (navel) of the body. Imagine in your mind's eye the navel is the center of a compass. You are extending in various directions from the arms, legs, and hips to create a well-aligned triangular shape in the body. As you focus on the navel, the lower back eliminates pressure. This aids the muscles of the leg to generate flexibility rather than tension, thus advancing the yoga aspirant into a space of triple peace. Never let your back feel pressured here. It is better to lift the hand higher on the front leg than to struggle to reach the floor. The drishti of the posture is set at the hands (hastagrai drishti). However, if this motion causes neck pain, then it is acceptable to gaze forward or even to the toes. Once the neck and shoulder gain strength and flexibility, the ability to hold the head in this position will become effortless. Allow a gentle spirit to flow as you merge with the rhythm of ujjayi pranayama.

English translation **Extended Triangle Pose**

UTTHITA TRIKONASANA (EXTENDED TRIANGLE POSE)

FEET: Set 3 to 4 feet apart. Front foot points forward and back foot points slightly in.

HANDS: Extend fully apart. Lower palm reaches flat to mat.

DRISHTI: Hand (hastagrai).

BREATH: Hold for 5 to 10 cycles of ujjayi breathing.

DO: Expand open through chest with arms apart. Upper shoulder stacks directly above the lower. Keep chest above the front extended leg. Extend comfortably through legs by firmly engaging quadriceps. Create proper alignment without forcing the pose.

DON'T: Slump forward or round the back. Don't strain neck or shoulder joint.

VARIATION 1:

FEET: Set 3 to 4 feet apart. Front foot points forward toward top of mat.

HANDS: Upper arm extends up. Lower hand rests on shin or ankle.

DRISHTI: Hand (hastagrai).

VARIATION 2:

FEET: Set 2 to 3 feet apart.

HANDS: Upper arm extends up. Lower hand rests on knee.

DRISHTI: Hand (hastagrai).

VARIATION 3:

FEET: Set 2 to 3 feet apart. Knee slightly bent.

HANDS: Upper arm extends up. Lower hand rests on knee or thigh.

DRISHTI: Hand (hastagrai).

PARVRITTA TRIKONASANA

Earth rotates as it revolves around the sun

Experience the rotation around the manipura (the inner sun). Watch it illuminate the core of the body through spinal bliss.

A personal revolution ignites in the center of the nervous system.

Deep rotation begins in the hips and less in the spine. Be active here. Deliver full-throttle breathing into the lungs as the tapas (liquid fire) begins to burn the impurities lying in the digestive system. The body will be fully purified now regardless of anything you have consumed in the last few days.

This pose deeply activates the digestive center of the body and supports the yoga student's practice of internal cleanliness (saucha). Allow yourself to focus fully inward. Give yourself over to grand insights as this pose offers an explosion of self-realization. Surrender and let your body melt into the space of the posture. Never utilise flexibility as a personal exhibition. Instead, let it develop slowly. Once flexibility develops, enjoy it! Welcome the impermanence of life in this revolution around the inner sun.

English translation   Revolved Triangle Pose

PARVRITTA TRIKONASANA (REVOLVED TRIANGLE POSE)

FEET: Set 3 to 4 feet apart. Front foot points forward and back foot turns in at a 45 to 60 degree angle.

HANDS: Lower arm crosses outside of the front foot. Palm flat to mat. Upper arm extends up, perpendicular to floor.

DRISHTI: Hand (hastagrai).

BREATH: Hold for 5 to 10 cycles of ujjayi breathing.

DO: Expand open through chest with arms apart and upper shoulder stacked directly above the lower. Keep spine elongated. The back leg should extend straight. When practiced correctly and with consistency this pose may aid in relief of sciatic nerve pain.

DON'T: Bend the back knee.

VARIATION 2:

FEET: Set 2 to 3 feet apart. Front foot points forward with a slight bend in front knee. Back foot turns in at a 45 to 60 degree angle.

HANDS: Lower hand reaches towards mat with pads of fingers.

DRISHTI: Hand (hastagrai).

VARIATION 3:

FEET: Set 3 to 4 feet apart. Front foot points forward. Back foot turns in at a 45 to 60 degree angle or balance on ball of back foot.

HANDS: Reach towards mat with pads of fingers.

DRISHTI: Nose (nasagrai).

PRASRITA PADOTTANASANA C

Lengthen in respectful submission to the inner self

Discover pliable living as the body and soul open into a space of surrender. Be filled with devotion

while divinity floats within anahata (heart) chakra.

Every time we bow is a time for deep inner reflection. The atmosphere of this pose is a space of solitude, silence, and reverence. The silence may be uncomfortable, yet it's required to elevate consciousness. Offer yourself over to a higher intention and pay attention to that authority. This authority is not a teacher outside of yourself, but is nestled inside the heart of your being. Reflect on this inner divinity guiding you to sublime existence.

Forward folds reflect the inner humbled self. Allow yourself to feel stretched open and pulled into exuberance. The elbows in this posture should not lock. Let the joints micro-bend with freedom. This posture is about squeezing the scapulas and ringing out the tension from the upper body. Instead of focusing on external beauty, focus on the beauty that dwells inside.

English translation Expanded Leg Forward Fold C

VARIATION 1:

FEET: Parallel, set 3 to 4 feet apart.

HANDS: Behind back with fingers interlaced, palms together. Bend elbows.

DRISHTI: Nose (nasagrai).

VARIATION 2:

FEET: Parallel, set 3 to 4 feet apart.

HANDS: Reach behind back for the opposite wrists or forearms.

DRISHTI: Nose (nasagrai).

PRASRITA PADOTTANASANA C (EXPANDED LEG FORWARD FOLD C)

FEET: Parallel, set 3 to 4 feet apart.

HANDS: Behind back with fingers interlaced. Palms together, pull towards floor.

DRISHTI: Nose (nasagrai).

BREATH: Hold for 5 to 10 cycles of ujjayi breathing.

DO: Maintain a long spine with the crown of head reaching the mat. Become active in the quadriceps. Firmly ground bottom of heels into mat. Avoid closing eyes and continue the correct ujjayi breathing technique.

DON'T: Struggle with an over extension in the arms. This prevents injury to elbow and shoulder joints.

MUKTA HASTA SIRSASANA

Let loose the grasp of illusion

Holding on to firm beliefs darkens the space of mind.

Meditate upon transcendent power.

Invert the feet towards the sun and ground the hands. When the head the turns upside down, the heart shines from within to without. These movements invite creative meditation into practice. Gravity naturally ages the body. This daily work of calming the unsteady spirit offers one an abundance of health. The use of ujjayi pranayama in inversions pushes forth the youthful elixir of divine love. One usually looks outward for love but this pose invites looking inward.

All yoga students should be mindful of placing too much weight on the head and cervical vertebrae. When lifting the legs in the pose one should feel stable in body and steady in mind. If the body is unsteady work instead on the modifications. Lift upward through the core of the body. This will ensure that you will eventually lift correctly without any strain.

English translation Free Hand Headstand

MUKTA HASTA SIRSASANA
(FREE HAND HEADSTAND)
FEET: Together with toes spread apart.
HANDS: Flat to the mat. Shoulder width apart under the elbows.
DRISHTI: Nose (nasagrai).
BREATH: Hold for 5 to 10 cycles of ujjayi breathing.

DO: Set foundation into hands. Keep arms at a 90 degree angle with power moving upward from arms and shoulders. Keep a long spine with the crown of head in contact to the mat. Create lightness through center of the body by utilizing uddyana bandha. Focus on developing core strength and uplift through strong quadriceps by practicing modified variations.
DON'T: Kick legs and feet up when entering the pose.

VARIATION 1:
FEET: Set 3 to 4 feet apart. Rise up on the ball of both feet.
HANDS: Flat to mat. Shoulder width apart under the elbows.
DRISHTI: Nose (nasagrai).

VARIATION 2:
FEET: Set 3 to 4 feet apart, flat onto mat.
HANDS: Set shoulder width apart, touching pads of fingers to mat.
DRISHTI: Nose (nasagrai).

VASHISTASANA

Master of every desirable object

Integral work of one's subtle nature imbues the body with magical truth. The process of self-discovery

intensifies prana throughout the body. Extend the body and open the mind with platonic prana propulsion.

This pose is named after the sage Vashista. He taught students to practice yoga through ahimsa (non-harming). In regards to asana, this means to be tranquil rather than muscle through the posture. This powerful tranquility supports the student's experience of challenge, balance, and steadiness. The breath in this pose should be powerful and steady. This steady breath stimulates the breakthrough of your self-discovery. Feel the energy pulse through the veins as the frontal body opens. Shower the body with prana.

English translation Side Plank Pose

VASHISTASANA
(SIDE PLANK POSE)
FEET: Extend one leg upward. Opposite foot grounded with leg straight.
HANDS: Bottom arm with hand flat to the mat. Upper arm extends up with first two fingers wrapped around the big toe or hand around outside of foot.
DRISHTI: Foot (padayoragrai).
BREATH: Hold for 5 to 10 cycles of ujjayi breathing.

DO: Root down into bottom hand and foot and move energy upward through the upper arm and leg. Stay open in the chest and remain energized through the center of the body by utilizing uddyana bandha and engaged quadriceps. Remain comfortably balanced and use the modified variations provided.
DON'T: Force the weight of the body into the bottom hand or wrist. Don't let the hips fall to the mat.

VARIATION 1:

FEET: Stacked on sides. Maintain strong stability in the quadriceps.
HANDS: Bottom hand flat to mat. Upper arm extends upward with palm facing open.
DRISHTI: Hand (hastagrai).

VARIATION 2:
FEET: Bottom knee on mat. Upper leg straight with foot grounded.
HANDS: Bottom hand flat to mat. Upper arm extends upward with palm facing open.
DRISHTI: Hand (hastagrai).

NATARAJASANA

The royal non-verbal communion

The body immerses into limitless bliss as anahata chakra lifts to the sky.

This lift increases the capacity to breathe in divinity.

Elevate the heart upward. Do not give up instead give into the movement. This asana initiates the dance of the cosmos to intermingle in your glowing anahata chakra (heart center). Feel the cosmos reach into your soul and lift you to higher states of being.

Witness the divine and transcend ordinary existence as the head and the foot meet in a graceful connection. The strength in the standing leg allows the spine to curve effortlessly. Connect to the experience of liquid fire flowing through the veins. Practice the modification that is well-suited to your physical dynamics.

English translation Royal Dance Pose

NATARAJASANA (ROYAL DANCE POSE)

FEET: Ground foot firm to mat. Maintain a straight and strong standing leg. Lifted foot moves back and up towards head.

HANDS: Both hands reach for lifted foot.

DRISHTI: Third eye (ajna chakra).

BREATH: Hold for 5 to 10 cycles of ujjayi breathing.

DO: Lift the chest and feel the radiance through the heart center. Gain stability from the strength in both legs. Avoid strain in the back and hip. Find your natural range of motion in the variations.

DON'T: Force reaching for the foot. This will prevent injury in the shoulders.

VARIATION 1:

FEET: Ground foot firm to mat. Lifted foot moves back and up towards head.

HANDS: Back hand reaches for inside of foot . Opposite arm upward in front.

DRISHTI: Hand (hastagrai).

VARIATION 2:

FEET: Ground foot firm to mat. Lift back foot behind lower back.

HANDS: One or both hands reach back for ankle.

DRISHTI: Upward (urdhva).

GARUDHASANA

The doorway to royal discernment

The magnificent king of feathers devours all worldly ignorance.

Spread the golden wings of the illuminated mind. Reverence of your microcosm

dispels any poison that attempts to invade your soul.

Take flight. Transform small desires into amplified courage. Connect with this intentional work as mula-bandha engages (root lock). This energetic up-liftment is similar to the lightness of a bird in flight.

This pose is named after the powerful bird Garudha. His wings were strong enough to create waves in the sea. Visualize this strength as you practice Garudhasana. This pose is a transformation from a small hatchling into a powerful bird. Find self-awareness as the obstacles are plucked away one by one.

Every breath is necessary and leaves no wasted energy in the body. Conjure sublime servitude internally to develop self-assurance. Take it slow, be patient, and have sharp discrimination.

English translation **Eagle Pose**

GARUDHASANA (EAGLE POSE)

FEET: Cross legs at the thighs with foot wrapped around ankle or calf.
HANDS: Cross arms with the hands and fingers in contact.
DRISHTI: Upward (urdhva).
BREATH: Hold for 5 to 10 cycles of ujjayi breathing.

DO: Ground firm into standing foot and use strength in both legs for the overall
stability in pose. Draw shoulders back while lifting arms upward. Allow the bind to occur effortlessly and abide with the calm presence of a perched eagle at the edge of a cliff.
DON'T: Be hasty in an attempt to bind arms and legs.

VARIATION 1:

FEET: Cross legs at the thighs with foot wrapped around ankle or calf.
HANDS: Anjali mudra (palm to palm) heart center.
DRISHTI: Upward (urdhva).

VARIATION 2:

FEET: Together. Bend knees.
HANDS: Hold elbow with opposite hand.
DRISHTI: Upward (urdhva).

DIGHASANA

Support from all directions

The peace of a gentle vayu (wind) flows inward from every direction.

Support comes from deep within and comes from far without.

O pen the eyes and fearlessly look inward. See the beliefs that bind you and the beliefs that open you. The ability to balance comes from a willingness to fall. No matter which direction you turn, no matter what challenges you face, support from all directions is attainable through the conscious breath.

With one leg grounded allow the rest of the body to soar. As your body takes flight, relax the mind and have trust in yourself. Engage the locks of the center and allow prana to fill your pose with boundless energy. Let Dighasana offer insight and self-transformation.

English translation **All Directions Pose**

DIGHASANA

(ALL DIRECTIONS POSE)

FEET: Standing leg straight. Foot firmly rooted to mat. Opposite leg lifts back, level to floor.

HANDS: Fingers spread with palms facing down. Extend arms back.

DRISHTI: Nose (nasagrai).

BREATH: Hold for 5 to 10 cycles of ujjayi breathing.

DO: Lift from the core center of the body by utilizing uddyana bandha. Draw outward from the center through all extremities, spine, and head in all directions. Use a wall for support by extending arms forward onto the wall with pads of fingers. When you fall from the position pick yourself up and immediately return to the position. This serves to eliminate any doubt.

DON'T: Give up if you have difficulty with balance on one leg.

VARIATION 1:

FEET: Front foot forward, firmly on mat. Back leg straight. Balance on ball of foot.

HANDS: Extend arms back with fingers spread and palms facing down.

DRISHTI: Nose (nasagrai).

VARIATION 2:

FEET: Front foot forward, firmly on mat. Back leg straight. Balance on ball of foot.

HANDS: Reach pads of fingers to mat, shoulder width distance apart.

DRISHTI: Nose (nasagrai).

URDHVA PRASARITA EKA PADASANA

Raise grounded vibrations

Expand the body into bold courage. Light bursts from the crown of your head as energy pulses through the glowing sushmna channel.

Lift the foot high to the stars. Can and can't are words of the past. The space around you is of complete surrender. Attune the soul. Transform the heart.

Beliefs hold you down. Erase false beliefs of the self and rest in luminous splendor. Don't worry, balance falls with grace into your heart.

If needed, bend the standing leg and defy gravity with the extended leg. Weightlessness comes from an intuitive understanding you are made of divine light.

English translation **One Leg Standing Split**

**URDHVA PRASARITA EKA PADASANA
(ONE LEG STANDING SPLIT)**

FEET: Standing leg straight. Ground foot firmly on mat. Opposite leg lifts perpendicular to floor.
HANDS: Placed on either side of standing foot, firmly on mat. Spread fingers wide.
DRISHTI: Nose (nasagrai).
BREATH: Hold for 5 to 10 cycles of ujjayi breathing.

DO: Elongate spine and allow head to fall. Feel a strong lift from the quadriceps. Press abdominals against the thigh. Draw shoulders upward. If breathing becomes labored, lessen the depth of the posture.
DON'T: Over stretch.

VARIATION 1:
FEET: Foot firmly on mat. Standing leg slightly bends. Elevate opposite leg within a comfortable range.
HANDS: Reach mat with pads of fingers, shoulder width distance apart.
DRISHTI: Nose (nasagrai).

VARIATION 2:
FEET: Foot firmly on mat. Standing leg straight. Opposite leg elevated level to floor.
HANDS: Reach along the standing leg as high as thigh.
DRISHTI: Nose (nasagrai).

TRIVIKRAMASANA

The great step to liberation

Three steps into yourself is the path towards liberation.

The fourth step is moksha.

Trivikrama translates to three steps. The light of divinity may be veiled in the three levels of mind. Through deliberate step-by-step work, the student can lift the veils dimming the conscious, unconscious, and subconscious mind. Once these veils have been lifted, liberation may be attained. Change the course of liberation from many steps to a path of three graceful steps. The energetic stance of this pose is like a great step.

English translation Grand Three Step Pose

TRIVIKRAMASANA
  (GRAND THREE STEP POSE)

FEET: Standing leg straight. Foot firmly on mat. Opposite leg lifts.

HANDS: Reach for upper foot.

DRISHTI: Nose (nasagrai).

BREATH: Hold for 5 to 10 cycles of ujjayi breathing.

DO: Elongate spine and press abdominals against the thigh. Feel a strong lift from the quadriceps. Draw upper leg towards head and maintain a comfortable opening. Draw shoulders down back and keep arms strong.

DON'T: Round back or force hamstring to stretch.

VARIATION 1:

FEET: Standing leg straight. Foot firmly grounded on mat. Extend opposite leg straight.

HANDS: Hold extended leg.

DRISHTI: Upward (urdhva).

VARIATION 2:

FEET: Standing leg straight. Foot firmly grounded on mat. Bend opposite leg to chest.

HANDS: Hold shin of lifted leg.

DRISHTI: Upward (urdhva).

SUPTA TRIVIKRAMASANA

Settle back into effortless liberation

Transform lilliputian existence in three steps and touch spiritual liberation.

The chakra discus kerfs away ignorance and illusion inaugurating awakened wisdom.

W hen liberation (moksha) is attained spontaneously it can sometimes leave as quickly as it came. Moksha attained through concentrated effort and divine intention will not slip away. Once awareness of divine intention develops the student becomes light, compassionate, and energetic.

In yoga, the entire length of the back body is referred to as the dark or west-facing. The frontal body is the light or east-facing. Lie with the dark-side to the floor and the light-side facing up. Draw one leg towards your head and anchor the opposite leg to the floor. While in this pose, experience the east-side of the body illuminate with intense refractions of brilliance. The practice of slow and conscious breathing demonstrates the breath-by-breath (krama) path to moksha. The breath is the link towards blissful nature. The student no longer questions how to attain moksha, it simply becomes a matter of when.

English translation Reclined Grand Three Step Pose

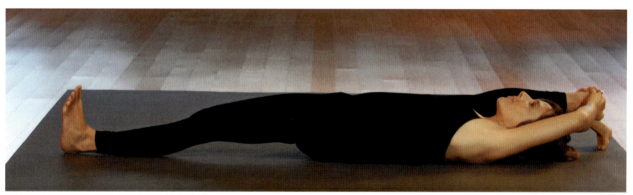

SUPTA TRIVIKRAMASANA (RECLINED GRAND THREE STEP POSE)

FEET: Move upper leg towards head with foot reaching to mat. Drive the opposite leg down with calf pressing to mat.

HANDS: Reach up for foot beside the head.

DRISHTI: Nose (nasagrai).

BREATH: Hold for 5 to 10 cycles of ujjayi breathing.

DO: Remain with the lower back on the mat. Maintain strength in both arms while drawing shoulders down. Keep the calf and heel of lower leg grounded to the mat. Allow the process to unfold comfortably and ease into the pose. Follow the natural movement your body will allow.

DON'T: Be too eager to master this position.

VARIATION 1:

FEET: Extend one leg upward. Opposite leg down with calf pressing to mat.

HANDS: Reach for the elevated leg on thigh or use a strap around bottom of foot.

DRISHTI: Upward (urdhva).

VARIATION 2:

FEET: Bend one leg into chest. Opposite leg down with calf pressing to mat.

HANDS: Reaching for the shin.

DRISHTI: Upward (urdhva).

HANUMANASANA

A high velocity leap of devotion

Brahmacharya (self-control) elicits the perfected siddhi (power) of moving mountains of suffering effortlessly. Devout and disciplined, this virtuous self restrains the wavering human tendencies. This gives way for the clouds of avidya (ignorance) to lift as loyal devotion moves in. Pull love in at speeds faster than the wind.

The leap of devotion is paramount for a deep yoga practice. Human nature can sometimes be half-hearted. Hanumanasana trains that shifting the half-hearted ways into whole-hearted ways, supports spiritual up-liftment. Restraint (brahmacharya) of the habitual tendencies creates clarity. This clarity allows one to feel pure heart-felt devotion. Loyalty and perseverance are the magical keys for unlocking this devotional yoga practice.

Choose the variation of the posture that helps you maintain a powerful and steady ujjayi pranayama.

English translation Royal Monkey Pose

HANUMANASANA (ROYAL MONKEY POSE)

FEET: Apart with legs fully extended front to back.

HANDS: Pressed together in exalted anjali mudra (palm to palm).

DRISHTI: Hands (hastagrai).

BREATH: Hold for 5 to 10 cycles of ujjayi breathing.

DO: Press down into the hamstring and calf of front leg and root down into the quadricep of back leg for good stability. Be cautious and feel comfortable in every part of your body when moving into this asana.

DON'T: Force this pose.

VARIATION 1:

FEET: Apart 3 to 4 feet, legs extended front to back.

HANDS: Reach with fingers in contact with the mat.

DRISHTI: Nose (nasagrai).

VARIATION 2:

FEET: Front leg straight with back knee bent onto mat.

HANDS: Reach with fingers in contact with the mat.

DRISHTI: Nose (nasagrai).

ARDHA CHANDRASANA

The illumination of darkness

Above the wandering star (earth) drifts the placid complexion of the moon.

Lightness and darkness in all its splendor.

Ardha chandrasana is the balance of opposites. One half of the body is grounded. The other half of the body is uplifted. This represents the balance of polar opposites that is the foundation of spiritual culture. The sun always reflects one side of the moon and the other side always resides in darkness. Like the moon, you are a perfect balance of light and dark. Open yourself to the light and the dark within and witness balance and illumination. Just as the moon reflects the light of the sun, divinity reflects in you.

Pull the warming energy of the quadriceps up into the solar plexus. Maintain this lift in the core and shine inwardly. Surrender to the exhilarating experience of Ardha Chandrasana. This pose is invigorating and requires patience in order to master. Remember, yoga asanas exist to support your quest of self mastery. Deep yoga practice honors the space of accepting where the body is today.

English translation   Half Moon Pose

ARDHA CHANDRASANA (HALF MOON POSE)

FEET: Standing leg straight with foot firmly rooted to mat. Opposite leg lifting skyward.

HANDS: Expand apart floor to ceiling. Pads of fingers of lower hand on mat. Palm of upper hand is faced open.

DRISHTI: Hand (hastagrai).

BREATH: Hold for 5 to 10 cycles of ujjayi breathing.

DO: Lift from the core center of the body by utilizing uddyana bandha. Draw outward from the center through all extremities, spine, and head. When you fall from the position pick yourself up and use the modifications to enjoy the balanced tranquility of half moon pose.

DON'T: Bear weight of body into the lower hand.

VARIATION 1:

FEET: Standing leg straight with foot firmly rooted to mat. Opposite leg extends back, lifted level to floor.

HANDS: Reach the mat with pads of fingers. Arms shoulder width distance apart.

DRISHTI: Nose (nasagrai).

VARIATION 2:

FEET: Standing leg straight with foot firmly rooted to mat. Opposite leg extends back, lifted level to floor.

HANDS: Reach for the knee of standing leg.

DRISHTI: Nose (nasagrai).

ARDHA MATSYENDRASANA

Awaken from the slumber of ignorance

The majesty of fish (Matsya) rescued the blueprint of mankind (manu) from great floods. The deluge

of discord is caused when the center of the self is askew. The encumbrance of avidya is replaced with

infinite space of auspicious vision. This primordial melody brightens the soul.

The waters of the body direct the emotional field of the student. This field of emotion is similar to the vastness of the sea. When thoughts merge with the vast sea, they are no longer yours. They are free and you are free. This freedom allows you to feel your most authentic self in the binding twist of Matsyendrasana.

Treat the midsection of the body with reverence. The emotional center resides at the base of the digestion. The digestive system works tirelessly for the health of the body. It extracts nutrients from food and stores nutrients for future use. An efficient and healthy digestion is important to maintain a strong mind and healthy body. Good digestion supports the heart beating stronger and the lungs breathing deeper. With a change in the type of foods absorbed, the practitioner of yoga will see a difference in the suppleness of the body as it binds and twists in Matsyendrasana.

English translation Half King of the Fish Pose

ARDHA MATSYENDRASANA
(HALF KING OF THE FISH POSE)
FEET: Place foot of bent leg firmly to mat outside of grounded thigh. Opposite foot up against hip.
HANDS: Forward moving arm crosses outside of upper bent leg as it reaches for foot.
DRISHTI: Side (parsva).
BREATH: Hold for 5 to 10 cycles of ujjayi breathing.

DO: Press the inner thigh of upper leg against the abdomen and create comfortable compression in the hip joint. Bring the chest as far outside of leg with reasonable rotation in spine up through the neck. Drop sit bone of bent leg down onto mat.
DON'T: Cross the foot outside the thigh if it throws you off balance.

VARIATION 1:
FEET: Foot crossing outside the thigh is pressed firmly to mat.
HANDS: The wrapping hand firmly pulls thigh towards abdominals. Opposite arm extends behind body with tips of fingers onto mat.
DRISHTI: Side (parsva).

VARIATION 2:
FEET: Grounded foot makes contact with ankle of opposite foot.
HANDS: The wrapping hand gently pulls thigh towards abdominals. The opposite arm extends behind body with tips of fingers onto mat.
DRISHTI: Side (parsva).

PURVOTANASANA

Develop invulnerability to the kleshas

Elevate the frontal body to the rays of Surya rising in the east.

The pinnacle of being no longer entertains latent impressions of malaise, anguish, or aversion again.

Confront the internal afflictions (the kleshas) and accomplish the blissful intoxication of existence.

Expand into greatness as you open the doors of the eastern body. As these doors open gain inner strength to stand up to the battles that are faced in daily existence. Feel empowered as anahata chakra (heart) lifts skyward. The mind and the body converge into sacred movement. Through deep breathing the frontal body releases decades of protection.

Dive into the life of devotion, letting go, and kaivalya (freedom through yoga). Summon the deep understanding of primordial existence. Allow your body to expand and surrender into the plank of least resistance.

English translation Eastern Plank Pose

PURVOTANASANA
(EASTERN PLANK POSE)
FEET: Together, plantar flexed and equally balanced. Legs straight.
HANDS: Under shoulders with fingers pointing toward feet.
DRISHTI: Nose (nasagrai).
BREATH: Hold for 5 to 10 cycles of ujjayi breathing.

DO: Lift with energy. Slightly tuck pelvis and feel the core of the body through utilizing uddyana bandha. Use the strength in both quadriceps with upward movement through the heart center. Use the modifications to build up to the full version of Purvotanasana.
DON'T: Lift the hips if it stresses the wrists, shoulders, or back.

VARIATION 1:
FEET: Hip width apart and firmly rooted into mat. Bend knees at 90 at degrees.
HANDS: Under shoulders with fingers pointing towards feet.
DRISHTI: Nose (nasagrai).

VARIATION 2:
FEET: Together, plantar flexed. Legs straight. Keep hips to floor.
HANDS: Down flat behind back at shoulder width apart. Fingers point towards feet. Elbows slightly bent. A slight lift upward through chest and chin.
DRISHTI: Upward (urdhva).

USTRASANA

The Infinite source of energy

The anatomy of the real self is exceptional. Traverse the desert dunes of illusion and ignorance with inner confidence.

Indefatigability is possible through brahmacharya (self-control).

Camels are a great wonder of the world. They have the ability to travel thousands of miles across harsh desert conditions with little water and food. They remind us of the message that less is more. In this pose, the feeling of the heart center opening is a tangible experience. Camel pose is extraordinarily powerful. It frees one from emotional pain and generates healing. It rinses the central nervous system and purifies the liver. Achievement of this pose can be a great challenge. Maintain the camels messages of endurance and temperance.

Slightly tuck the pelvis for protection of the lower back and surrounding anatomical structure. Conserve your energy as you work through this pose. Revel in the space of humility and elevate with tranquility.

English translation Camel Pose

USTRASANA (CAMEL POSE)

FEET: Tops of feet pressed to the mat. Knees hip width apart.

HANDS: Reach comfortably back for feet.

DRISHTI: Nose (nasagrai).

BREATH: Hold for 5 to 10 cycles of ujjayi breathing.

DO: Use the strength in the quadriceps and back muscles to support you in this position. Allow an organic conversion to take place in this posture and tap into your body's reservoir of energy. Follow variations for your comfort level and range of motion.

DON'T: Compress the lower back or engage the glutes. Don't force an external rotation of the shoulder joints.

DRISHTI: Nose (nasagrai)

VARIATION 1:

FEET: Knees hip width apart.

HANDS: Press into lumbar region of back. Point fingers down or in contact with the backs of thighs.

DRISHTI: Upward (urdhva).

VARIATION 2:

FEET: Knees hip width apart. Use a folded blanket or extra padding for feet and knees if necessary.

HANDS: Pressed together in Anjali mudra (palm to palm).

DRISHTI: Nose (nasagrai).

RAJA EKA PADA KAPOTASANA

The raja path of inspiration

The royal path is one of illumination.

It sends the message that divine love and devotion lead to spiritual ascension.

Strongly develop in yourself the qualities of masculine tranquility and maternal intuition.

Kapotasana translates to pigeon pose. Pigeons or doves may be small in size but they have powerful meaning. These birds are known for their amazing navigational skills and their nurturing spirit. No matter how far off course you may be, the power of pigeon pose will navigate you back on the right path. Use the pigeon as your guide and experience heightened levels of awareness. With this inner awareness you will be determined to find your way back to the true self.

The origin of this asana is truly a back bend. It creates up-liftment from the navel to the crown of the head. This posture encourages sacrifice of the ego and desires. Practice this back bend with a grand gesture of devotion.

English translation One Leg King Pigeon Pose

VARIATION 1:

FEET: Front leg with knee bent forward. Back foot pulled towards hip.
HANDS: Forward arm lifted up and other reaches for back foot.
DRISHTI: Hand (hastagrai).

VARIATION 2:

FEET: Front leg with knee bent forward. Back knee bent.
HANDS: Forward arm down with finger tips in contact to mat. Opposite hand reaches for back ankle.
DRISHTI: Nose (nasagrai).

VARIATION 3:

FEET: Front leg with knee bent forward. Back leg and foot extends to the back of mat.
HANDS: On mat with pads of fingers reaching back to support an arched back.
DRISHTI: Third eye (ajna chakra)

RAJA EKA PADA KAPOTASANA
(ONE LEG KING PIGEON POSE)

FEET: Front leg with knee bent and foot placed near opposite hip. Back knee bends as foot lifts towards head.
HANDS: Both reaching for foot behind head.
DRISHTI: Third eye (ajna chakra)
BREATH: Hold for 5 to 10 cycles of ujjayi breathing.

DO: Ground down into sit bone of the front leg with knee bent forward. Draw down into the top of the back thigh. Feel a comfortable extension in the main hip flexor. The backbend should feel natural. Enjoy an uplifted and expanded heart center. Remain calm in the asana and practice the modifications. Use of a yoga block under sit bone of front leg will assist with equal balance.
DON'T: Distress the hips, knees, or back.

SETU BANDHASANA

Bridge of possibility

A yogi is destined to a life of humbleness. Practice satya and the bridge of possibility shall never fall. Devoid of half-hearted discipline, the yogi encounters the concentrated truth that lies within the whole heart.

Setu Bhandasana translates to bridge pose. It bridges the gap between the impossible and the possible. The bridge to blissful existence reminds you that the moments of life are precious and should not be squandered. Dwell in grace and allow prayerful discipline (tapas) to be your daily work.

This pose offers an opportunity to reflect upon the initial intention of your practice. A slight tuck of the pelvis eliminates pressure in the back. The deep bending of the spine relieves multiple pressure points and softly heals the whole being with splendor. Purity will come with practice.

English translation **Bridge Pose**

SETU BANDHASANA (BRIDGE POSE)

FEET: Backs of your heels together with toes turning out. Outside of feet press down to mat. Legs fully extended.

HANDS: Reach for opposite shoulder as arms are crossed over heart center (anahata chakra).

DRISHTI: Nose (nasagrai).

BREATH: Hold for 5 to 10 cycles of ujjayi breathing.

DO: Feel grounded into the fifth metatarsals (outsides) of the feet. Press into bottoms of feet as much as your body allows. Keep abdominals firm. Create a slight tuck of the pelvis and push forward into the legs and feet for a strong foundation. Follow modifications to aid in building strong shoulder and neck muscles. Allow legs to bear the body weight.

DON'T: Push higher up in the hips than your body's natural range of movement will allow. Don't hold entire body weight on the head.

VARIATION 1:

FEET: Backs of your heels together with toes turning out. Outside of feet press down to mat. Legs slightly bent.

HANDS: Interlaced. Engage triceps with balanced weight on shoulders.

DRISHTI: Upward (urdhva) or nose (nasagrai).

VARIATION 2:

FEET: Backs of your heels together with toes turning out. Outside of feet press down to mat. Legs bent.

HANDS: Stretched alongside body, palms press to floor.

DRISHTI: Nose (nasagrai).

VARIATION 3:

FEET: Hip width apart. Firmly planted beneath the knees.

HANDS: Palms flat to mat and shoulder width apart. Fingers reach toward heels.

DRISHTI: Upward (urdhva).

YOGANIDRASANA

Evolve into spiritual liberation

Within the depth of the unconscious mind there is an awareness of the breath.

This restful awareness is the shape and form of one who knows the divine.

This deep state of pratyahara (sensory withdrawal) liberates your soul.

Wrap the soul in divine warmth. Feel this moment of peace and of solitude. The mind settles down. The reactions stop. Aloneness. Kaivalya. Kaivalya is the experience of being alone with divinity. Mind, soul, and body effortlessly witness the light of divinity. Let the inner agni softly burn the fluctuations of consciousness that prevent deep rest. This liquid fire flows in a slow rhythm. It tones the bladder, the kidneys, and the abdominal organs. It deeply massages the nerves.

Enter this pose gently and draw the legs towards the body. With regular practice the hip joints move with greater ease. Take care and move into this posture with a restful and contented mind.

English translation Sleeping Yoga Pose

YOGANIDRASANA (SLEEPING YOGA POSE)

FEET: Move behind the head, one at a time. Cross ankles.

HANDS: Wrapped underneath lower back.

DRISHTI: Upward (urdhva) or third eye (ajna chakra).

BREATH: Hold for 5 to 10 cycles of ujjayi breathing.

DO: Follow your natural range of motion when you bring the legs up. Settle the head comfortably back into the feet. Avoid aggressive pressure in the external rotation of the thigh. This prevents unnecessary pressure on the back. Experience effortlessness in this asana while it fuels the internal agni (fire). Maintain mental steadiness when you practice this movement and use the variations most suitable for your body.

DON'T: Force the feet behind the head.

VARIATION 1:

FEET: Directly above knees. Thighs move towards mat.

HANDS: Wrapped around feet with arms reaching from inside both legs.

DRISHTI: Upward (urdhva).

VARIATION 2:

FEET: One foot presses to mat. The opposite lifts towards head.

HANDS: Reach for lifted foot with shoulder inside of knee or thigh. Opposite hand presses lower leg down. Slightly lift torso toward upper leg.

DRISHTI: Nose (nasagrai).

VARIATION 2:

FEET: Touch together with knees apart and bent.

HANDS: Wrapped around knees to open hips.

DRISHTI: Upward (urdhva).

URDHVA DHANURASANA

The magnificent arc

The channel of chakras illuminates with dazzling intensity.

Curvature of the physical body effortlessly elevates the aspirant to liberation.

U rdhva translates to move upward. In this case, up towards the heavens. Dhanur translates to bow, to shape, or to curve. Urdhva Dhanurasana is an uplifted salutation of reverence. The eastern side of the body moves in the direction of the cosmos. Surrender to the power of the sun resting brightly in the center of your heart. Explore inner awareness beyond your daily perceptions.

The grounded feet support the foundation for the upward movement of prana. The slightly tucked pelvis eliminates any spinal pressure. Move the body effortlessly up into the ethereal space of unbounded consciousness.

English translation Upward Bow Pose

URDHVA DHANURASANA (UPWARD BOW POSE)

FEET: Set hip width apart. Firmly planted with toes forward.

HANDS: Flat to mat. Shoulder distance or wider.

DRISHTI: Nose (nasagrai).

BREATH: Hold for 5 to 10 cycles of ujjayi breathing.

DO: Point fingers toward feet. Use the legs to lift. Use uddyana bandha as your core strength for an effortless upward movement. Avoid unnecessary strain on the lower back.
Practice keeping hands and feet as a firm foundation for this asana.

DON'T: Move the feet once you have lifted into position.

VARIATION 1:

FEET: Set hip width apart. Firmly planted with toes forward.

HANDS: Flat to mat. Shoulder width distance or wider. Bear weight into the arms set at 90 degrees. Place crown of head to mat.

DRISHTI: Nose (nasagrai).

VARIATION 2:

FEET: Set hip width apart. Firmly planted with toes forward.

HANDS: Interlaced. Engage triceps with balanced weight on shoulders.

DRISHTI: Upward (urdhva).

ADHO MUKHA VRKSASANA

Shine upside down

Point the arrow of disciplined practice to the target of oneness.

The aspirant and the Self unite under the spell of unbreakable unity.

Flip upside down and flip the veil of illusory existence on its head. The new gravitational pull of the body changes the practitioner's inner world view. Transform the whirling thought patterns into the perfected mode of sharp shooting devotion. Sharp. Razor sharp is the path of yoga for the devotee. With this grand shift of perspective the goals of yoga are at your fingertips. This supports the development of prajna (illuminated wisdom).

With this new inner view the student of yoga positively glows with radiant skin and bright eyes. Inverted tree pose tones the internal organs and supports healing the body of disease. It also enhances balanced hormone production. In this pose the blood flows into the realm of your mind and increases your internal awareness and vigor. Any student of yoga can practice this inverted pose. Modifications are an important aspect of learning yoga postures. You can still enjoy the benefits even if you aren't fully flipped upside down.

English translation **Inverted Tree Pose**

ADHO MUKHA VRKSASANA (INVERTED TREE POSE)

FEET: Together with toes spread apart.

HANDS: Shoulder width apart. Root down firmly to mat.

DRISHTI: Nose (nasagrai).

BREATH: Hold for 5 to 10 cycles of ujjayi breathing.

DO: Set foundation into hands and arms perpendicular. Move power upward from arms and shoulders. Maintain lightness in the body by utilizing uddyana bandha. Focus on developing core strength and a strong center. Uplift slowly with strong quadriceps. Practice modified variations.

DON'T: Jump or kick legs and feet up into pose.

VARIATION 1:

FEET: Standing leg straight with heel of foot lifted. Opposite leg lifts skyward.

HANDS: Palm of hands in contact with mat. Shoulder width distance apart.

DRISHTI: Nose (nasagrai).

VARIATION 2:

FEET: Standing leg straight with foot firmly rooted to mat. Opposite leg lifting skyward.

HANDS: Pads of fingers in contact with mat. Shoulder width distance apart.

DRISHTI: Nose (nasagrai).

PASCHIMOTTANASANA

The guardian of the liquid fire

In the star studded sky the thousand eyes of heaven witness the dark side of the sun.

Bask in great health and be courageously incorruptible.

Revere the liquid fire as it illuminates your dark side.

Paschimottanasana is the heart of the Liquid Fire Yoga® sequence. It is a posture of self-inquiry and divine awakening. This favorable approach will fuel the liquid fire forming from within. Connection to this fluid energy sustains the illumination of your path to liberation.

Agni (digestive fire) brings light to the depths and shadows of the body. The level of concentration affects the student's capacity to stoke this digestive fire. One who generates this fire has the ability to burn physical stressors of the body. This calms the practitioner and enhances the atmosphere for sacred movement (asana). Gentleness toward the back and hamstrings is strongly urged. Bend the knees if there is back pain or limited range of hip movement. The focus of this pose is on activating the inner agni rather than looking for the feeling of a good stretch.

English translation   Intense West Stretch Pose

PASCHIMOTTANASANA (INTENSE WEST STRETCH POSE)

FEET: Together and dorsiflexed. Legs straight.

HANDS: Wrapped around bottom of feet. Palms face out with one hand clasping wrist of opposite hand.

DRISHTI: Nose (nasagrai).

BREATH: Hold for 5 to 10 cycles of ujjayi breathing.

DO: Maintain strength in both legs by rooting them firmly down into the mat. Hold space for a straight spine with abdominals pressed firmly against the thighs. Bend knees and straighten back to minimize any strain to hips, knee joints, or lower back.

DON'T: Force, struggle, or slump.

VARIATION 1:

FEET: Together and dorsiflexed. Legs straight.

HANDS: Reach for sides of feet.

DRISHTI: Nose (nasagrai)

VARIATION 2:

FEET: Together and dorsiflexed. Knees bent.

HANDS: Rest onto shins or thighs.

DRISHTI: Nose (nasagrai)

VARIATION 3:

FEET: Together and dorsiflexed. Legs straight.

HANDS: Rest onto knees.

DRISHTI: Nose (nasagrai) or feet (padayoragrai).

PADMASANA

Expand primordial purity

Deliberately and silently from the benevolent waters the lotus grows. Surya sparks rays upon the water inspiring growth. The meniscus of the water gives as the lotus bud moves toward the rays of light. The stem bends and sways as the enlightened being blossoms into perfect peace.

Padmasana (lotus pose) represents the delicate flower of knowledge. The lotus bud is a reminder that knowledge is not something to force but something you allow to blossom. It's the blossoming of all the elements of your world into a singular stem of bliss.

Seal the fingers into jnana mudra (the seal of wisdom) by joining the index finger and thumb. This mudra is symbolic of the love inside of you connecting with the love outside of you. These two divine forces uniting generates wisdom. Wisdom allows you to use your intellect for perceiving the source of divine love. This decelerates the intellects desire for material objects and increases its desire to explore divinity. Sit peacefully and silently. Breathe deliberately and slowly. Allow yourself to move through the stages of transformation unhurried and unobstructed.

English translation Seated Lotus Pose

PADMASANA (SEATED LOTUS POSE)
FEET: Over the opposite thigh towards the creases of hips. Soles face upward.
HANDS: Jnana Mudra. Thumb and index finger connect creating a circle. Last 3 fingers extend out.
DRISHTI: Nose (nasagrai).
BREATH: 33 cycles of ujjayi breathing.

DO: Sit on a cushion. Gently sit as tall as you can without any strain. Have a lifted center so that you hold a beautiful space for breathing deeply with minimal movement. Keep the hands relaxed with a little energetic pulse moving through the fingers.
DON'T: Slump forward or hold a pose that is uncomfortable.

VARIATION 1:
FEET: Legs crossed simply.
HANDS: Jnana Mudra. Thumb and index finger connect creating a circle. Last 3 fingers extend out.
DRISHTI: Nose (nasagrai).
PELVIS: Sits bones onto mat or cushion.

VARIATION 2:
FEET: Soles of feet together.
HANDS: Jnana Mudra. Thumb and index finger connect creating a circle. Last 3 fingers extend out.
DRISHTI: Nose (nasagrai).
PELVIS: Sits bones onto mat or cushion.

VARIATION 3:
FEET: Bottoms of feet grounded with ankles crossed.
HANDS: Jnana Mudra. Thumb and index finger connect creating a circle. Last 3 fingers extend out.
DRISHTI: Nose (nasagrai).
PELVIS: Sits bones onto blocks or cushions.

SAVASANA

Dissolution of i

The small self dissolves and the sacrosanct relationship begins.

This is an offering. A sacrifice. This sacrifice of the small self allows you to recognize the real Self.

Savasana translates to corpse pose. Traditionally, savasana is the practice of dissolving the old self and connecting with the real Self. However, in today's culture the state of savasana is more commonly known as deep rest.

To conclude the Liquid Fire Yoga® session surrender the body into stillness. Observe the heart rate slow. Breathe soft and naturally. Rest into a quiet space. The work of pratyahara (sensory withdrawal) is the state of ceasing material desires through resting the five senses. Thoughts, emotions, and fears may rise up. Look upon these vacillations (vrittis) of the mind without any reaction toward them. Practice of this inner silence will slowly dissolve the emotional swings that come from an unconscious rest. Eliminate all need for sleep and stay attuned to the present moment. Utilise this time to train the mind to become sattvic (pleasant).

Awaken from this rest with deliberate deep breathing. Enjoy this time and wake up slowly. Stretch your body mindfully. Press yourself up to a seated position and remain with the eyes closed. Sit tall and place the hands into anjali mudra (the seal of honor). Conclude the asana practice with the three sounds of OM .

English translation **Corpse Pose**

SAVASANA (CORPSE POSE)

FEET: Set wider than hip-width externally rotating out.

HANDS: Softly relaxed open with arms set apart from trunk of body.

DRISHTI: Eyes softly closed, attention inward.

BREATH: Slow the breathing pattern to full long deep inhalations and longer exhalations. Allow the sound of the breath gradually become silent.

DO: Remain in this posture for 5-10 minutes. Set up in a comfortable position and become perfectly still. Softly close the eyes. Allow yourself to become tranquil and calm in the body as well as in the mind. Settle into physical stillness. Avoid moving out of habit. Become cognizant of the movements you create by choice.

DON'T: Move mindlessly. Refrain from sitting up quickly from posture.

VARIATION 1:

FEET: Set wider than hip width apart. Flat to mat with bent knees.

HANDS: Softly relaxed open with arms set apart from trunk of body.

DRISHTI: Eyes softly closed, attention inward.

VARIATION 2:

FEET: Set wider than hip-width externally rotating out. Bent knees propped up with blankets and bolsters. Cushion or padding under shoulders, head, and neck.

HANDS: Softly relaxed open with arms set apart from trunk of body.

DRISHTI: Eyes softly closed, attention inward.

LIQUID FIRE YOGA® PRACTICE - ASANA SEQUENCE CHARTS

INSTRUCTIONS TO FOLLOW FOR ASANA CHARTS
When following the charts refer to the directions below each picture.   Directives will indicate:
The right or left side you are applying the posture. The number of cycles of breath and if the posture is a transitional pose. Please refer to previous asana pages for modifications and for expanded instructions of postures.

SURYA NAMASKARA A and SURYA NAMASKARA B - CHART 1
Practice each pose one breath at time. Practice three to five cycles each of the Surya Namaskara A & B (sun salutation A & B). Build endurance slowly and take your time learning this practice.

STANDING ASANAS - CHART 2
Practice each standing pose on the right side when indicated. After completing the movements on the right side, take a vinyasa. Then repeat the same sequence of postures on the left side. The chart will state which poses to practice on both sides and if they have a transition or a connecting vinyasa sequence in between.

SEATED ASANAS - CHART 3
Practice each asana in the order of the sequence. After holding each pose for five to ten breaths, take a vinyasa or simply switch sides. At the conclusion of asana practice, take a five to ten minute rest in Savasana.

LIQUID FIRE YOGA® - SURYA NAMASKARA A - CHART 1

SAMASTHITHI

5 to 10 cycles of
ujjayi pranayama

**URDHVA
VRKSASANA**

INHALE

UTTANASANA

EXHALE

ARDHA UTTANASANA

INHALE

CHATURANGA DANDASANA

EXHALE

URDHVA MUKHA SVANASANA

INHALE

ADHO MUKHA SVANASANA

EXHALE

5 to 10 cycles of ujjayi pranayama

ARDHA UTTANASANA

INHALE

UTTANASANA

EXHALE

**URDHVA
VRKSASANA**

INHALE

SAMASTHITHI

5 to 10 cycles of
ujjayi pranayama

LIQUID FIRE YOGA® - SURYA NAMASKARA B

SAMASTHITHI

5 to 10 cycles of
ujjayi pranayama

UTKATASANA

INHALE

UTTANASANA

EXHALE

ARDHA UTTANASANA

INHALE

CHATURANGA DANDASANA

EXHALE

URDHVA MUKHA SVANASANA

INHALE

ADHO MUKHA SVANASANA

EXHALE

5 to 10 cycles of ujjayi pranayama

VIRABHADRASANA I

RIGHT SIDE

INHALE

CHATURANGA DANDASANA

EXHALE

URDHVA MUKHA SVANASANA

INHALE

ADHO MUKHA SVANASANA

EXHALE

5 to 10 cycles of ujjayi pranayama

VIRABHADRASANA I

LEFT SIDE

INHALE

CHATURANGA DANDASANA

EXHALE

URDHVA MUKHA SVANASANA

INHALE

ADHO MUKHA SVANASANA

EXHALE

5 to 10 cycles of ujjayi pranayama

ARDHA UTTANASANA

INHALE

UTTANASANA

EXHALE

UTKATASANA

INHALE

SAMASTHITHI

5 to 10 cycles of
ujjayi pranayama

**URDHVA
VRKSASANA**

INHALE

Vinyasa -

UTTANASANA

EXHALE

ARDHA UTTANASANA

INHALE

CHATURANGA DANDASANA

EXHALE

URDHVA MUKHA SVANASANA

INHALE

ADHO MUKHA SVANASANA

EXHALE

5 to 10 cycles of ujjayi pranayama

ANJENAYASANA

RIGHT SIDE

INHALE

Transition

VIRABHADRASANA II

RIGHT SIDE

5 to 10 cycles of
ujjayi pranayama

UTTHITA PARSVAKONASANA

RIGHT SIDE

5 to 10 cycles of
ujjayi pranayama

VIPARITA VIRABHADRASANA

RIGHT SIDE

5 to 10 cycles of
ujjayi pranayama

PARVRITTA TRIKONASANA

RIGHT SIDE

5 to10 cycles of
ujjayi pranayama

CHATURANGA DANDASANA

EXHALE

URDHVA MUKHA SVANASANA

INHALE

ADHO MUKHA SVANASANA

EXHALE

ANJENAYASANA

LEFT SIDE

INHALE Transition

VIRABHADRASANA II

LEFT SIDE

5 to 10 cycles of ujjayi pranayama

UTTHITA PARSVAKONASANA

LEFT SIDE

5 to 10 cycles of ujjayi pranayama

VIPARITA VIRABHADRASANA

LEFT SIDE

5 to 10 cycles of ujjayi pranayama

PARVRITTA TRIKONASANA

LEFT SIDE

5 to10 cycles of ujjayi pranayama

CHATURANGA DANDASANA

EXHALE

Vinyasa - transition

URDHVA MUKHA SVANASANA

INHALE

Vinyasa - transition

ADHO MUKHA SVANASANA

EXHALE

Vinyasa - transition

UTTHITA TRIKONASANA

RIGHT SIDE

5 to 10 cycles of ujjayi pranayama

ARDHA CHANDRASANA

RIGHT SIDE

5 to 10 cycles of ujjayi pranayama

DIGHASANA

RIGHT SIDE

5 cycles of ujjayi pranayama

URDHVA PRASARITA EKA PADASANA

RIGHT SIDE

5 cycles of ujjayi pranayama

TRANSITION

INHALE

Transition to next pose

CHATURANGA DANDASANA

EXHALE

URDHVA MUKHA SVANASANA

INHALE

ADHO MUKHA SVANASANA

EXHALE

233

ANJENAYASANA

LEFT SIDE

5 cycles of

ujjayi pranayama

UTTHITA PARSVAKONASANA

LEFT SIDE

5 to 10 cycles of

ujjayi pranayama

UTTHITA TRIKONASANA

RIGHT SIDE

5 to 10 cycles of

ujjayi pranayama

ARDHA CHANDRASANA

LEFT SIDE

5 cycles of

ujjayi pranayama

DIGHASANA

LEFT SIDE
5 cycles of
ujjayi pranayama

**URDHVA PRASRITA
EKA PADASANA**

LEFT SIDE
5 cycles of
ujjayi pranayama

TRANSITION

INHALE
Transition to next pose

CHATURANGA DANDASANA

EXHALE
Vinyasa - transition
to next pose

URDHVA MUKHA SVANASANA

INHALE
Vinyasa - transition
to next pose

ADHO MUKHA SVANASANA

EXHALE

Vinyasa - transition

to next pose

ARDHA UTTANASANA

INHALE

UTTANASANA

EXHALE

**URDHVA
VRKSASANA**

INHALE

Vinyasa -

transition to next

SAMASTHITHI

5 to 10 cycles of
ujjayi pranayama

MUKTA HASTA SIRSASANA

Prep. Pose

MUKTA HASTA SIR-

5 cycles of
ujjayi pranayama

TRANSITION

Transition to next
pose

PRASRITA PADOTTANASANA C

5 cycles of
ujjayi pranayama

SAMASTHITHI

INHALE
Vinyasa - transition
to next pose

**URDHVA
VRKSASANA**

INHALE

UTTANASANA

EXHALE

ARDHA UTTANASANA

INHALE

CHATURANGA DANDASANA

EXHALE

URDHVA MUKHA SVANASANA

INHALE

Vinyasa - transition
to next pose

ADHO MUKHA SVANASANA

EXHALE

Vinyasa - transition
to next pose

ARDHA UTTANASANA

INHALE

UTTANASANA

EXHALE

UTKATASANA

INHALE

RIGHT AND LEFT SIDE
5 to 10 cycles of
ujjayi pranayama

SAMASTHITHI
5 to 10 cycles of
ujjayi pranayama

RIGHT AND LEFT SIDE
5 to 10 cycles of
ujjayi pranayama

TRIVIKRAMASANA
RIGHT AND LEFT SIDE
5 to 10 cycles of
ujjayi pranayama

SAMASTHITHI
5 to 10 cycles of
ujjayi pranayama

**URDHVA
VRKSASANA**
INHALE
Vinyasa -
transition to next

UTTANASANA
EXHALE

ARDHA UTTANASANA
INHALE

CHATURANGA DANDASANA
EXHALE

URDHVA MUKHA SVANASANA
INHALE

ADHO MUKHA SVANASANA
EXHALE
Vinyasa - transition
to next pose

TRANSITION
TO NEXT POSE

VASHISTASANA
RIGHT SIDE
5 to 10 cycles of
ujjayi pranayama

TRANSITION
TO NEXT POSE

VASHISTASANA
LEFT SIDE
5 to 10 cycles of
ujjayi pranayama

TRANSITION

TO NEXT POSE

CHATURANGA DANDASANA

EXHALE

URDHVA MUKHA SVANASANA

INHALE

ADHO MUKHA SVANASANA

EXHALE
Vinyasa - transition
to next pose

HANUMANASANA

LEFT SIDE
5 to 10 cycles of
ujjayi pranayama

ADHO MUKHA SVANASANA

EXHALE
Vinyasa - transition
to next pose

HANUMANASANA

LEFT SIDE
5 to 10 cycles of
ujjayi pranayama

CHATURANGA DANDASANA

EXHALE

URDHVA MUKHA SVANASANA

INHALE

ADHO MUKHA SVANASANA

EXHALE
Vinyasa - transition
to next pose

TO NEXT POSE

USTRASANA

5 to 10 cycles of
ujjayi pranayama

CHATURANGA DANDASANA

EXHALE

INHALE

ADHO MUKHA SVANASANA

EXHALE
Vinyasa - transition
to next pose

SETU BANDHASANA

5 to 10 cycles of
ujjayi pranayama

URDHVA DHANURASANA

3 TIMES
5 to 10 cycles of
ujjayi pranayama

YOGANIDRASANA

5 to 10 cycles of
ujjayi pranayama

SUPTA TRIVIKRAMASANA

RIGHT AND LEFT SIDE
5 to 10 cycles of
ujjayi pranayama

CHATURANGA DANDASANA

EXHALE

URDHVA MUKHA SVANASANA

INHALE

ADHO MUKHA SVANASANA

EXHALE
Vinyasa - transition
to next pose

PASCHIMOTTANASANA

5 to 10 cycles of
ujjayi pranayama

PURVOTANASANA

5 to 10 cycles of
ujjayi pranayama

CHATURANGA DANDASANA

EXHALE
Nose

URDHVA MUKHA SVANASANA

INHALE

ADHO MUKHA SVANASANA

EXHALE
Vinyasa - transition
to next pose

RAJA EKA PADA KAPOTASANA

RIGHT SIDE
5 to 10 cycles of
ujjayi pranayama

ARDHA MATSYENDRASANA

RIGHT SIDE
5 to 10 cycles of
ujjayi pranayama

CHATURANGA DANDASANA

EXHALE

URDHVA MUKHA SVANASANA

INHALE

ADHO MUKHA SVANASANA

EXHALE
Vinyasa - transition
to next pose

RAJA EKA PADA KAPOTASANA

RIGHT SIDE
5 to 10 cycles of
ujjayi pranayama

ARDHA MATSYENDRASANA

RIGHT SIDE
5 to 10 cycles of
ujjayi pranayama

CHATURANGA DANDASANA
EXHALE

URDHVA MUKHA SVANASANA
INHALE

ADHO MUKHA SVANASANA
EXHALE
Vinyasa - transition
to next pose

ARDHA UTTANASANA
INHALE

ADHO MUKHA VRKSASANA
RIGHT AND LEFT
Prep. Pose

ADHO MUKHA VRKSASANA
5 to 10 cycles of
ujjayi pranayama

UTTANASANA
EXHALE

ARDHA UTTANASANA
INHALE

CHATURANGA DANDASANA
EXHALE

URDHVA MUKHA SVANASANA
INHALE

ADHO MUKHA SVANASANA
EXHALE
Vinyasa - transition
to next pose

PADMASANA
33 cycles of
ujjayi pranayama

SAVASANA
Rest deeply for 5 to 10 minutes

BEYOND**ASANA**

Reach divinity through stillness. The way of a sattvic yogi.

Meditation is the unteachable medium. The practice of it opens the doorway to sacrifice.

Sacrifice is a devotional state of giving up all actions of personal self service.

All personal actions are directed to the whole world of humanity.

Dhyana is an inclination to exist perfectly for others.

Meditation (dhyana) is an experience of being absorbed with the Divine. The experience of meditation cannot be taught. According to Patanjali, one will naturally move into meditative absorption after they have mastered pratyahara (sensory withdrawal) and dharana (learning to meditate). The work to achieve meditation should be practiced daily with concentrated focus. Students are advised to approach the practices of pratyahara, dharana, and dhyana with a calm mind and body. They should also have the ability to sit comfortably without any strain or sleepiness. The practice of sitting upright with a mudra (seal) and a mantra (prayer or chant) is the practice of dharana (learning to meditate). The mudra and the mantra are not the actual meditation experience but are the tools one may use to achieve meditation (dhyana). They help to focus the mind on one object at a time. Gradually the mind will effortlessly find stillness and dhyana becomes possible.

The desire to work daily toward meditation is the effort expected from a yoga student. Eventually the student will have the ability to apply pratyahara, dharana, and dhyana to their daily lives.

DHYANA

FEET: Over the opposite thigh towards creases of hips. Soles face upward.
HANDS: Anjali mudra (palm to palm)
DRISHTI: Nose (nasagrai) or softly closed.
PELVIS: Resting onto mat or props (cushion, blanket, or block).

DO: Create a peaceful atmosphere in a silent room. Refrain from using music during this time. Turn off the television and the cell phone. Perform this practice during a time of day without any distractions. Let family and friends know this is your personal quiet time. Each day is a practice and the removal of ego is a constant practice. This is work that one must do consistently. It is a life long endeavor to peace.
DON'T: Allow yourself to become prideful of practicing this work.

VARIATION 1:
FEET: Over the opposite thigh towards creases of hips. Soles face upward.
HANDS: Ganesha Mudra. Set in front of solar plexus. Left palm faces out. Right hand faces in. Clasp fingers together.
DRISHTI: Nose (nasagrai) or softly closed.

VARIATION 2:
FEET: Over the opposite thigh towards creases of hips. Soles face upward.
HANDS: Ashvaratna mudra. Interlace index and middle finger. Extend the thumb, ring, and pinky finger.
DRISHTI: Nose (nasagrai) or softly closed.

VARIATION 3:
FEET: Legs folded back while sits bones are resting onto heels. For more cushion and elevation of hips use a block or blanket directly under sits bones.
HANDS: Anjali mudra (palm to palm)
DRISHTI: Nose (nasagrai) or softly closed.

ABOUT US

Feel the LUV.

Calvin and Theresa Curameng (C & Lokah Luv) practice, teach, and live their yoga discipline daily. They can be found directing an award winning yoga studio in the city of Orlando, located in the heart of the sunshine state, Florida. This little haven (stood as the back-drop for many of the pictures in this book) goes by the name College Park Yoga® (established in 2001). Calvin and Theresa's approach to the ancient discipline of yoga is original, clear, and easy to understand. Students and yoga teachers travel from all over the nation to their studio, to participate in their unique yoga classes known as Liquid Fire Yoga®. Since 2002, they have been training and teaching students of yoga about the benefits and importance of raw food and vegan cuisine and how these foods affect yoga practice.

Liquid Fire Yoga® system is based on the Yoga Sutras of Patanjali. This devotional practice encompasses five easy to do daily practices (pancha vahanas) to help the current day yoga student glimpse the pure state of yoga. They inspire students to develop and sustain a practice to advance towards the high state of bliss, while living in a busy and sometimes chaotic world.

Calvin and Theresa are intrinsically devoted to the well-being of their students. They have made it their life mission to create bright and welcoming spaces for people to have a pleasant atmosphere for the development of yoga practice.

Currently, they reside in Orlando, with their dog Indra. They have been the directors of College Park Yoga® since its inception in 2001. They also enjoy surfing, stand-up paddle boarding, mountain biking, hiking, glamping, gardening, and being one with nature. Their heart is in everything they do: teaching yoga classes and workshops, graphic design, photography, creating books, websites, and videos. It is with great graciousness they share BURN Kitchen Vegan Cuisine and Liquid Fire Yoga® with you!

SHARE BLESSINGS AND LOVE

"When you are inspired by a great source, share the source of that inspiration!

We look forward to meeting you on the yoga mat!" With divine love - C & T .

GLOSSARY OF YOGA TERMS

Abhyasa

Repetition; method of practice.

Agni

The sacred digestive fire created through ujjayi pranayama.

Apana

Downward moving wind (vayu) energy. This relates to all reproductive and elimination systems of the body.

Anjali mudra

The seal of honor. Palm to palm mudra. Used to demonstrate openness and respect for the teachings of sacred work.

Annapoorna

The perfect food. The giver of food and nourishment.

Ananda

Blissful.

Asana

Sacred movement. Pose of reverence. In reference to seated meditation practice, it is the actual seat upon which one sits.

Ashtanga/Astanga Yoga

Refers to the astanga sutra in Patanjali's Yoga Sutras. This sutra outlines what is needed to prepare aspirants for the state of blissful union. It outlines the following practices:

1. Yamas - Ethics
2. Niyamas - Self-restraint
3. Asana - Postures
4. Pranayama - Controlled movement of energy
5. Pratyahara - Withdrawal from the senses
6. Dharana - Concentration
7. Dhyana - Deep meditation
8. Samadhi - Euphoria

Asmita

Egoism. Self-forgetting. Misunderstanding.

Bhagavad Gita

The chapter about yoga practice in the Indian epic, Mahabharata.

Bhakti yoga

The yoga path of devotional practice.

Bhodisattva

A person who practices selfless actions for the welfare of humanity.

Citta

Consciousness. It creates awareness in the physical body and makes the body come alive with life, perceptions, and memories.

Dharana

Concentration. Learning to meditate.

Dhyana

Deep meditation. Steady unbroken focus.

Drishti

To look outward while turning attention inward. The drishti points for asana practice:

Nasagrai- Tip of nose
Urdhva- Upward
Ajna Chakra- Third Eye
Angustha Madyai- Thumbs
Hastagrai- Hands
Parsva- Side
Nabhi- Navel
Padayorgarai- Foot

Dukha

Distress, pain, and suffering.

The Gunas

The Three Tendencies of Nature (prakriti)

Tamasic - delusional, inattentive, weary, conceited, sleepy.
Rajasic - dynamic, desirous, dissatisfied, impatient, greedy, grief
Sattvic- naturally devoted to good deeds, tranquil mind, rapture, joyful, blissful.

Guru

Gu means darkness. Ru means light. The guru is the one who dispels darkness and illuminates the student of yoga.

Hatha Yoga

Ha means the sun. Tha is the moon. Hatha is balancing both the left and right hemispheres of the body through many devotional disciplines. Asana is the most familiar discipline of Hatha yoga.

Ishvara

The supreme guru of yoga. "The omniscient teacher of all teachers, expressed by the sound of OM." (Yoga Sutras 1.24-1.27). The unchanging soul.

Jnana

Insightful knowledge. Knowledge of the spirit, the small self, and the Divine.

Karma Yoga

The yoga of right action. Also called Kriya yoga.

Kevala Kumbhaka

The restraint of the unconscious breath.

Klesa (Klesha)

The five afflictions of humans.
1. Avidya - Ignorance of the Self.
2. Asmita - Egoism.
3. Raga - Attachment.
4. Dvesha - Aversion.
5. Abhinivesa - Clinging to bodily life.

Koshas

The 5 sheaths of energy that make up man.
1. Annamaya Kosha- the physical
2. Pranamaya kosha- the physiological
3. Manomaya Kosha- the psychological.
4. Vijnamaya Kosha- the wisdom mind.
5. Anandamaya Kosha- the blissful sheath.

Maya

The illusions of existence.

Mudra

To seal.

Niyama

The second branch of Ashtanga Yoga. The internal renunciation:
1. Saucha - Purification
2. Santosha - Contentment
3. Tapas - Desire for practice
4. Svadyaya - Study of self and texts
5. Ishvara Pranidhana - Divine love

OM

Infinite Peace. Om is the pranava (all pervading sound). Phonetically chanted as A-U-M.

Pancha Vahana

The five vehicles of Liquid Fire Yoga® that support the development of disciplined and focused yoga practice.

1. Consumption of fresh food
2. Liquid Cleansing - hydration
3. Asana - sacred movement
4. Pranayama - movement of energy.
5. Wisdom - the application of studies and practice.

Prana

Upward moving energy and the vital life-force. This energy can restrict and expand.

Pranayama

Prana is life-force. Yama is to restrain. Controlled breathing.

Pratyahara

Withdrawal from the senses.

Prajna

Illumined wisdom. Supports the achievement of meditation. This is not intellectual knowledge, it is the knowledge of the true Self.

Prajnaparadha

To sin against wisdom.

Pratipaksha Bhavanam

Is two parts. Redirecting negative thoughts and actions to become thoughts and work for the Divine. The second phase is self-reflection of what caused the negative thought or action to rise.

Prakriti

Nature. Shakti. The natural world.

Rajas

A tendency of nature that animates activity. The etymology of rajas (rajasic) is unrelated to raja- illumination.

Raja Yoga

Patanjali's Yoga. Raja translates to illuminated or royal. It is the path of yoga where the yoga student does the internal work to conquer their mind.

Sadhaka

Spiritual aspirant.

Samadhi

Euphoria. Complete immersion with the divine Self.

Sattva

A tendency of nature. Naturally devoted to good deeds.

Sukha

Joyful space.

Tamasic

A tendency of nature that is delusional, inattentive, weary, conceited, and sleepy.

Tapas

Literally means to burn. Burning impurities. Zealous learning of Self. Intensity for deep practice. Prayerful discipline.

Ujjayi Pranayama

Literally means the expansion of prana. The walking breath. The wave breath.

Upanishads

A Vedic literature that means to devotedly sit close. The texts express the ways one may experience yoga (union with the divine).

Vahana

Vehicles, chariots, and that which carries. Can also be translated to mean having power over evil.

Vinyasa

To place or set down mindfully.

Vinyasa Krama

To place or set down mindfully breath by breath.

Viveka

Discernment of the real from the unreal. Recognizing the divinity in all.

Vritti

The actions of individual consciousness (citta).

Yama

Restraint. The first limb of the astanga sutra in Patanjali's Yoga Sutras.

1. Ahimsa - Non-violent
2. Asteya - Non-stealing
3. Satya - Truthfulness
4. Brahmacharya - Self-control
5. Aparigraha - Non-greediness

Yoga

Perfection in action. Union with divinity.

Vayu

Air or wind. The wind energy of the body.

GLOSSARY OF FOOD TERMS, TOOLS & TECHNIQUES

Asian Pear

Also called nashi. It is a Japanese Pear. The fruit resembles a large yellow apple. It has crisp juicy flesh and is cultivated in Japan, Korea, the US, and New Zealand.

Agave Nectar

Usually in a liquid form. Similar in texture to maple syrup or honey. Not considered as a healthy alternative to other sweeteners and not safe for diabetics. Due to the current controversy over this food source, it is not recommended to use in BURN recipes.

Almond Flour

Fresh ground raw almonds. To make fine almond flour, grind almonds ¼ cup at a time in a food processor. This process will prevent nuts from turning into a butter and also create a finer flour. Use a flour sifter or wire mesh strainer to separate the fine flour from larger granules. Store in refrigerator in an airtight container.

Amino Acids

Protein enzymes that help process, assimilate, and digest foods. Found in many raw and vegan foods.

Bok Choy

An Asian plant of the cabbage family. It has a loose cluster of edible, dark-green leaves on white stalks. The leaves and stalks of this plant are usually cooked as a vegetable or eaten raw in salads.

Blender

VitaMix® is a high-powered blending tool. It is necessity to for the raw food kitchen. It is the only blender on the market currently that can transform a dense nut into a silky smooth treat.

Brown Rice

A wonderful grain used for many of our SolFood dishes. Brown rice is a highly nutritious food source. We suggest to consume it in small amounts and always pair with fresh greens and veggies.

Brown Rice Noodles

Brown Rice Noodles are made with 100% whole grain, are usually gluten- free, and are a good source of dietary fiber. This is a great alternative to other pastas. It should be consumed in moderation. There are no known health benefits to this pasta.

Calcium

A nutrient that is found in many dark leafy greens, broccoli, and in all nuts and seeds. In particular it is prominent in hemp and sesame seeds.

Cacao

Chocolate beans in their pure raw form. One can order it in chips called nibs or fine ground. Usually imported from Dominican Republic and South America.

Capers

Are edible flower buds of the caper. Usually consumed pickled.

Cashew Nuts

A fantastic source of antioxidants. They are also a source of trace minerals copper, manganese, magnesium, and phosphorus. Commonly used in cuisine from the East, Central and South America.

Celtic Sea Salt®

A special salt processed in a clean natural environment. Celtic Sea Salt® contains many micro nutrients: magnesium, iodine, iron and many more. These nutrients support the body's cellular functions.

Ceramic Knife

A very sharp knife that never needs sharpening. Also, they are fantastic for cutting soft skinned fruits and veggies.

Chia Seeds

Is a food that is rich in omega-3 fatty acid and a good source of the mineral, manganese. This mineral benefits the body's absorption of calcium. Chia seeds also regulate blood sugar levels and supports the metabolism of fats and carbohydrates.

Chinese Cabbage

Is the common name for bok choy. However, there is another variety of this cabbage whose leaves are lighter in color and form a nice cabbage head. Also goes by the names Napa cabbage, celery cabbage, or Chinese cabbage.

Chipotle Peppers

Are red jalapeno peppers smoked to give them a distinctive smoky flavor. These peppers are a delicious way to add heat and smoky flavor to sauces and salsa.

Chopping board

There are many chopping boards to choose from. A bamboo chopping board is the best one to choose as it will not dull your knives or crack ceramic knives. Bamboo is also naturally antimicrobial and is environmentally sustainable.

Cilantro

Is the Spanish name used in North America for the spice coriander. We use these nutritional fresh leaves as an ingredient in Indian, Thai and Mexican cuisine.

Coconut

Thai young coconuts are the best nutritive source for desserts. The water of young coconuts is purifying for the body and great for liquid cleansing. Young Thai coconuts are usually in a white or green shell and are most easily found in Asian food markets.

Coconut Sugar Crystals

Coconut sugar is a natural occurring sugar from the flower of coconut. We also suggest to use other natural sugars from raw dates and date sugar.

Coconut Oil

Is an edible oil extracted from the kernel or meat of matured coconuts, harvested from the coconut palm. Virgin coconut oil (VCO) is composed mainly of medium-chain triglycerides, which do not carry the same risks as other saturated fats.

Corn

We suggest to eat corn that is organic and farm fresh. Many USA organic farms grow colorful corn that is high in nutrition.

Coriander Seed

The seed is traditionally used in cooked dishes. Coriander is common in South Asian, Indian, Middle Eastern, Central Asian, Mediterranean, Latin American, Portuguese & Chinese foods. The seeds provide significant amounts of calcium, iron, magnesium, and manganese. Coriander has been documented as a traditional ayurvedic treatment for type 2 diabetes.

Dehydrator

Dry fruits, veggies, crackers, chips, and desserts. The best brand to buy is the Excalibur®. It evenly dries food horizontally across all the trays. This ensures even heat distribution for the food. This is a feature that is essential when preparing raw food patties or desserts.

Dragon Fruit

A bright pink and green skinned fruit that grows from a cactus. Originally from Mexico but also thrives in the Philippines. Pitaya is another name for this juicy sweet fruit of divine pleasure.

Date Sugar

Is made from dried dates and adds a rich sweetness to recipes. It is a healthy replacement in recipes that call for brown sugar.

Dijon Mustard

Whole, ground, or cracked mustard seeds are mixed with water, salt, lemon juice, or vinegar to create a sauce ranging in color from bright yellow to dark brown.

Cumin

Its seeds are used in the cuisines of many cultures east to west. Cumin is used in its whole seed form or ground into a powder. In Sanskrit, cumin is known as jira. Jira means "that which helps digestion". In the Ayurvedic system of medicine, dried cumin seeds are used for medicinal purposes.

Cutting techniques

Chop, dice, slice, mince, and julienne

Daikon Radish

A mild-flavored winter radish (Raphanus sativus) usually characterized by fast-growing leaves and a long white root.

Dill Weed

Fresh and dried dill leaves are widely used as herbs for sauces and salads in Europe, Russia, and central Asia.

Dulse

Dulse is a sea vegetable that is a good source of minerals and vitamins compared with other vegetables. It contains all trace elements needed by humans and has a high protein content. Suggested to have daily for those who have hormonal imbalances.

Fenugreek

Is a traditional Indian spice used mostly in curries and masalas. This seed in ayurvedic medicine, is used to help with obesity, type 2 diabetes, constipation, and high cholesterol. It has a strong flavor. Only a little should be used at one time.

Food Processor

They make food prepping a breeze. They chop, mince, dice, and puree foods with ease. Cuisinart® brand is an affordable and reliable food processor that we suggest to have on hand.

Forbidden Rice

A black rice with protein and heart strengthening nutrients. This rice is a powerful source of antioxidants. It is known by some sources to be the one of the most healthful foods on the planet. It is used in many traditional medicines as a heart attack preventative staple.

Goji Berries

A moderately sweet berry. Great for use in both salads and desserts. They contain 11 essential vitamins and 22 trace minerals including potassium, copper, riboflavin, zinc, and iron. They support hormone balance particularly in men.

Habanero

A supremely hot pepper used in many international cuisines that measures 100,000 to 500,000 Scoville units. They contain a beautiful nutrient called capsicum. This nutrient helps the body fight obesity and mental disorders. It also naturally lowers blood pressure and cholesterol.

Heirloom Tomatoes

Often referred to as ugly. They are some of the most nutritious form of tomatoes on the planet. Many different varieties exists. The yellow heirloom tomato is known for relieving pain in chemotherapy patients.

Hemp Seed

These seeds are also called, the victorious. This little seed has the ability to help conquer disease in the body. It is an anti-inflammatory and has a perfect balance of omegas 3,6, and 9.

Herbal Coffee

A great healthful coffee alternative usually made from carob, barley, and chicory root. This beverage should be consumed in moderation. In small amounts, chicory root is known to support strong liver function and has a stimulating effect on the mind.

Himalayan Salt

A highly nutritious salt mined in the Himalayan mountains of India. It is an ancient variety of salt that supports healthful heart functions. It is great for patients who suffer from high blood pressure. This perfect salt still should be used in moderation.

Honey

It is a sweetener made from nectar collected by the honey bee. It has many medicinal uses, from soothing sore throats to eliminating bags under the eyes—a product not often consumed by (strict) vegans due to it being a by-product of a sentient being.

Italian Parsley

Often referred to one of the worlds most healthiest foods. A beautiful variety of parsley whose leaves are flat and wide and is often mistaken for cilantro. Italian (flat leaf) parsley has a lighter flavor than the curly parsley commonly used.

Juicer

A raw food kitchen essential. The Omega® brand juicers are affordable high-power juicers that can handle the demands of a raw food kitchen. The Omega® Nutrition Center Juicer model comes with the feature of the blank plate. This allows you create fresh fruit ice creams and nut butters.

Jungle Peanuts

This peanut is not a nut. It is a legume of the pea family. They are grown in the wild of the amazon jungle. Packed with nutrients and tons of protein these legumes will keep you happily full and physically toned.

Kalamata Olives

Beautiful almost purple brown olives. Filled with nutrients that support good bone health. And, their anti-inflammatory properties help keep allergies at bay.

Mandoline

A kitchen tool that slices and shreds fruits and vegetables with ease. Great for creating different sizes and textures of apples, cucumbers, and carrots.

Mung Bean

Also called Moong dal. A small green colored bean used in soups or sprouted for salads and wraps. Mung beans are filled with protein. When sprouted the benefits of mung beans is increased.

Mixing Bowls

Stainless steel is suggested for daily use. Ceramic, glass or wooden bowls are also good choices. Avoid plastic bowls and containers.

Miso

This fermented soy bean is known as a miracle food. In the east it is used to battle breast cancer. Filled with zinc, phosphorus, vitamin K, manganese, copper, and an array of other nutrients, this food is a must have. We suggest refrigerated brands for their flavor and quality.

Medjool Date

Dates have B-6, niacin, and have traces of almost every mineral the body needs. When they are dehydrated the benefits are increased.

Millet Bread

Clouted as one of the most nutritious foods on the planet. The millet grain offers manganese, copper, phosphorous (great for muscle repair), and magnesium. Millet bread is a nice alternative to other traditional breads.

Maple Syrup

A great source of manganese and zinc. Zinc is fantastic for the health of your skin. Maple syrup is a liquid sweetener made from the sap of a maple tree. For a sugar, maple has the least amount of adverse affects on the brain. Use in moderation.

Maca Powder

A nutty flavored powder. Maca packs in nutritional value. It is most known for its ability to normalize hormone function and relieve muscle soreness.

Macadamia Nuts

Cultivated on islands like Hawaii and Australia. These beautiful tropical nuts offer a significant amount of protein and lipids necessary for healthful absorption of nutrients. For vegans, the macadamia nut is necessary for maintaining good protein levels in the body.

Lipids

Necessary fats the body needs in order to process and absorb nutrients found in fresh food. First cold press and organic oils, nuts, and seeds are excellent sources of lipids.

Liquid aminos

A great replacement for nama shoyu or soy sauce in recipes. Liquid aminos have no wheat and are celiac friendly.

Kombucha Tea

A fermented tea beverage that offers a nice source of healthful bacteria. This increases the digestive systems ability to absorb nutrients from food. Usually made from live yeast cultures. Most yeast is vegan (yeast is a fungi) but check with distributor of kombucha tea to be sure.

Kelp Noodles

Raw noodles made from the seaweed, kelp. A delicious and wonderful raw food treat donning the same nutritional properties of kelp sea weed. Kelp is known to balance hormones and has cancer fighting properties. Enjoy raw or slightly cooked. Can be found in the Pancit Noodle Dish in the SolFood section.

Kim Chi (chee)

Kim chi is a household favorite. A flavorful fermented salad of the east. It is a great addition to all Asian, Korean and Filipino cuisine. An amazing food that supports good digestion.

Mustard Seed

High quantities of selenium is found in mustard seeds. Selenium is a nutrient that increases the metabolism. Omega 3 and manganese are only a couple reasons why this medicinal seed should be a food staple. Use sparingly; it is a medicine.

Nama Shoyu

A fermented, almost raw, soy sauce. The base is wheat and salt. Therefore, it should be avoided if you have celiac disease. We suggest to use gluten free tamari, amino acids, or coconut aminos for wheat sensitive diets.

Napa Cabbage

See Chinese Cabbage.

Nori

Has the equivalent amount of omega -3's as 2 avocados. Beneficial for the skin as it reduces acne and a whole host of other facial complications. It also balances hormone function and is an anti-inflammatory food.

Nutritional Yeast Flakes

A vegan dried yeast. It has a cheddar cheese-like flavor. Excellent for a vegan food plan, this food is rich in B-12. B-12 is a nutrient more commonly found in animal food products.

Oils

Purchase first cold pressed and organic oils. Flax, chia, and black sesame oil are great alternatives to the standard cooking oil. Oils are essential for a vegan food plan as lipids are necessary for the body to process and absorb nutrients from fresh foods.

Pickled Vegetables

Fermenting vegetables is a great way to store and preserve garden grown vegetables. Plus, fermented foods are beneficial for the entire digestive system.

Pine Nuts

Are an amazing small package of nutrients. These tiny nuts have iron and vitamins A, C, and D. They also contain high quantities of magnesium and protein. Their flavor is similar to a sharp cheese and is a great substitute for cheese in Italian dishes.

Pomegranate

Has a roaming history covering Iran, China, California and Florida. The pomegranate is also mentioned in the book of exodus. It is known to be one of the first five cultivated foods in the world. This berry has a thick reddish skin and the seeds have vitamins C and K. The seeds, when eaten whole, are a good source of dietary fiber.

Processed food

Are usually boxed, canned, bagged or frozen. They are loaded with preservatives and have a high sodium or sugar content. They are also made with dyes and chemicals and are very difficult for the body to digest.

Protein

A vital nutrient which effects energy levels. It can be found in dark leafy greens, nuts, seeds, and legumes.

Raw

Food in its most natural nutrient dense state with minimal alternation. Raw food can be pressed, steamed, dried, blended and juiced. Raw food is filled with natural enzymes that help with the digestion process. Cooking food over 118 degrees cooks out these vital enzymes.

Sea Vegetables (seaweed)

Sea vegetables are a tremendous source of B vitamins. They stabilize hormonal imbalances and should be a part of daily diet.

Sea Salt and Himalayan Salt

Celtic Sea Salt and Himalayan Salt are the only 2 salts used in our recipes. Both offer full nutrient and micro-nutrient replenishing the body needs. These salts regulate blood pressure and are good for the heart. Even though this salt is beneficial, one should still consume in moderation.

Shallots

Look like miniature onions but with a lighter and sweeter taste. They have iron, potassium, and dietary fiber. Great replacement when the flavor of onion is needed in recipes.

Soaking and Sprouting

An important water process for nuts, legumes, whole grains, and seeds that opens up the enzymes, reduces starch, and increases the nutritional value of the food. This process makes food easy to digest and supports nutrient absorption.

Spiralizer

An Asian kitchen tool that makes various noodle sizes and styles out of fruits and vegetables.

Spirulina

A nutrient dense food with B-12. It has cancer fighting nutrients and is filled with manganese, iron, potassium, zinc, fatty acids and over 18 amino acids. Include this miracle food into a weekly food plan.

Star Fruit

Amazing low calorie fruit. It is a yellow tropical fruit with steep crevices. When sliced the fruit takes on the shape of star. Rich in dietary fiber, B-6, and vitamin C.

Sun Flower Seeds

Big things always come in small packages and this seed marks the height of that. Rich in vitamins (especially E) and minerals. Also high in magnesium which helps with reducing asthma and heart disease.

Sun Flower Sprouts

A complete plant protein. A micro-green that has the all the essential amino acids to help repair muscle tissue and it has a 100 times the enzymes of other salad greens. They reduce high blood pressure and are part of a heart attack preventive food plan.

Super Food

Raw foods that have an unusually high vitamin and mineral content. These foods are not supplements. They are pure raw food and are usually dried and ground for ease of use.

Supplements

Supplements come in a various shapes and forms. They are an unnatural concentration of nutrients that are unnecessary for the body. We advise very strong caution when selecting a supplement source.

Sweet Potato

Rich in nutrients; vitamin A, C, B1, 2, 3, & 6. A powerful antioxidant and a great anti-inflammatory food. Sweet potatoes come in many varieties. Our favorite is the Okinawa and Japanese sweet potato.

Swiss Chard

Swiss chard has highly nutritious leaves and is considered to be one of the most healthful vegetables available. It is rich in minerals, dietary fiber, and protein.

Tamari

A soy sauce and nama shoyu replacement that is wheat free.

Tahini

Sesame seeds ground into a creamy texture. These seeds are used in eastern medicine. The tiny seeds are filled with essential proteins. Eat tahini for amazing health, glowing skin, strong bones, and muscles.

Tamper

A baton shaped tool designed to move ingredients into blade of VitaMix® container during the blending process. .

Turmeric

Has been used as a spice and medicine in India for thousands of years. Turmeric has antioxidant power, is an anti-inflammatory, and has been known to lower risk of heart disease.

Vegan

A person whose chosen lifestyle does not harm any sentient being on the planet. Vegans do not support the use of any animal food products. They use cosmetics that are not tested on animals and that have no animal ingredients. Their clothing and accessories are also made without animal by-products.

Vinegars

Apple cider vinegar is the chosen form of vinegar for many raw foods. Another alternative to vinegar is liquid aminos (see liquid aminos). We use also small amounts of coconut, balsamic, and champagne vinegar more for flavor. Use vinegar sparingly.

Wasabi

Great for the liver, bone strength, and good digestion. It has a strong flavor and heat. Use in small quantities.

INDEX OF YOGA ASANAS AND TERMS

Yoga Asanas & Terms - BURN Kitchen - Vegan Cuisine - Index

REFERENCE LIST

Keep your fire burning and keep studying

Iyengar, BKS

Light on Yoga.

New York, Shocken Books, 1994

Light on The Yoga Sutras of Patanjali.

Hammersmith, London. Thorsons, 2002

Mallison, James

The Shiva Samhita.

 Woodstock, NY, Yoga Nidya, 2007

Easwaran, Eknath

The Upanishads.

Tomales, CA, Nilgiri Press, May 2006

Sri Swami Satchidandna

The Yoga Sutras of Patanjali.

Yogaville, Integral Yoga Publications, 1990

The Living Gita.

Yogaville, Integral Yoga Publications, 1990

Brotman, Juliano

With Lenkert, Erica.

RAW the UNcook Book.

New York, Harper Collins, 1999

ACKNOWLEDGEMENTS

BURN Kitchen Vegan Cuisine came to fruition with the help of a few divine wonders. This page is dedicated to those light-filled beings of unwavering support. Our gratitude extends to you beyond measure!

To our supreme Guru (teacher), The Sage Patanjali. With great adoration, we dedicate our entire life's work, practice, and breath to you. Your profound and inspiring teachings of yoga naturally create equanimity within. We are devoted to continuing to share this tradition with yoga students.

To Theresa's Mom, Yvonne, Thank you for the tall mountain of support you give us daily. Your love, light, and pleasantness serve as one of the great sources of our peace and keep us strong. I have never known a woman as fascinating, patient, generous, or as loving as you. I am eternally grateful to have the incredible fortune to have you as my mother, friend, and one of the most outstanding teachers I have ever known. Thank you for all your love and undying support. I love you, and Calvin loves you. - T.

To Theresa's Dad, Thomas, I was 14 when you passed from lung cancer. The loss of your breath inspired me to work on my breath. Witnessing your suffering encouraged me to devote my life to helping remove the suffering of others. When I see the sunset and the colorful rays of light, I can feel you cast your light of support each day. - T.

To Calvin's Mom, Cheryl, The everlasting love you give us is felt no matter how far away you are. Your easygoing nature and welcoming personality serve as an inspiration for us and everyone who meets you. Theresa and I are grateful for you and love you deeply. - C.

To Calvin's Dad, Morie, My fondest childhood memories are of you and me chopping, dicing, and slicing in the kitchen. Acting as your sous-chef for the fantastic meals you created was an honor. I will never forget these meals and memories. - C.

To Beryl Bender Birch, You are a heartfelt teacher of the classical 8-limbed yoga path who advocated our approach toward teaching physical modifications for the practice. We will always be grateful for the day you told us after witnessing firsthand how amazing our students practice yoga, "Keep doing what you're doing. It's great work".

To BKS Iyengar, Our first exposure to yoga stemmed from your powerful words about Patanjali in the book Light On Yoga. This book was a great inspiration and showed us yoga was a dance of life and a compelling discipline. Because of you, we have a deep, resounding dedication and devotion to the meditative work of yoga. Thank you for inspiring us to love all aspects of yoga and your illuminating teachings.

To Caiti and Tim, Caiti, this version of BURN Kitchen Vegan Cuisine came about after you visited Florida to help us edit and play with words. Thank you for your delightful sense of humor and for finally seeing the lightning bolt in fierce pose, LOL. And thank you, Tim, for coming out for a weekend adventure of photography and vegan pizza! We send you both tons of gratitude and love.

To Our Students, who have supported our studio and the teachings of yoga through thick and thin - you inspired us on deep levels to mix our spiritual ingredients with material ingredients and allowed us to share with you how to create the food we love.

We are deeply honored to be blessed with so many gentle, pleasant, and dedicated students devoted to the discipline of yoga practice. You are our fuel on many levels, giving us the energy to keep sharing, even when it may be uncomfortable or challenging. You know the result will be better than good!

May your love for yoga practice and divine food inspire many others to practice beyond the pose, too!

To our readers, Our heartfelt devotion to yoga fuels us to continue serving humanity through the teachings of yoga. Thank you for reading this book. We are honored to share the teachings of yoga from our unique perspectives with you!

With blessings and love, Calvin and Theresa

NAMASTE

The luminous light inside of me
bows to the luminous light inside of you.